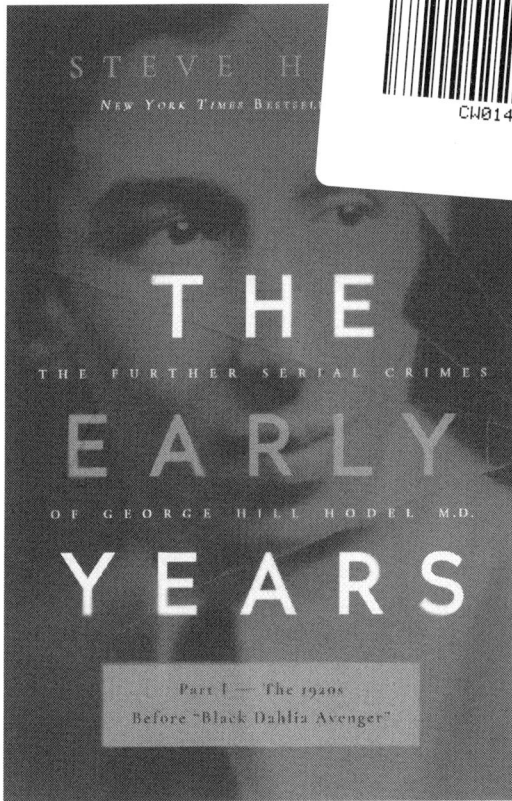

STEVE H[...]
NEW YORK TIMES BESTSEL[...]

THE

THE FURTHER SERIAL CRIMES

EARLY

OF GEORGE HILL HODEL M.D.

YEARS

Part I — The 1940s
Before "Black Dahlia Avenger"

The Early Years - Part I
Copyright 2021 - Steve Hodel

All Rights Reserved

ISBN: 13-9780996045773
Printed in the United States of America 4321098765
Cover design: Hannah Linder

Thoughtprint Press Los Angeles, California

Steve Hodel

Dedication:

For the victims, living and dead

~

When I despair, I remember that all through history the way of Truth and Love has always won. There have been tyrants and murderers and for a time they can seem invincible, but in the end they always fall. Think of it, always.

—Mahatma Gandhi

Contents

George Hodel 1925 Photographs

The two self-portraits (bottom of page 3) taken by George Hodel circa 1925.

The original photograph, in my possession, has on the back, in my father's handwriting, the title: "*Merlin gazes at cracked mirrors.*"

On the second photograph (shown below, top) again on the reverse side of the picture, the then 18-year-old crime reporter for the *Los Angeles Record* newspaper, has written, "*Portrait of a chap suddenly aware of the words of Sigmund Freud.*"

Both of these self-portraits were displayed in a "One Man Show" at an art gallery in Pasadena, California in he mid twenties.

(**SKH Note** - The handwriting [printing] shown beside the two photos below was included in more than a dozen samples used by court-certified QDE [Questioned Document Expert] Hanna McFarland to positively identify George Hodel's handwriting as a "positive match" to multiple notes written by the "Black Dahlia Avenger" in 1947 postings the killer mailed to the newspaper press and police in Los Angeles, California.)

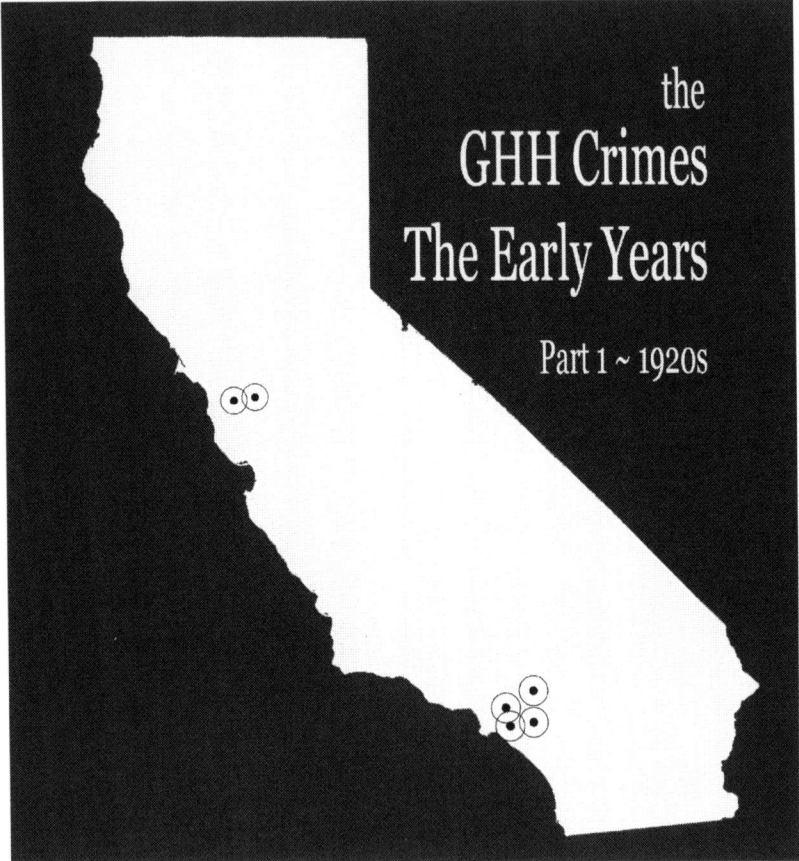

the
GHH Crimes
The Early Years

Part 1 ~ 1920s

Introduction

In writing *George Hill Hodel: The Early Years*, my original intent was to present all of my father's *suspected* crimes from the 1920s and 1930s in one edition.

I have found this simply is not possible as it would require a book that would dwarf Dostoevsky's nearly seven-hundred-page opus, *Crime and Punishment*.

Therefore, I will collate *The Early Years* in two parts, two editions.

This edition is Part 1 and presents my investigations of his **suspected** crimes in the 1920s.

Note that I said, "*suspected* crimes."

I want to be crystal clear on this point.

My two-part, *The Early Years* investigations are just that—a search for the truth.

Investigation - {dictionary.com]

Investigation is the noun form of the verb investigate, which derives from the Latin verb *investigare*, meaning "to follow a trail" or "to search out."

...

The '*vestig*' part of the word *investigare* can be traced back to the Latin word *vestigium*, meaning "**footprint**." (This is also the basis of the English word *vestige*, meaning "a trace or visible evidence of something.")

In the presentation of these crimes from long ago (the first one goes back *one hundred years*), I make no claim to a "solution." I do not and am not saying that my father, George Hill Hodel, committed any of these crimes, beyond a "reasonable doubt"—which would be the legal requirement to find him guilty.

Several of these crimes, without the introduction of hard physical evidence or DNA, are not solvable.

Other cases have been claimed to be "solved" by law enforcement, and each considered, "Case Closed."

In several of them, it is my position that 1) the wrong man was convicted or 2) the suspect committed the crime, but had an unidentified accomplice(s) or 3) the suspect has never been identified, and the case remains an *ice-cold whodunit* that was filed and forgotten long ago.

I can hear the hardcore skeptics' voices now—their minds made up even before the books are published.

"Jesus, now Hodel is saying his dad killed _____ and ____! Every famous unsolved murder in California and beyond. Where is he going next? The Grassy Knoll in Dallas?"

To be clear:

These crimes from the Twenties and Thirties did not present themselves to me post-*Black Dahlia Avenger* published in 2003.

I was aware of them and his possible involvement in them as early as the year 2000, *a full three years* before I presented my father to the world as the killer of Elizabeth "Black Dahlia" Short and responsible for the other LA Lone Woman Murders.

In 2003, I thought my first book *Black Dahlia Avenger* would be followed by a second book presenting crimes as *suspected* "early years" offenses committed in his youth.

I had no idea that by "following the evidence," I would be led to George Hodel's crimes as: Chicago's "Lipstick Killer" and Manila's "Jigsaw Murder" and then to his pre-retirement serial crimes in the San Francisco Bay Area as "Zodiac."

So, here we are, some twenty years and six books and twenty-five murder victims later.

What I thought would be "Book II" has now become **Book VII** followed by **Book VIII**.

For those who are coming across my investigations for the first time, I would strongly urge you to read the pre-"early years" books in the below-recommended order.

Steve Hodel's: 6 True-Crime Books (in reading order left to right)

In truth, it is *one ongoing investigation* very much like an actual Homicide Progress Report, which chronologically updates new findings and linkage as the new evidence is uncovered.

This is where
The Early Years ~ Part 1
begins:

Chapter 1

Our Russian Roots

My paternal grandmother, Esther Leov Hodel, died before I was born. She contracted tuberculosis and passed away in a sanitarium in Los Angeles in 1935.

My brothers, Michael and Kelvin, and I did have sporadic contact with our paternal grandfather, George Hodel, Sr., I have fond memories of riding the Red Car from Hollywood to visit him in Santa Monica.

[SKH Note: To differentiate between George Hodel, my grandfather, and George Hill Hodel, my father—Senior or Sr. is used for my grandfather, and Junior or Jr. is used to represent my father.]

We called him our "1-2-3 Grandfather" because on the rare occasions we saw him, he would reach out, grab us by the waist, and lift us high into the air as he called out the words, "1,2,3."

My memories of George, Sr. are few. As young children, I doubt that my brothers and I saw him more than three or four times. Unlike our father, who was over six feet tall, grandfather at five-foot six was quite small in stature. He was dark complexioned, and I recall him being quite introverted. He died in Los Angeles in 1954 at the age of eighty-one.

My mother attended his funeral and I remember her remarking on several occasions how surprised she was at the number of people that came to the service.

Mother's words, told to me as a teenager:

"When your 1-2-3 grandfather passed away, you would think it was like a Hollywood star or some very famous person had died. Hundreds of people attended his funeral. I was shocked. I never really understood why so many people came. All I knew about your father's father was that he sold insurance."

From my newest research, I now know that my grandparents were strong supporters of the arts in early Los Angeles and had some very influential friends who they either knew from pre-revolutionary Russia, or had met in Paris.

These "connections" paint a very different picture of my grandparents. Clearly, my grandfather's life and sphere of influence extended far beyond my mother's impression of him being a clerkish and unassuming "insurance salesman."

Let's go back to the turn of the twentieth century and examine some of the "thoughtprints" that my grandparents have left behind.

My grandparents were both Ukrainian immigrants. Our original family name was Goldgefter. My father's father, George Goldgefter, was born on February 5, 1873, in the seaport city of Odessa. His father, Eli Goldgefter, was an accountant and a German scholar.

My paternal grandmother, Esther Leov, was born in the same year on April 15, 1873, in Sharhorod, Ukraine, which lies some 275 miles northwest of my grandfather's birthplace. Esther's family was rumored to be related to either Russian or French nobility.

Steve Hodel

George Goldgefter and Esther Leov birth cities 1873

It is believed that George, Sr. and Esther met in Paris, shortly after his arrival circa 1894. At the time of their courtship Esther was a practicing dentist in Paris, a highly unusual profession for a woman of that period.

Information related to my grandparents early lives is extremely sketchy. No real family history is known other than a few word-of-mouth anecdotes. Some information was handed down to me thanks to my grandfather's third wife, Alice Hodel, who I first met briefly as a young boy while living at the Sowden/ Franklin House.

In the early 1950s, when I was about twelve, our mother would take my brothers and me on the Red Car (LA's then go-to mass transit system of electrically powered streetcars) to make occasional visits to see grandfather and Alice in their small apartment in Santa Monica, California.

Alice, circa 1945, had met and married the widowed George Hodel, Sr., while working as a lab technician at my father's *First Street Clinic* in downtown Los Angeles. While we had no real contact over the years, after grandfather's death, Alice kept in touch by sending a UNICEF Christmas card which like clockwork arrived each year.

In the late Seventies after the birth of my first son, Michael, she came to visit our home and brought a number of personal family photographs which included both of my paternal grandparents along with other "unknown relatives." It was at this time that Alice informed me that "Esther Leov was somehow related to royalty," but could not (or would not?) provide any additional details.

Also included with the pictures was a typewritten essay, written by my grandfather describing his life in Russia and his "escape" out of the country in 1894. I think it is a remarkable description of the life and times in pre-revolution Russia and I present it here in its entirety without any editing or changes from the original. [NB: *ESCAPE* is by grandfather George Hodel, Sr.]

ESCAPE

By George Hodel

(as told to Alice Hodel - pages 11-17)

An "iron curtain" extended around the borders of Russia in the time of the Czars for the young man of military age. The seven years of military service was dreaded for the officers were tyrannical and the men treated like slaves. In a time when pogroms were common, the regime was especially severe in the treatment of the Jewish people.

It is very different in the United States, for here the young soldier is treated like a human being.
In my home in Odessa, a seaport on the Black Sea, the subject was frequently discussed, for I was one of five sons. Ways of leaving the country were known, but all were dangerous.

My father, an accountant by profession, was a German scholar. On his desk were always books and magazines in the German language. He, even, studied astronomy, his favorite subject, in German.

As I approached the dreaded age of 21, we talked of my future. I was surprised when my father declared, "If it were my life to live, I would go to France."

"Not Germany?" I asked.

He shook his head, "I have great respect for the German learning, but France is the freest, most interesting part of the world."

"But what about America?"

"It is easier to make money in America," he said. "But for the young man, a hard row to walk, is better. When you are older you might go to America. Then you will be more mature and will appreciate how hard life is in other places."

My mother listened to the discussions. She agreed that I should plan to go away.

Nodding her head, she said, "Yes, it will be better for you than the army. I should not want to think of you in the army."

In February, I was 21. There was still a small chance that I might escape the military service, for each year when the class was called up, a drawing of numbers was held, and a few men would be excused from military service. This could be called a human lottery.

As I waited for the day of the drawing, I began my preparations for escape, if I should not be one of the lucky ones. Ways of crossing the border were frequently discussed with friends by families with sons of military age. All of these ways required money to be used to bribe police and military officials.

Passports could be borrowed or bought using an assumed name. If a traveler with a borrowed passport was discovered, it meant trouble for the owner of the passport as well as the traveler. This was a risk I was not willing to take.

Soon after my birthday, I bought a passport, made out in the name of Peter Lubkin, from a police official, known to be open to bribery, at the police headquarters.

The letter, demanding my presence at the military headquarters in Odessa on the day of the drawing, arrived in April.

Early on the appointed day the young men, many accompanied by their families and friends, assembled in a huge hall in the massive stone building which was the military headquarters. Already it was a tragic scene. The eyes of the mothers were misty as they foresaw the departure of their sons. The faces of the fathers and friends were somber, and there was an atmosphere of dread and fear, sharpened by the presence of uniformed officers with their stern faces. My family did not accompany me.

Finally, as all eyes watched, an officer brought out the fatal box. As each man drew his number, it was easy to see from the reaction of his family and friends what his fate had been. Usually the women broke into loud weeping and the men rubbed their eyes with the back of their hands.

Rarely a group would dry their eyes and laugh unsteadily. The men would clap each other on the back and some would break into song as they left the hall.

My turn came. My number was one, which was not a lucky number. I was instructed to report to a doctor for the physical examination and to have a tailor make my uniform. Now, I must act fast.

Not wishing to worry my family, I did not tell them the details of my plan, but a code word was selected which I would send them by wire when I was safe.

Knowing that it was easier for the rich to pass through the inspections I must face, I decided to play the part of a rich young man.

The first step was to buy three pieces of expensive luggage. One was a small case for razor and brushes, the other two were large suitcases. As the luggage cost, so much, there was not enough money left to buy much to put in it, but it certainly looked impressive.

Next, I bought a first-class ticket to the Polish frontier. I could have purchased a ticket to Vienna, which was my immediate destination, but decided not to waste money until I knew I would not be turned back.

The next night I boarded the train. It was not easy to be nonchalant, as on my way back to my compartment from the first-class dining car, I passed one of the several uniformed officers on the train and I noticed that his eyes narrowed as he looked at me.

As the train rumbled its way toward the frontier, I slept at intervals. In the morning I carefully arranged my luggage so that a visitor would be sure to see it and appreciate its value.

The same officer I had passed in the corridor, a middle-aged man with a stern face and questioning eyes, knocked on the door of the compartment, entered and seated himself beside me.

"Where are you going, young man?" was the first question asked in a deep voice.

"Vienna," I answered.

"Why do you go there?"

To still the trembling of my legs, I pressed my knees together, as I told the story I had invented.

"My mother is sick in a hospital there and I go to be with her."

He rubbed his nose with the back of his hand as he asked, "How long do you plan to stay?"

"That will depend upon how well she gets along. I hope to bring her back with me."

Then he snapped, "Why didn't you buy a ticket to Vienna instead of the frontier?"

"There may be a telegram for me at the frontier. If the operation has been postponed, I will return to Odessa and come back next week."

He relaxed a bit as he said, "This is miserable work assigned to me. I have to question all men of military age, so that I may send home those who are running away from military service."

"How can you tell which ones are running away?"

Raising his head proudly, he said in a superior tone of voice, "I never make a mistake."

I continued my questioning, "But how can you know?"

"Well," he said, "they are usually nervous."

Hoping my voice would not betray how nervous I was, I said, "You must be very clever."

He smiled in agreement.

"I hope your mother gets along all right," he said as he handed me the pass which would allow me to cross the frontier and board the train for Vienna.

After he was gone, I breathed easier, but was thankful when the train stopped in a muddy field which was the end of its run. The Austrian train was waiting across the frontier.

The only building was a big shed-like structure. Here military officers collected the passports for the final inspection. At long tables, they examined them one by one. Restlessly the passengers walked about. As each passport was approved, the name of its owner was called.

"Peter Lubkin," a harsh voice called.

"Peter Lubkin," was called again.

As other names were being called, a brusk officer with a strident voice approached me, "Why didn't you answer when your name was called?"

My heart dropped to my boots. How could I have been so careless as not to recognize my assumed name, when I was so near victory?

"I am sorry, sir," I answered, "you see my mother is very sick in Vienna. Even, now, she may be under a knife on an operating room table. I was so troubled, I didn't hear."

Without a word, he turned and briskly walked away. I saw him talking to the officer who had questioned me that morning, the man who never made a mistake. Just as briskly he came back and handed me my passport.

I wanted to run, but deliberately I picked up my expensive luggage and walked over the frontier to FREEDOM.

On the Austrian train, I wrote the telegram to send to my parents.

"Blago," it said, which means Thankfulness.

The End.

Upon his arrival in Paris, grandfather decided he needed a new name. Dropping the "Peter Lubkin" pseudonym, he would henceforth be known as "George Hodel." (Why Hodel? I don't know, other than being informed it was and remains a fairly common Swiss name.)

Nothing is known about George Hodel's early years in France from 1894 to 1900, however, we do know that during that time he met, courted, and then married the practicing dentist, Dr. Esther Leov on May 5, 1901.

Less than a month later, the newlyweds entered the United States through Ellis Island on May 31, 1901.

George and Esther resided in New York for several years, then came west to California, and established residency in the Garvanza District in northeast Los Angeles.

My father, their only child, George Hill Hodel [Jr.] was born on October 10, 1907, at the Clara Barton Hospital at the corner of Fifth Street and Grand Avenue in downtown Los Angeles. On the birth certificate George, Sr. listed his occupation as "banker" and Esther listed her profession as "dentist."

George, Esther and newborn George, Jr. and their French *au pair* circa early 1908 in front of their then LA residence.

(Photo courtesy of Donald Lomas family—Esther Hodel was a first cousin on Lomas' grandparent's side who were also from and a prominent family in Sharhorod, Russia)

1-George Hodel Sr. 2-Esther Hodel 3-Walter Hodel 4-George Hodel Jr.

This photograph shows an early family gathering of relatives, cousins on my grandmother Esther's side of the family. Based on George Jr.'s appearance (No. 4) the photo was likely taken circa 1910. Walter Hodel (No. 3 lower right) followed his older brother, George Hodel, Sr. to the US in 1903 and would eventually retire to Santa Barbara, California, where he died in 1976 at the advanced age of 95.

(Photo courtesy of Donald Lomas Family)

George, Sr. in a "goodbye photo" taken just before his
wife and son's departure to Europe.

In 1912, **Esther Leov Hodel** with her five-year-old
Georgie in hand, departed from her home in Los
Angeles and sailed to Europe where she enrolled her
budding genius in Madame Montessori's newly
opened school in Paris, France.

Just several years before his passing, Father, in an
after-dinner reminiscence with June and me,
affectionately reflected on this period of his
childhood.

"My first language as a young boy was French, so I felt very much at home in Paris, which remains to this day, one of the great cities of the world. My mother and I lived in Paris for about a year and stayed at the home of a Prince Troubetzkoy and his wife." Smiling he added, "I even remember rolling a large hoop through the streets of Paris on my way to school."

Father continued his narrative:

"About a year later, my mother and I returned home on the passenger ship, *Kaiser Wilhelm*. As we pulled into New York harbor I was talking to my mother, and from behind me came a familiar voice that called out, "Hello George. Welcome home." I turned around to see my father standing on-deck in the presence of two US Customs officers. It turns out my father wrote a letter to Theodore Roosevelt, the former President of the United States and informed him that I was returning home and asked if he might be granted permission to ride out with the Customs Officers so he could give me a surprise "Welcome Home." I don't know how my father managed it, but he was granted permission and there he was onboard our ship."

I found this information received piecemeal from my father and June to be most curious. Why did he return from Paris in less than a year? How and why would a former US President grant my grandfather permission to ride out with the New York Customs Officers to greet his son? What was my grandmother's connection to a Russian Prince and Princess? These questions were initially placed on hold, but now many years later, I have at least found some of the answers.

Paris 1912 - Prince and Princess Troubetzkoy

The nature of the Troubetzkoy/Hodel relationship remains a mystery. To this day, I am uncertain if my grandmother was a distant relative or merely a close friend.

Regardless, I have discovered a wealth of material on the Russian Prince and his circle of friends, which obviously included my grandmother, Esther Leov Hodel. Let's examine some of what I have discovered on this Russian Royal.

Paul Troubetzkoy and Coat of Arms and Seal

Here is a short biography excerpted from a 2009 article published in the Moscow Tretyakov Gallery Magazine, and written by Svetlana Domogatskaya.

The son of a Russian prince and an American woman, Paolo (Pavel Petrovich) Troubetzkoy

(1866-1938) was born, grew up, received education and started a career in art in Italy. In Russia he worked, with intervals, from 1898 through 1906. By 1898 he already created a considerable number of works that can incontestably be called masterpieces, participated in many international exhibitions, and reached maturity as an artist. Twice, in 1906-1914 and in 1921-1932, he kept a studio in France, near Paris; from 1914 through 1921 he lived and worked in Hollywood, where he bought a small house and built a spacious studio.

In Russia at the turn of the centuries, Paolo Troubetzkoy became a cultural landmark. Strange as it may seem, it was his carefree attitude that helped finally reveal the impotence of the outdated academic forms and relieve the artists from the obligation to heed this canon such as it had become by the late 19th century. This alone is sufficient to love Troubetzkoy "with a special love."

The following excerpt is from the Foreword of a 1919 art catalog, *Portraits In Bronze and Marble* by Paul Troubetzkoy, written by Arthur Hoeber. The brochure indicated Troubetzkoy's works were exhibited February 16-28, 1919, at the Galleries of M. Knoedler & Company, 556-558 Fifth Avenue, New York.

An American mother, a Russian father, a life of wide cosmopolitan experience, a master of many languages, circumstances have singularly favored Paul Troubetzkoy in equipping him for the profession he pursues with such splendid enthusiasm. His statues are all over the world, in the museums of Paris, Rome, Berlin, St. Petersburgh, Moskow, Venice, Milan, Buenos Ayres, and here in America at Toledo, Buffalo, San Francisco, Chicago, though, alas, not in New York, and he has given the world many portraits of prominent people of two continents. These works in bronze, in marble, and in plaster, speak for themselves, for his is a talent of a unique order and intensely personal, reflecting the man himself in his varying moods. As such they will, I venture to predict, make a wide and serious appeal. - Arthur Hoeber

Troubetzkoys arrive in New York, January 1914

Portrait of Angelina Troubetzkoy

Paul Troubetzkoy's painting of his wife 1914

Paul Troubetzkoy's equestrian statue of Alexander III (Alexander Alexandrovich Romanov 1845-1894) was erected in St. Petersburg on May 23, 1909. Many consider this to be his greatest work. In the photo above, taken some years later, the artist is seen standing in front of the monument.

TOLSTOY 1898

RODIN 1906

VANDERBILTS 1911

G.B. SHAW 1928

Troubetzkoy bronzes of Tolstoy, Rodin, G.B. Shaw, George and Edith Vanderbilt family, and Benito Mussolini (on next page - 28)

MUSSOLINI (1926)

In July 1913, for unspecified reasons my father's Montessori early education in Paris was abruptly cut short. After spending less than one year in the company of the Troubetzkoy's mother and son booked passage on the *S.S. Kaiser Wilhelm*, and returned home to the US. They departed from Cherbourg, France, on 2 July 1913, and arrived at the Port of New York, on 8 July 1913.

This was the port arrival that my father, just a few years before his death, had described to June and me, where he "heard his name called out, had turned around to see his father on deck in the company of two Customs Officers." (Presumably with the letter granting permission from former President Theodore Roosevelt in his pocket.)

As a point of interest,my original research into ship passenger records showed Esther and Georgie Hodel listed and booked aboard the *S.S. Imperator* showing they were returning to the US in the company of George and Edith Vanderbilt (also close friends of the Troubetzkoys in Paris). Records showed they had departed from Cherbourg 10 July 1913 arriving in NY 16 July. Initially, I assumed my father's normally "perfect memory" in recounting the voyage claiming he had returned on the *Kaiser Wilhelm* rather than the *S.S. Imperator* was simply incorrect. Understandable, since he was recalling events from eighty years prior. Not so. In rechecking a copy of the handwritten passenger list, I discovered that though still named as having crossed on that date, Esther and Georgie Hodel's names had a line drawn through them. (The Vanderbilts did not.) I then rechecked and found Esther and Georgie's *names also listed* on the *S.S. Kaiser Wilhelm*, which had departed one week earlier. However, in that document there was no strike through. Father's memory had not failed him. They had merely decided to book passage one week earlier.

S.S. Imperator 1913

S.S. Kaiser Wilhelm

Esther Hodel
Georgie Hodel

Original Passenger Lists of the *S.S. Imperator* and *S.S. Kaiser Wilhelm* both show "Esther and Georgie Hodel" returned to the US from France in July 1913. On the *Imperator* list, the Hodels show returning home with George and Edith Vanderbilt who were also close friends of the Troubetzkoys and had separate sittings with the artist for bronze portrait sculptures. An examination of the documents shows that the Hodels were "scratched" from the *Imperator* as they had in fact sailed home on the *Kaiser Wilhelm* one week earlier.

(Historical Note—The *S.S. Kaiser Wilhelm* was pressed into German service at the start of WWI, and just one year after my father's return to America, was sunk by the British in "The battle off Rio de Oro," in the Spanish Sahara, on August 26, 1914.)

A Roosevelt-Troubetzkoy Connection

Additional research has now shown that there existed a further direct link between Prince Troubetzkoy and Franklin D. Roosevelt, cousin to the former President Theodore Roosevelt. (FDR's wife, Eleanor, had a closer relationship to Teddy, as she was his niece.)

I quote from a press briefing by Mike McCurry dated October 23, 1995, on the occasion of a meeting between President Clinton and Russian President Yeltsin at the Roosevelt family library in Hyde Park, New York.

"**As the two Presidents entered** the house, President Clinton showed President Yeltsin a life-sized bronze sculpture of Franklin Roosevelt at the age of 29 that was completed in 1911 by a Russian sculptor, Prince Paul Troubetzkoy. You can—there are probably different ways to transliterate that—Prince Paul Troubetzkoy, who is the son of a Russian diplomat, if memory serves me right. The artist's brother, Pierre, painted a portrait of Sarah Roosevelt, Franklin Roosevelt's mother, which President Clinton also showed to President Yeltsin as they walked into the library. (The bronze statue was commissioned by Roosevelt's grandmother, Nelly Blodgett, on the occasion of FDR's entrance into politics as a New York state legislator.)"

BIRD COLLECTION and bust stand in hall. F.D.R. began collecting birds at 11, built up collection of 300 North American birds. He shot most of them, mounted some himself. Bust was done by Prince Paul Troubetzkoy in 1911 but may be removed because daughter Anna wants it.

Photo from LIFE Magazine, April 15, 1946, shows FDR bust sculpted by Paul Troubetzkoy in 1911

On 27 December 1913, just six months after Esther and Georgie Hodel returned to America with war clouds rapidly darkening over Europe, the Troubetzkoys booked passage on the *S.S. France*, and arrived in the US on 4 January 1914.

Prince and Princess Troubetzkoy would remain in America for the next six years and not return to France until 1921.

After spending several years sculpting and exhibiting his art in New York, the couple came West to Hollywood, where they purchased a small home and the artist opened a studio and began sculpting Hollywood's royalty including: Mary Pickford, Douglas Fairbanks, Sr., and Sessue Hayakawa. (Hayakawa lived in the US from 1911-1923, and was one of the most popular and highest paid stars in Hollywood, earning over two million a year.)

My early 2001 research into the documented historical recounting of the political corruptions of Los Angeles during the Mayor Porter and Shaw Era (1930s) led me to a remarkable book entitled *Angel City In Turmoil: A Story Of The Minute Men Of Los Angeles In Their War On Civic Corruption, Graft and Privilege* (American State Press). It was written by Guy W. Finney, a newspaperman and political historian of that day and was published in 1945. The book primarily provides us with a detailed chronicle of a decade of corruption during the Shaw Administration, up and through the mayor's eventual recall by the citizens of Los Angeles, after the planted bombing and attempted murder of retired LAPD Detective, Harry Raymond by his brother officers. Also detailed are the many corruptions and crimes of LAPD Chief of Police James Davis with his forced retirement and the eventual indictment of District Attorney Buron Fitts. These need not be repeated here.

However, in reviewing the author's historical description of early Los Angeles and its power brokers, which naturally included mention of the Otis Chandler, *Los Angeles Times* dynasty, the following incredible *thoughtprint* lay hidden in a single paragraph!

In an early chapter of the book Finney discusses a historical scandal (1931) which involved negotiation between Harry Chandler and the City of Los Angeles over the sale of the *Los Angeles Times* original building at First Street and Broadway. (The scandal involved the over-inflated appraisal of the building by some $600,000 a cost passed on to the taxpayers.)

The scandal is not of import to us, but here is what reporter Finney had to say about the building and what does relate to our present-day investigation. I quote from page 53:

Many Los Angeles citizens viewed the crusty building as a spiritual portrait of the late walrus-mustached Gen. Harrison Gray Otis, Publisher Chandler's lamented father-in-law, whose martial deeds in the Philippine insurrection of the Filipino patriot Emilio Aguinaldo are well immortalized in a statued Dumasian glamorization of the three manly virtues (valor, nobility, wisdom) which stands heroically at the west side of MacArthur (Westlake) Park. Elder Angel City residents regard this statue with considerable veneration as a fitting symbol of past grandeur rewarded.

The records, however, would seem to indicate that this memorial was more of a social than a civic service to Los Angeles, inasmuch as the cost ($50,000) was raised by the hat-passing method among the deceased warrior's social and business legatees. Oddly enough, the sculptor, as might have been expected, was not one distinguished for his military memorials, as, for example, Daniel Chester French or Gutzon Borglum, but was a salon favorite of that day—**Prince Troubetzkoy.** (Emphasis mine.)

Paul Troubetzkoy's 1920 statue of General Harrison Gray Otis (1837-1917) erected near downtown Los Angeles, in Westlake Park (renamed MacArthur Park after General Douglas MacArthur in the 1940s). Otis was appointed a Brigadier General in the Philippine-American War. After relocating to Los Angeles, he rose to become owner/publisher of the powerful *Los Angeles Times-Mirror* newspaper.

Troubetzkoy's statues also depict a flag-draped soldier and a young boy selling newspapers. The plaque inscription reads: "General Harrison Gray Otis, 1837-1917. Soldier, journalist, friend of freedom. Stand fast, stand firm, stand sure, stand true."

(**Note** - A current visit by me to the statue revealed the soldier is AWOL from the monument. Research indicated that he was hit by a car and his last known location waa reported to be "in the basement of the Otis Art Institute.")

"When I study and reproduce a living thing, it is not the thing itself I wish to represent, but life—that life which vivifies and animates all things alike."

Paul Troubetzkoy

Bronze Horses statue signed 'Paul Troubetzkoy 1926'
(From Steve Hodel personal collection)

The Hodels, Alexander Zelenko
The Monterey Road Residence

In Black Dahlia Avenger *(Arcade 2003)* I included the following anecdote from my father's boyhood:

By the age of nine, George had become recognized throughout Southern California as a future concert pianist; his teacher predicted a great musical career for him. An old family photograph captures the image of the Russian composer Rachmaninoff visiting the Hodel home in South Pasadena, where he, accompanied by the Russian minister of culture and his wife, attended a private recital given by Father when he was only nine.

My father's fame as a prodigy spread, and soon the newspapers were writing articles about him.

On July 14, 1917, for example, the *Los Angeles Evening Herald*, alongside a photo of my father wrote:

A little boy, 9 years old, has been chosen by the French committee to play before the Belgian mission at the French celebration at Shrine Auditorium today.

The lad thus chosen above scores of adult musicians is George Hodel, son of Mr. and Mrs. George Hodel of 6440 Walnut Hill Avenue. He is a pupil of Vernon Spencer and is regarded in the world of music as a genius.

Though a mere youngster, he has studied music for years and he was selected as a piano soloist by the French committee entirely because of his great talent.

While he has composed several musical works, he will play Massenet and Chaminade selections when he appears before the Belgian mission.

This 1917 article went on to describe my father's intellectual abilities, which I did not include in the earlier publication, but will here add to the narrative.

> This little French boy* is declared by his friends to be a genius along several lines. At the age of 9 he is in the seventh grade at school and has already written many poems. Recently his verses have been on the European war. One of them, written a short time before the fall of the Russian Czar reads:

Armies; scattered; withered—what for?
What has Europe gained by war?
When will cannon's mouth be cold
From killing by the hundredfold?
German's strength and England's flower
Ruthlessly destroyed for lust and power!
Rulers' jealousy, monarchs' hate;
Not the sudden turns of fate,
Has made this murderous field!
When will Kaiser, King, and Tzar
Be no more, human lives to mar?

* George Hill Hodel - *American born, not French*

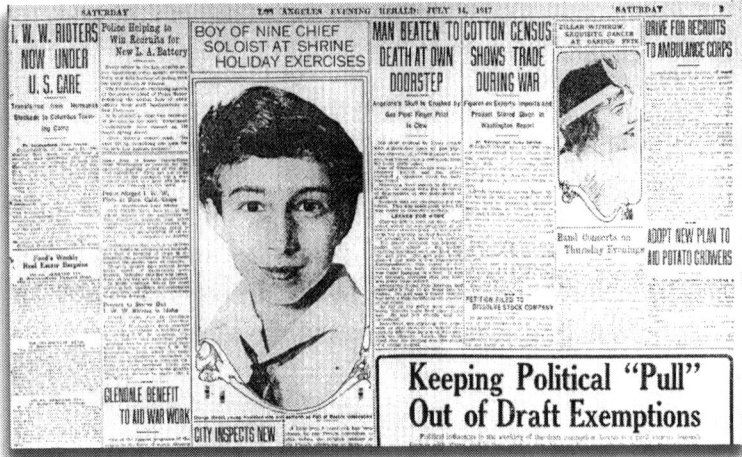

Los Angeles Evening Herald July 14, 1917

George Hodel, age nine, a musical prodigy, was selected to play a piano concert at the L.A. Shrine Auditorium in honor of Bastille Day.

Author's Note - An investigative irony that I simply cannot ignore is shown in the above reproduction of the original article. The headline immediately to the right of my father's reads, "Man Beaten To Death At Own Doorstep; Angeleno's Skull is Crushed by Gas Pipe; **Finger Print is Clew**."

As we now know, young George Hodel whose photo is seen immediately adjacent to the murder reportage, will grow up not to become either a concert pianist or poet, but rather—a serial killer. One of his favorite *modus operandi* being to crush his victims skulls by way of blunt force trauma. (Elizabeth "Black Dahlia" Short, Jeanne "Red Lipstick Murder" French, 1950 tape-recorded assault victim Jane Doe at the Franklin House *using a pipe,* etc.)

Also, note the journalist's use of the **then common spelling of** the word "**Clew**." George Hodel in his later employment as a crime reporter for the *L.A. Record* newspaper in the Twenties, **will use this same spelling** and even continue its use in some of his mailings to the press through the 1960s and 1970s as Zodiac. (November 9, 1969, "Death Machine Letter" sent to San Francisco Chronicle: "If you wonder why I was wipeing (sic) the cab down I was leaving fake clews for the police to run all over town with...")

Further note the *Evening Herald's* description of Georgie as "this little French boy..."

French was the Hodel family's first language at home and obviously because of his fluency, the reporter assumed he was born in France rather than America.

Both of his parents, though Russian-born, spoke fluent French from living in France before coming to the US through Ellis Island in 1901. (Recall, that in the Jeanne French murder in 1947, the waitress/ witness, the last person to see her alive, informed police that "when I served them dinner, the suspect was speaking French with the victim just before they left the restaurant together.")

Russian Architect Alexander Zelenko
A Birthday Present

Los Angeles Times
October 15, 1922

(article on next page 42)

BOY'S HOME IS PLANNED BY RUSSIAN

Famous Architect Decides to Remain in City After Completing Work

BY ALMA WHITAKER

Not many boys can boast that a famous architect came over from Russia to build them a house as a fifteenth birthday present.

This was the distinction which fell upon young George Hill Hodel, who attained his fifteenth birthday on the 10th inst. and fell heir on the same day to a beautiful Swiss-Russian residence high on the hill at 6512 Walnut Hill avenue, built and completed by M. Alexander Zelenko of Moscow to the day.

M. Zelenko, life-long friend of M. and Madame G. Hodel, was invited to come to this country six months ago for this purpose—to build a worthy house for their son. The result is a most interesting structure comprising nine rooms, and two oriental outdoor rooms. Terraced gardens lead up to the house, which is a last-word model of modern efficiency although outwardly having all the charm of the old Russian and Swiss architecture.

Everything inside, including the heating arrangements, work by electricity—a mere pressed button warms any room. An unusual feature is a sunken fireplace with inglenooks, framed in Russian carving.

M. Zelenko is an artist as well as an architect, and four hand-painted panels of great beauty bear witness to his skill in the main living-room.

M. Zelenko is not a stranger to the United States, having been deputied with a mission from the Czar's government in 1913 to visit Europe and America to study educational methods. His report in book form graces the Russian archives today. When the Bolsheviks came into power M. Zelenko was offered the portfolio of the Ministry of Education, but being out of sympathy with the Bolsheviks, he declined in favor of Maxim Gorky, his friend, who now holds it.

And now he is so enamored of California that he has built a home in the Japanese style, replete with faithful detail, where he intends living with his charming wife on Walnut Hill—never to return to Russia as a subject.

On October 15, 1922, just five days after my father's fifteenth birthday, the following article (column on 243 and retyped below) appeared in the *Los Angeles Times*. Written by Alma Whitaker, the newspaper's immensely popular and nationally syndicated columnist whose career with the paper would span some thirty-three years.

BOY'S HOME IS PLANNED BY RUSSIAN

Famous Architect Decides to Remain in City After Completing Work

By Alma Whitaker

Not many boys can boast that a famous architect came over from Russia to build them a house as a fifteenth birthday present.

This was the distinction which fell upon young George Hill Hodel, who attained his fifteenth birthday on the 10th inst. (sic) and fell heir on the same day to a beautiful Swiss-Russian residence high on the hill at 6512 Walnut Hill Avenue. Built and completed by M. Alexander Zelenko of Moscow to the day.

M. Zelenko, life-long friend of M. and Madame G. Hodel, was invited to come to this country six months ago, for this purpose—to build a worthy house for their son.

The result is a most interesting structure comprising nine rooms and two oriental outdoor rooms. Terraced gardens lead up to the house, which is a last-word model of modern efficiency although outwardly having all the charm of the old Russian and Swiss architecture.

Everything inside, including the heating arrangements, work by electricity—a mere pressed button warms any room. An unusual feature is a sunken fireplace with inglenooks, framed in Russian carving.

M. Zelenko is an artist as well as an architect, and four hand-painted panels of great beauty bear witness to his skill in the main living room.

M. Zelenko is not a stranger to the United States, having been deputed with a mission from the Czar's government in 1913 to visit Europe and America to study educational methods. His report in book form graces the Russian archives today. When the Bolsheviks came into power M. Zelenko was offered the portfolio of the Ministry of Education, but being out of sympathy with the Bolsheviks, he declined in favor of Maxim Gorky, his friend, who now holds it.

And now he is so enamored of California that he has built a home in the Japanese style, replete with faithful detail, where he intends living with his charming wife on Walnut Hill—never to return to Russia as a subject.

(**Author's Note - Ms. Whitaker** gives the Hodel residence address as "6512 Walnut Hill Avenue." The street name would later be changed to its current address of, 6512 Monterey Road.)

Left: Esther Leov Hodel, George Hodel's mother and the author's grandmother, circa 1912.

Below: This Hodel family photograph was taken circa 1917 at the Hodel residence in South Pasadena. It depicts composer Sergei Rachmaninov seated between the Russian minister of culture and his wife (possibly the Zelenkos).

**Georgie Hodel played piano for composer
Sergei Rachmaninov at Hodel residence**

[Left] **Alexander Ustinovich Zelenko (1871-1953)**
[Right] **George Hodel, Sr. (1873-1954)**

"M. Zelenko, was a life-long friend of
M. and Madame G. Hodel"

L.A. Times Columnist Alma Whitaker, 1922

Here is a brief biography of the Russian architect, Alexander Zelenko. (Excerpted from Wikipedia)

Alexander Zelenko grew up in Saint Petersburg, Russia. Graduated from Saint Petersburg Civil Engineers Institute in 1892, and trained in Vienna and Moscow. In 1899 he relocated to Samara, where he brought Art Nouveau to the town and received numerous commissions as "Town Architect."

"After the Russian Revolution of 1917, and until his death in 1953, Zelenko worked in various Soviet educational institutions, notably in setting architectural standards for schools and kindergartens. Zelenko collaborated in the Museum Commission (1919-1931) designing exhibitions for children (1925-1929). He died in Russia in 1953."

French Government Bldg, Moscow

Society House, Moscow

Recreational Hall, Moscow

Syrian Embassy, Moscow

A few Alexander Zelenko designed buildings in Moscow

The 1922
Zelenko Built Hodel Residence
and "Tea House"

So, from the early *L.A. Times* newspaper article, we learn that Alexander Zelenko, one of Russia's most admired architects is a "lifelong friend of the Hodel's." He has come to Los Angeles to build the main home and **a separate "tea house"** specifically **built as** the **private residence of fifteen-year-old, Georgie who** *has graduated from high school* **and is enrolled and has** *just begun his studies* at one of the world's most prestigious universities (then and now), Pasadena's *California Institute of Technology* (*Caltech*).

Let's take a look at both the exterior and interior of my grandfather's home as it appeared a decade ago.

In 2005, the home was listed for sale and was unoccupied and "on the market." At that time I was able to take a quick walk through and obtained some photographs. Though in disrepair, the eighty-three-year-old home still had a feeling of grandeur and remarkably, some of Zelenko's personal paintings yet remained on the walls and ceiling and his original highly decorative fireplace appeared unchanged. Let's take a look.

Hodel Residence and Tea House, 6512 Monterey Road (City Cultural Monument No. 802)

Main House. Black arrow marks front deck of George Jr.'s elevated separate "Tea House" residence

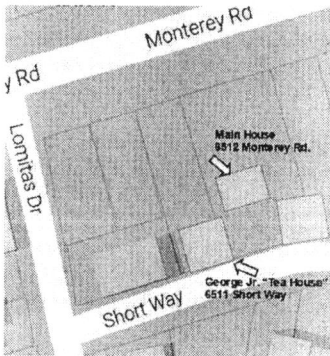

In another, "You can't make this stuff up" irony, my father's 1922 "Tea House" residence (built behind the main house) had its own street address of 6511 SHORT WAY! (Short being the name of George Hodel's most famous victim, Elizabeth "Black Dahlia" Short, whom he will brutally murder some twenty-five years later.)

L.A. Historian/Preservationist Charlie Fisher
L.A. City Cultural Designation at street front.

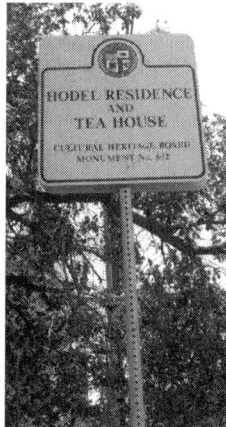

Thanks to the hard work and tireless effort of CHARLIE FISHER, a Northeast L.A. historian and preservationist, and president of the *Highland Park Heritage Trust*, the "Hodel Residence and Tea House" was declared Historic-Cultural Monument No. 802 by the Los Angeles City Council on June 1, 2005. The exterior/interior photos of my grandfather's home and my father's "Tea House 15th Birthday Present" were taken by me in 2005. (To be clear, the cultural designation was approved by Los Angeles City solely due to the fame and world class status and to honor Russian architect, Alexander Zelenko, *and not* because of the later infamy of Dr. George Hill Hodel as a world-class serial killer.)

The Tea House - 6511 Short Way (Built higher on the hillside with an entrance off Short Way.)

George Hodel, Jr.'s "Tea House" 6511 Short Way (street fronts rear of the large land parcel). Gifted to my father on his fifteenth birthday. (Photos were taken by the author in 2005. The home was in disrepair and on the market in "as is" condition pending future remodel by potential new owners.)

View of Main House from George Jr.'s "Tea House" deck

Main House viewed from street level on Monterey Road

Unique Zelenko-designed chimney atop Main House

Main House Interiors (Zelenko Art)

Original Alexander Zelenko 1922 decorative panel paintings remain on walls and ceiling of the main house as well as unique tiled fireplace in living room. The artist/architect's use of beautiful soft pastel colors (green, blue, pink) to enhance his artwork sadly are lost in these black-and-white photographs.

To my eye, Zelenko's paintings are highly fantastical. Colorful peacocks, a winged creepy-crawly, and a snakelike creature with initials, lettering, or a sentence that has become unreadable over time.

Zelenko's artwork is so unusual that I find myself questioning its meaning and its signage. Is it Whimsy, Fantasy, Mythology, a secret fraternity such as Freemasons or the Order of Rosicrucian's? Quite mysterious.

In attempting to decipher the letters on the body of the "snake" they appear to read:

A DRE - -- -- C ------n S-----R R O +

Sun/Moon House on a Hill painting on the wall in Tea House. I believe this is also a Zelenko original. However, I cannot rule out the possibility that fifteen-year-old George Jr., painted it?

In further researching Alexander Zelenko, I chanced upon the following additional Los *Angeles Times* article, *Activities and Interests of Women, in and Outside of Homes.* It was written by Myra Nye and dated, December 20, 1922. This article, following my father's "Birthday Present" article by just two months, underscores the close friendship between the Zelenkos and the Hodels.

Three puppet plays, adapted from folk and fairy stories, charmed an invited audience of persons prominent in club and art circles Sunday at the home of Mr. and Mrs. George Hodel, 6512 Walnut Hill Avenue. The doll folk, under the direction of Mr. Alexander Zelenko, formerly of the University of Moscow, Russia, went through their parts as if they enjoyed their drolleries, and with the artistic and characteristic heads and costumes, and elaborate scenery, all suited to the background of each act, brought forth much enthusiastic applause.

In a preliminary talk, Mrs. Clara V. Winlow, author of children's books, briefly sketched the history of puppets, and emphasized their educational value.

The Petrushka puppets (Petrushka is Russian for Punch) as they call themselves promise something new to those interested in children's entertainment.

Nuestro Pueblo (Our Town)
Charles Owens and Joe Seewerker

Nuestro Pueblo was a popular weekly column that ran in the *Los Angeles Times* from 1938 to 1940.

The column was a team effort by staff writer Joe Seewerker and artist/illustrator Charles Owens. Owens did the art and Seewerker provided the research and wrote the historical text.

The column featured various notable locations throughout Los Angeles ("Our Town") and provided a short folksy and conversational history lesson along with Owens' fabulous illustrations.

So popular was the duo's column that two years later, *Nuestro Pueblo: Los Angeles, City of Romance* (Houghton Mifflin Co. 1940) was published in book form which included a compilation of 184 of their 1938-1940 historic stories and sketches. (Though now long out-of-print, I highly recommend all Angelenophiles and history lovers, try and obtain a copy of the book. Charles Owens' sketches complemented by Joe Seewerker's research are pure magic.)

L.A. *Times* **columnist's two-year series of historical text and sketches published in book form in 1940**

On September 7, 1938, my grandfather's home was featured in their *Los Angeles Times* column, entitled, *A Russian Architect in Action.*

The original article is reproduced below. Note that Owens' sketch also includes George Jr.'s "Tea House".

NUESTRO PUEBLO

By JOE SEEWERKER and CHARLES OWENS

A RUSSIAN ARCHITECT IN ACTION

Some years ago a gentleman with banking connections looked over the thousand and one types of houses which have been constructed in Los Angeles and decided he wanted something different from all of them.

So he imported a Russian architect, showed him a plot of ground in the 6500 block on Monterey Road and told him to go to it.

The result was a house which passers-by still view with awe. Believing he should make some concessions to the warm Southern California climate, the architect stuck a half-dozen balconies on various outside sections of the house, then threw in a few cupolas for good measure.

Inside, remembering the cold of Siberia, he built two huge sunken fireplaces which were —and are—capable of warming a barracks. For a delicate touch he went out and bought a truckload of man-sized grapevines and used the vines in decorating the inner walls. Then

he hired twelve carpenters and kept them busy for three months cutting filigree patterns which he placed where his fancy dictated.

The finished house was surprisingly attractive, but rather startling to anyone entering it unwarned. The present owner, Stanton Fraser, says the result stunned the original owner somewhat so that he did not protest when the Russian architect, imbued with the building fever, pointed to a lot of lumber which was left over and said: "Now I'll build you another house from that."

The second house was as unusual in design and as full of queer gadgets as the first. Built close to the first, it is of Chinese design. Or at least Mr. Fraser thinks it is Chinese.

"The Russian again took up the grape motif," says Mr. Fraser. "Only in the Chinese house he used a growing grapevine to decorate the living-room. He must have had an erotic eye also, because he decorated the bathroom with paintings of nude women."

In reading Mr. Seewerker's history lesson on the house, we learn the name of the present (1938) owner is "Stanton Fraser." Fraser obviously bought it from my grandfather just a few years prior, whom Seewerker refers to as, "a gentleman with banking connections."

I have not conducted a property search on the house, but expect my grandfather likely sold the home around the time of his wife, Esther's death in 1935. (Grandmother died in a rest home after suffering some years from tuberculosis.)

At the close of the article the present owner, Mr. Fraser, comments on "The Russian" (George Hodel, Sr.) and the separate residence which he calls the "Chinese House." As follows:

> "He [Hodel Sr.] must have had an erotic eye also, because he decorated the bathroom with paintings of nude women."

Of course, we now know, what Mr. Fraser did not— that the paintings in the bathroom would not have come from the "erotic eye" of the father, *but rather, the son.*

 The boy genius with the erotic eye who had recently had the sex scandal with the Caltech professor's wife and after one year had been asked to leave the university. The same boy with the erotic eye who at seventeen and editor-in-chief, had just penned his Dedication to his about-to-publish magazine, *Fantasia,* which read:

> To the portrayal of bizarre beauty in the arts, to the delineation of the stranger harmonies and the rarer fragrances, do we dedicate this, our magazine.

Such beauty as we may find in a poem, a sketch, or a medley of colors; ...or the noises of a city street; in a temple or a brothel or a gaol, in prayer or perversity or sin.

Introduction to Rod Serling's *Twilight Zone*

There is a fifth dimension beyond that which is known to man. It is a dimension as vast as space and as timeless as infinity. It is the middle ground between light and shadow, between science and superstition, and it lies between the pit of man's fears, and the summit of his knowledge. This is the dimension of imagination. It is an area which we call...*The Twilight Zone.*

Just three weeks following the *Nuestro Pueblo* (September 7, 1938) publication (shown on pages 57-58) that featured my grandfather and my father's private homes in the Northeast section of Los Angeles, the article (shown on page 61) appeared in the same column.

On October 3, 1938, Messrs. Owens and Seewerker presented Angelenos with another remarkable home, this time a "Hollywood Showplace."

NUESTRO PUEBLO

By JOE SEEWERKER and CHARLES OWENS

HOLLYWOOD SHOW PLACE

There is an edifice at 5121 Franklin avenue which sure makes persons from the hinterland stop and stare on their trip to Hollywood.

The edifice—you might call it a mansion, if you favor words like that—was built in 1927 by Lloyd Wright, the architect, for a retired gentleman of means who wanted something different. He got it.

"It's the sculptural style of architecture," explains Mr. Wright.

Sculptural architecture, it seems, fits the building right into the landscape.

One of the striking features of the Franklin-avenue structure is the mass of stone and cement which projects out from the roof line.

"My goodness, I wouldn't want to live in a place like that," one viewer gasped. "That darned stuff might come tumbling down on you while you was trying to open them gates to get in the house."

"Them gates" are huge, iron affairs constituting what would be the door into an ordinary home. There is no danger of the mass of stone and cement tumbling down. The entire building is constructed of steel placed both horizontally and vertically.

The inside of the building is as striking as the outside. One of its features is a huge patio with a fountain in the center. Rooms in the building are built around the patio and the fountain.

When this article was written in 1938, the Sowden House was already a famous Los Angeles landmark. Built a decade earlier in 1926 by Frank Lloyd Wright, Jr. (Lloyd Wright), it was a real show stopper.

A huge Mayan Temple in an upscale part of Hollywood. Passersby both on foot and in their vehicles literally stopped and stared in wonderment at this magnificent home. Truly, something right out of a Hollywood Set.

However, far more amazing is what lay hidden in this Hollywood Show Place's future. The house was just entering its teens, still innocent and naïve. However, in another decade it would reach its manhood and be forced to silently witness some unimaginable horrors.

Seven years forward, in 1945, the "Hollywood Show Place" would be purchased by one of Los Angeles's most prominent physicians, Dr. George Hill Hodel.

Dr. Hodel, at that time was Chief Venereal Disease Control Officer for the L.A. County Health Department and owner of the *First Street Clinic* at First Street and Central in downtown Los Angeles.

That same year, his beautiful screenwriter wife, Dorothy Huston Hodel, now divorced from the famous film director and married to George, (Huston's longtime friend) along with George's three sons, Michael, age six, Steven (myself), age four, and our younger brother, Kelvin, age three, all moved into what we would call, "The Franklin House."

Two years later, on January 15, 1947, this Hollywood Show Place, now just entering manhood at age twenty-one, would be forced to watch in cold stone silence as its owner, George Hodel performed a surgical torture-murder and committed what would become Los Angeles's most infamous crime: The slaying and bisection of Elizabeth "Black Dahlia"

Short. (Later secret DA Files would reveal that Dorothy and we three sons were away and stayed with her brother, our uncle, for that three-week period, leaving our father ostensibly alone at the home.)

Another two years would pass and a new crime would be committed inside its walls. This time child molestation and incest. George, with three adults (his lifelong friend, Fred Sexton, who was a regular visitor at the Franklin House, along with two adult females), would have sexual intercourse in the master bedroom with his daughter, and my half-sister, Tamar. (Three months later, in October 1949, George Hodel would be arrested by LAPD for incest and child molestation. He hired criminal defense attorney Jerry Giesler, the Johnny Cochran of that day, and would "beat the case" in a three-week O.J.-like jury trial. Fifty-three years later, my investigation would uncover hidden DA Files that suggested that a $15,000 payoff was made to the DA's office to gain his acquittal.)

A *Twilight Zone* scenario? Absolutely.

In 1971 this "Hollywood Show Place" was added to the National Register of Historic Places and in 2003 it was designated a Los Angeles Historic-Cultural Monument No. 762.

Again, the historic designation did not derive from the fact that it was the actual crime scene location of LA's most infamous murder of the "Black Dahlia" and the fact that its owner was her killer. No, the cultural designation for our former home, both locally and nationally, was to honor its architect/builder, Frank

Lloyd Wright, Jr., for his "striking and innovative style."

At Wright's death in 1978, Ted Thackery, Jr., staff writer for the *Los Angeles Times* in writing the obituary *"Services Pending for Lloyd Wright, 88, Creator of Diverse L.A. Landmarks"* recognized the Franklin House as one of Wright's most accomplished designs, writing, "the cultic, brooding Sowden house which critics have hailed as the apogee of his residential work."

A Late-Night Call
Rumors Inside the Palace Walls

In March 2001, I received a telephone call from my half-sister, Tamar. It was late in the evening and Tamar called to tell me that she had just spoken to our brother, Kelly. She had called to ask him if he was going to attend the special tribute to the singer John Phillips. (Former husband of Tamar's close friend, Michelle Phillips, who is godmother to Tamar's three sons.) The tribute had been hastily scheduled at the Roxy Theatre in Los Angeles after his sudden death from a heart attack, just days earlier.

We spoke of various things, and the subject then turned to family. Armed with the new information related to grandfather, I realized in our previous talks, I had never really discussed our grandfather George, Sr., or his wife, Esther, with Tamar.

This led to other questions and what follows is a verbatim summary of Tamar's remarkable statements related to me on that March night in 2001. (Keep in mind that at the time of this conversation, though I had been conducting my ongoing investigation approaching two years it yet remained completely secret from family and friends. All Tamar and the others knew and believed was that I was in the process of gathering information for a book about my career with the LAPD.)

Tamar Nais Hodel circa 2001
(Tamar passed away on October 3, 2015, at age 80)

The Tamar conversation / her words:

"I didn't like grandfather, Steven. He was a bad man. He always reminded me of a little fat toad. He molested me at the Franklin House when I was eleven. Yes, it's true. He was touching me and then he took out his penis and was playing with himself."

"I don't really know a lot about him. I just didn't like him. I think he was born in Turkey. You know Hodel isn't our real name. When he went to Paris he picked it. I remember they were talking once and I heard the name, but I don't recall what it was. It sounded kind of like a Russian name, but I think it was Turkish. My middle name, Nais, is Turkish. No, I think you're wrong about him coming from Russia. Maybe we could get a birth certificate and find out for sure?"

(**SKH Note**: As I indicated, in 2001, I was keeping my ongoing investigation secret from everyone, including Tamar, but had already obtained our grandfather's birth certificate.)

"I remember something about him [George, Sr.] and others taking money from the Czar's Treasury. They sneaked it out of the country or something. Grandfather supposedly opened a bank in New York with the money they got from the Czar. That's what I remember, something about getting money out of Russia. I don't remember who I heard it from. Maybe dad or him or someone, but it was supposed to have happened.

"Do you remember his second wife? Her name was Andre. She played the piano at the Franklin House. You don't remember? How can you not remember Andre? Yes, I know where my name came from. Father chose it from the writings of the poet Robinson Jeffers. Jeffers wrote this poem called, *The Roan Stallion and Tamar*.

"It's all about incest. In the poem that *Tamar* has sex with both her father and her brother."

The Tamar conversation / I learned:

So then, within a brief thirty-minute telephone conversation with my half-sister, I learn dramatic new disclosures about the Hodel family history. She informs me that her namesake *Tamar* originates from a poem involving incest with a father and brother! That Tamar was molested by our grandfather at age eleven. That George, Sr. may have been involved with others in a scheme to steal money from the Czar's treasury, and have it smuggled out of Russia, possibly to France, where he and his confederates may have devised a plan to get the money and or jewels from Europe to New York where it was possibly used to fund and open a bank! (What seemingly adds weight and validity to Tamar's unexpected revelations is the fact that to my knowledge, I was the only living Hodel relative that possessed the knowledge and documentation that grandfather, shortly after arriving in Los Angeles, listed his profession on his son's 1907 birth certificate as "Banker," which prior to Tamar's disclosure simply made no sense.)

Tamar's disclosures force us to question what exactly were the Goldgefter-Leov-Hodel-Troubetzkoy-Zelenko-Rachmaninov connections? Friends certainly, but what else? Was the connection fiduciary? Were these prominent Russians, known to be high-ranking members and several of them actual "ministers" of the monarchy, involved in some secret cabal? Did they conspire and were they successful in helping smuggle out some of the royal treasury from

Russia, before the revolution and the Czar's execution in 1918? Did these same men reunite in Paris for some certain years, then proceed with a second plan to get some of the Czar's treasury out of Europe and into the United States?

Did my grandfather, as a respected Los Angeles businessman and supporter of the arts, help influence the decision and tilt the scale to ensure that the $50,000 commission for the Harrison Gray Otis statue was awarded to his close friend, Prince Paul Troubetzkoy?

Tamar's disclosures coupled with the deeper knowledge we now have of my grandparents' friendships and connections to people of wealth and power could well explain his ability to:

1. Immigrate to and through Ellis Island accompanied by his household servants.

2. Commission one of Russia's leading architects, A.U. Zelenko, to design and build him an opulent home in the prestigious Garvanza section of Los Angeles. A man of such influence that he was offered the position of Russian Minister of Education.

> "When the Bolsheviks came into power M. Zelenko was offered the portfolio of the Ministry of Education, but being out of sympathy with the Bolsheviks, he declined in favor of Maxim Gorky, his friend, who now holds it."
>
> Alma Whitaker
> *L.A. Times* article (October 15, 1922)
> "Boys Home Is Planned By Russian"

3. Obviously, grandfather, George Hodel Sr. in his letter to ex-President Theodore Roosevelt would have mentioned his close friendship with Prince Paul Troubetzkoy and that George Sr.'s son and wife had been in residence with them in Paris, and were now returning home on the *Kaiser Wilhelm*. George Sr.'s request, to be allowed to ride out on the US Customs boat to meet and surprise his son, when coupled with the Troubetzkoy entrée, would not have seemed that unusual particularly since Paul had just sculpted the bust of Teddy's cousin, the young FDR, the year prior (see page 33).

(Backgrounded as we now are, one must wonder could this short-lived adventure of a school boy's return from Paris, actually itself have been a "cover" for smuggling in more stolen goods from the Czar's Treasury? With grandfather's letter in hand from Theodore Roosevelt, the former President of the United States, does anyone think for a moment that his son's or wife's personal effects would be searched by the Customs' Officers?)

In this connection, additional research has now shown that there existed a further direct link between Prince Paul Troubetzkoy and Franklin D. Roosevelt, cousin to Teddy. I quote from a press briefing mentioned earlier by Mike McCurry dated October 23, 1995, on the occasion of a meeting between President Clinton and Russian President Yeltsin at the Roosevelt family library in Hyde Park, New York.

> As the two Presidents entered the house, President Clinton showed President Yeltsin a life-sized bronze sculpture of Franklin Roosevelt at the age of 29 that

was completed in 1911 by a Russian sculptor, Prince Paul Troubetzkoy. You can—there are probably different ways to transliterate that—Prince Paul Troubetzkoy, who is the son of a Russian diplomat, if memory serves me right. The artist's brother, Pierre, painted a portrait of Sarah Roosevelt, Franklin Roosevelt's mother, which President Clinton also showed to President Yeltsin as they walked into the library." (The bronze statue was commissioned by Roosevelt's grandmother, Nelly Blodgett. on the occasion of FDR's entrance into politics as a New York State legislator.)

4. Grandfather's ability to finance father's education first at Caltech, then pre-med at Berkeley, and finally medical school at the University of California at San Francisco. All of these vast expenses occurring at the height of the Great Depression!

5. The below pictured family photograph was given to me by my grandfather's third wife, Alice Hodel. It shows George Sr.'s (white arrow) attendance at a formal white tie dinner. Written on the back of the photo, "1500 delegates from the world over, seated at table #47, next to the President's table." The photograph was presumably taken in Paris, as it bears a stamp, "*The New York Times*, Wide World Photos, 37 Rue Caumartin, Paris." (With the mention of "1500 delegates and the President" I assumed it referred to the Paris Peace Talks of 1920. However, Grandfather at that time would have been forty-seven, and in this photo to my eye, he appears considerably older?)

6. Grandfather's large, and as my mother told it, "Celebrity-like funeral" in 1954, where a large gathering of unknown mourners came to pay their final respects. Was this unexpected homage by so many friends their way of recognizing and turning out to pay respect to a man who had been their friend and more? Perhaps, a man who also provided some secret but very silent service?

With this inclusion of my grandparents' circle of prominent friends from the turn of the century forward, we shall see if any new truths surface, or perhaps, like so many other questions, these will simply remain unanswered as *enigmatic riddles wrapped in mysteries.*

Grandparents George (1873-1954) and Esther Hodel (1873-1935) gravesite at Forrest Lawn Cemetery in Glendale, California. Gravestones laid side by side read, "Until the day break, and the shadows flee away" a partial quote from *Song of Solomon.*

Until the day break and the shadows flee, turn, my beloved, and be thou like a roe or like a young hart on the mountains of Bether.

Song of Solomon 2:17
(King James Version)

Before the day breeze blows and the shadows flee, turn about, my love; be like a gazelle or a young stag upon the jagged mountains.

Song of Solomon 2:17
(Common English Bible)

Chapter 2

George Hodel - South Pasadena High 1922-23

As the workmen feverishly hammered away on the two new homes under construction on Monterey Road, hoping to meet the October deadline of George, Jr's fifteenth birthday—the young genius had other matters on his mind.

In **June 1923** he had **graduated from South Pasadena High School** and just two months later the **fifteen-year-old,** after having **achieved** the *highest public education test scores in all of California,* was enrolled and would be **beginning** his **freshman year at** the *California Institute of Technology* (**Caltech**) in Pasadena.

His junior and senior high school years had been good ones. Active, with lots of pressure, but he had persisted and won!

As a fourteen year old junior, holding the 1922 South Pasadena High School Yearbook, *Copa De Oro* in his hand, he could page through to his name and read the printed description of his many accomplishments.

> "Honor Roll, Latin Club, Debating, Short Story Contests, Spelling Contests, Economics Club, Senior Class Play, Staff Reporter for the school's newspaper, *The Tiger*."

I can see him smiling as he read his classmates' description of him:

"Adjective that best describes him - INTELLIGENT."

"By-word that best describes him - MYSELF."

South Pasadena Year Book 1922 George Hodel age 14

**George Hodel (lower left) three-year member of the
high school Debating Team**

George would have been particularly proud of the fact that he had entered and won not one, *but two* Short Essay contests, both of which were published in successive yearbooks.

Free to choose his subject, in his Junior year young George opted to write about-DEATH.

Here is that first essay as published in the Year Book.

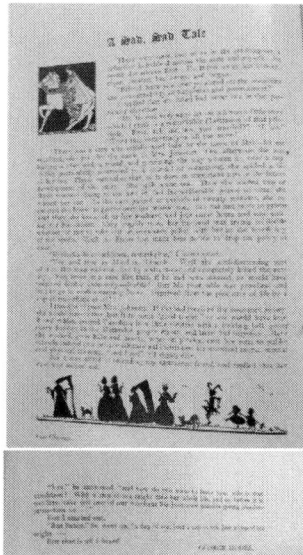

South Pasadena High Yearbook

A Sad, Sad Tale

There were only two of us in the smoking-car, a reflective individual across the aisle and myself. He broke the silence first. He threw away his five-cent cigar, crossed his knees, and began:

"Friend, have you ever pondered on the instability and commutability of happiness and contentment?"

I replied that my mind had never run in that particular direction.

"Ah, 'tis sad, very sad—let me tell you a little story which I think is a remarkable illustration of that principle. First, tell me, are you married?"

"I am."

"Then this concerns you all the more."

"There was a very nice middle-aged lady by the name of Mrs. —let me recollect, oh—yes—by the name of Mrs. Johnson. One afternoon she was having a visit with a friend, and gossiping, the way women do, over a cup of her tea. Please remember that, as it does an important part in the future development of the story. She spilt some tea. Thus she waited two or three minutes fixing it up, and in this inconsiderable period of time, she missed her car. As the cars passed at periods of twenty minutes, she reentered the house to grieve over her misfortune. But she had more to grieve over than she knew of, as her husband had just come home and was waiting for his dinner. Very angrily now, her husband was trying to decide whether or not to take out an insurance policy with her as the beneficiary of the spoils. Well, no dinner had made him decide to drop the policy at once."

"Remarkable coincidence, remarkable," I interrupted.

"Yes, and true as Abraham Lincoln. Well, the soul-distressing part of it is, this man was run over by a street-car and completely killed the next day. You know in a case like that, if he had been insured, he would have received double indemnity—double! But his poor wife was penniless and had to go to work sweeping floors. Deprived from the pleasures of life by a cup of tea—think of it."

I thought of poor Mrs. Johnson. If she had received the insurance money, she would have either lost it to some "good tipper," or she would have kept it and ridden around Pasadena in a little electric with a tinkling bell, going every Sunday to the Methodist prayer meets, and lived 'till fifty-five. Here she worked, grew hale and hearty, went on picnics, sent her sons to public schools instead of a private educational institution for excellent moral, mental and physical training," "and lived" 'til eighty-five.

But I was afraid of offending my distressed friend and replied that her case was indeed sad.

"Yes," he answered, "and now do you want to leave your wife in that condition? Why a cup of tea might ruin her whole life, and so, before it is too late, take out one of our excellent life insurance policies giving absolute protection to—

But I started out.

"But listen," he went on, "a cup of tea, just a cup of tea, just a cup of tea might—

But that is all I heard.

GEORGE HODEL

And here is George Hodel's second winning short story published this time in the 1922 Senior Class Yearbook.

As before, free to select his own subject matter young George Hodel chose *again* to write about—DEATH.

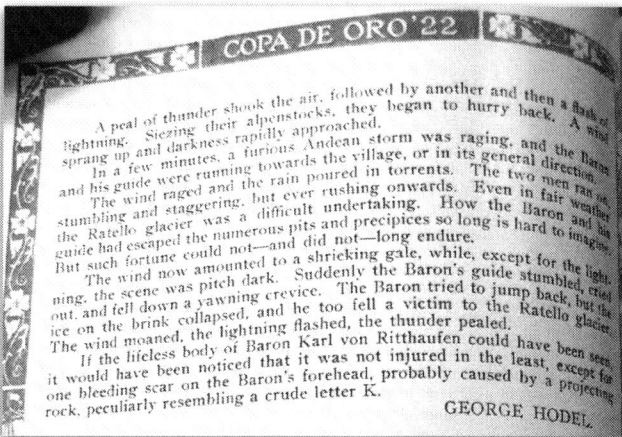

A peal of thunder shook the air, followed by another and then a flash of lightning. Siezing their alpenstocks, they began to hurry back. A wind sprang up and darkness rapidly approached.

In a few minutes, a furious Andean storm was raging, and the Baron and his guide were running towards the village, or in its general direction. The wind raged and the rain poured in torrents. The two men ran on, stumbling and staggering, but ever rushing onwards. Even in fair weather the Ratello glacier was a difficult undertaking. How the Baron and his guide had escaped the numerous pits and precipices so long is hard to imagine.

But such fortune could not—and did not—long endure.

The wind now amounted to a shrieking gale, while, except for the lightning, the scene was pitch dark. Suddenly the Baron's guide stumbled, cried out, and fell down a yawning crevice. The Baron tried to jump back, but the ice on the brink collapsed, and he too fell a victim to the Ratello glacier.

The wind moaned, the lightning flashed, the thunder pealed.

If the lifeless body of Baron Karl von Ritthaufen could have been seen, it would have been noticed that it was not injured in the least, except for one bleeding scar on the Baron's forehead, probably caused by a projecting rock, peculiarly resembling a crude letter K.

GEORGE HODEL

South Pasadena High Yearbook, 1922

Untitled Second Essay

A peal of thunder shook the air, followed by another and then a flash of lightning. Siezing (sic) their alpenstocks, they began to hurry back. A wind sprang up and darkness rapidly approached.

In a few minutes, a furious Andean storm was raging, and the Baron and his guide were running towards the village, or in its general direction.

The wind raged and the rain poured in torrents. The two men ran on, stumbling and staggering, but ever rushing onwards. Even in fair weather the Ratello glacier was a difficult undertaking. How the Baron and his guide had escaped the numerous pits and precipices so long is hard to imagine.

But such fortune could not—and did not—long endure.

The wind now amounted to a shrieking gale, while, except for the lightning, the scene was pitch dark. Suddenly the Baron's guide stumbled, cried out, and fell down a yawning crevice. The Baron tried to jump back, but the ice on the brink collapsed, and he too fell a victim to the Ratello glacier.

The wind moaned, the lightning flashed, the thunder pealed.

If the lifeless body of Baron Karl von Ritthaufen could have been seen, it would have been noticed that it was not injured in the least, except for one bleeding scar on the Baron's forehead, probably caused by a projecting rock, peculiarly resembling a crude letter K.

GEORGE HODEL

(**SKH Note** - I did not discover the yearbooks until making a trip to *South Pasadena High* circa 2006. In first reading this short story, and discovering my father's use of irony to connect Baron Karl's death injury made to form the letter "K" (for Karl) my mind immediately jumped forward from the fourteen-year-old's 1922 essay some twenty-five years to his 1947 murder of victim Jeanne French. In that crime, as the "Black Dahlia Avenger," after beating her to death with a tire iron, and posing her nude body in a vacant lot, he removed a red lipstick tube from her purse and wrote the letters, "Fuck You, B.D." As we know, this same need to leave special taunting and ironic messages on or near his victims' bodies would become a major crime signature throughout his serial killings.)

Senior Class Play

The Yellow Jacket

"Craft, guided by cruelty, outweighs vulgar manliness.
I must contrive to destroy his honesty and cleanness of life."

Wu Fan Din (Daffodil)
(From Play, *The Yellow Jacket*)

The South Pasadena High's Drama Instructor had made the decision.

The Senior Class would perform *The Yellow Jacket: A Chinese Play Done in A Chinese Manner in Three Acts*. Written by George C. Hazelton and Benrimo, the play had opened a decade earlier in New York.

Though much younger than his classmates, cast in one of the lead roles would be George Hodel who would play Wu Fan Din (Daffodil). Though there was no way the drama teacher could have known it, as we shall soon learn, George was perfect typecasting.

Here is a brief description of the play from *Opera in a Multicultural World: Coloniality, Culture,*

Performance (Routledge 2015) Edited by Mary Ingraham, Joseph So, Roy Moodley...

The trope of "Chinese opera" was used often in yellowface dramas, which became popular toward the end of the nineteenth century. George Hazelton's play *The Yellow Jacket,* was particularly famous for its depiction of Chinese theater in San Francisco. Premiered in 1912 in New York, it soon won critical acclaim in Europe, with more than two hundred performances in London alone; it was also performed and revived in the subsequent decades frequently in the rest of the US (Harbeck 1996; Kim 2010). Advertised as a "Chinese Drama Played in [the] Chinese Manner," it purportedly employed the "stage convention" of the Chinese opera such as huge lanterns, an orchestra of cymbals and gongs, a "Property Man", etc. Not surprisingly, one of the two most popular characters in *The Yellow Jacket* was an effeminate male role, Wu Fan Din (Daffodil), whose opening lines are "I advise this honorable audience that I am a man, though I possess a daffodil nature. I go to view delightful embroideries, but retard my footsteps, that you may observe my charm...I possess feminine qualities of great luxuriance" (Hazelton *et al* 1913, 62-63). A review of the premiere considered him "a creature of such rarefied culture and delicacy that he seemed almost too frailly flowerlike to be human" (The New York Times 1912). Schuyler Ladd perfected this effeminate role and returned regularly in nearly every revival well into 1930s such that a New York Times article featuring him was entitled "The Perennial Daffodil" (1929).

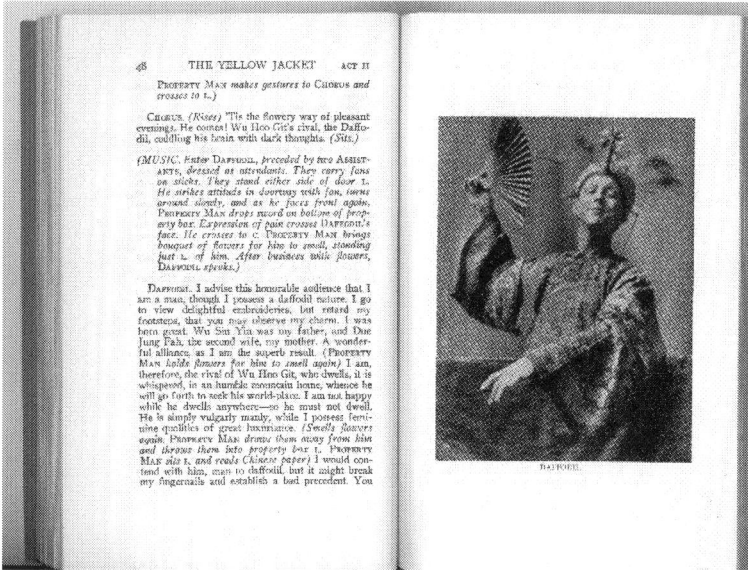

Unnamed actor (possibly Schuyler Ladd) seen here in the role of Daffodil from an early printing of the play.

Let Daffodil introduce himself to us directly from his entrance lines in the original play, **Act II**:

> (MUSIC. *Enter* **DAFFODIL**, *preceded by two* ASSISTANTS, *dressed as attendants. They carry fans on sticks. They stand either side of door L. He strikes attitude in doorway with fan, turns around slowly, and as he faces front again,* PROPERTY MAN *drops sword on bottom of property box Expression of pain crosses* DAFFODIL'S *face. He crosses to c.* PROPERTY MAN *brings bouquet of flowers for him to smell, standing just L of him. After business with flowers,* DAFFODIL *speaks.*)

DAFFODIL:

I advise this honorable audience that I am a man, though I possess a daffodil nature. I go to view delightful embroideries, but retard my footsteps, that you may observe my charm. I was born great. Wu Sin Yin was my father, and Due Jung Fah, the second wife, my mother. A wonderful alliance, as I am the superb result.

> (PROPERTY *MAN*
> *holds flowers for him to smell again.*)

I am, therefore, the rival of Wu Hoo Git, who dwells, it is whispered, in a humble mountain home, whence he will go forth to see his world-place. I am not happy while he dwells anywhere—so he must not dwell. He is simply vulgarly manly, while I possess feminine qualities of great luxuriance.

> (*Smells flowers again.*
> PROPERTY MAN *draws them away*
> *from him and throws them*
> *into property box* L.
>
> PROPERTY MAN *sits* L.
> *and reads Chinese paper*)

I would contend with him, man to daffodil, but it might break my fingernails and establish a bad precedent. You may think the match unequal, because of my delicacy in a contest with brawn; but I assure you that it is not so. Craft, guided by cruelty, outweighs vulgar manliness. I must contrive to destroy his honesty and cleanness of life.

> (*Shuts fan with click.*
> ASSISTANT *fans him with large fan.*)

I will call to my aid Yin Suey Gong, whom you will meet and know by the hump on his back. I will have him present his porcelains to the unsuspecting Wu Hoo Git. He deals deliciously in porcelains. He shall drop flowers of pleasure in Wu Hoo Git's path, that my rival may inhale their odors of vice. Observe how I contend with brawn.

(Shuts fan with click. MUSIC. ASSISTANTS exit r. DAFFODIL goes up toward R. door as he speaks) Cut the flowers in my path that I may walk. *(Exits door r.)*

Clearly, the drama teacher's choice of George Hodel to play Daffodil, a true Flower of Evil, was a stroke of genius. *(Pun intended)*

**South Pasadena High 1922 Yearbook
showing cast of Senior Class Play
"Yellow Jacket"
[Unable to identify George Hodel (Daffodil)
in photo above due to costuming and makeup]**

George Hill Hodel

Chronological Timeline (1922-1940)

What follows is my attempt to piece together an *approximate* chronology of events in my father's life from his high school graduation, until his appointment as L.A. County Health Department Venereal Disease Control Officer, in the early 1940s.

I emphasize *approximate*, because my source material derives from: family anecdotes, interviews with friends/acquaintances, his prior employment records, letters of recommendation, government documents and newspaper accounts.

Many gaps appear in this eighteen-year attempt to track my father's movements, and will likely remain unknown and unknowable.

One final caveat—The actual order of events in the timeline may be slightly out of line with the true chronology, simply because, in most cases, I have only been provided the year or span of years.

Let us begin where we left off—George Hodel has just graduated from South Pasadena High School—the year is 1923.

1923

GHH graduates from high school in June and matriculates to *California Institute of Technology*, Pasadena on September 26, 1923 at age fifteen. His stated goal was to "become a chemical engineer."

Has an affair with a professor's wife who becomes pregnant. The affair results in a break-up of her marriage and she leaves California and travels to the East Coast where she gives birth to George's child whom she aptly names "Folly."

The university, while keeping the scandal quiet, expels George Hodel after the completion of his first year of schooling. My review of his transcripts show during his freshman year at *Caltech* he took the following courses: English & History, Physics, Chemistry, Math, Drawing, Military Science.

1924-1928

GHH engages in social activities in and around Pasadena. Experiments with drugs and attends opium dens in LA's Chinatown, and is hanging out with young intellectuals, poets, artists.

Apparently, George's initial acting debut as "Daffodil" blossomed, as my research showed that several years later, the wannabe thespian joined and performed in two separate plays with the Pasadena Community Players, (aka The Pasadena Playhouse).

Two separate articles in the *Los Angeles Times* mention George's on-stage performances. The first was a part in William Congreve's five-act play, *The Way of the World*. The *LA Times* article of November 30, 1924, in describing the play wrote, "...gives a lively picture of English high life, following the age of Puritanism. All of the characters created by Congreve save one are very worldly."

Fourteen months later, on January 17, 1926, George is again mentioned in the *LAT*, this time with a part in the Potboiler Art Theatre performance of, *The Man Who Ate the Popomack*. (Described as a "tragic-comedy of love in four acts by W.J. Turner, the play had opened on Broadway two years earlier, in 1924.)

George Hodel:

A Portrait of the Artist as a Young Man—

During this same period, the mid-to-late 1920s, George Hodel hobnobbed in elite Pasadena social circles, engaged in intellectual debates, and developed an interest in photography and exhibited his "one man show" at an unknown Pasadena Art Gallery.

My source on this was my stepmother, June Hodel, who shortly after my father's death, in May 1999, showed me these original 1925 photographs. At that time, I simply used my camera in hand, which was an early model Sony digital video, to seize the moment and quickly take some stills. Consequently, the reproduction quality as presented here is somewhat lacking, but not bad considering the spontaneity of the moment.

As we have seen from his early endeavors, acting, writing, poetry, and now photography, it is clear that my father had at a very early age, developed a strong desire to be creative.

Still in his teens, he wanted to be recognized and accepted as an artist.

Candidly speaking, I did not receive my father's "art genes." My worst grade in high school was a "D" which I received in my junior year in an art appreciation class.

However, I do have friends who are recognized as accomplished artists and professional photographers and do possess the ability to see and understand and interpret the works of a kindred spirit, such as George Hodel.

One such friend is Bill Crump.

Bill works and lives in the Dallas/Fort Worth area and has been a professional photographer for more than fifty years. He received his BA from Texas Tech University.

In describing himself on his website, Bill says, "I am self-taught as a photographer. My art background and the art history background are the most valuable part of my photographic success."

His stunning portfolio includes a broad range of subjects: "Heavy Industry, Energy Technology, High Tech and Communications, Aviation and WWII Aviation Heroes, Texana, Portraits, and People, Places, and Things."

In March 2017, I approached Bill and asked if he would be willing to take a look at my father's early photography and render his opinion.

Bill graciously agreed and his professional comments appear along with each photograph.

I believe that all of George Hodel's photographs were taken by the then seventeen-year-old in and around the Los Angeles area circa 1925.

Steve Hodel

Untitled

Untitled

~

BCrump: These two (untitled photos pages 88 & 89) are from a refinery. Since there was an oil boom in California, they were probably made around the Wilmington area near Long Beach.

The photograph on (page 88) allowed GH to use the parallax of the lens to use the vertical perspective to his advantage. Leaving a very small area between the two tanks to allow more depth and using the cylindrical shapes to keep the photograph interesting.

The second (page 89) is possibly old "bubble towers" or stabilizer towers for gasoline. I really don't know for sure. The guy in the foreground gives it some scale.

Might be the same guy in the very vertical photograph with the pole.

~

BCrump: These three photographs seem to be of the same person. The first one uses more dramatic light to give a more sinister look. The second dramatic and more posed and the third, the subject is lit nearly full-face. Just some cross light to define the subject's jaw-line.

(**SKH Note** -Possibly a photo of Tom Evans at age, 26 a known rum-runner, drug-smuggler of that day, who will be questioned by LAPD in 1949 as possibly knowing several of the *LA Lone Woman Murder* victims. (Mimi Boomhower and Jean Spangler))

~

BCrump: Again, these three are of the same person. I believe it was a single light source that was not moved, but GH had the subject move a bit. The lighting in the 1920s was pretty primitive. Probably GH had a strong photo light bulb in a reflector to light his subjects. The lighting was harsh and dramatic, which he used successfully. I don't believe there was any diffusion as there is today. Even the Great George Hurrell didn't use a lot of diffusion even in the 30's and 40's when he shot his Hollywood Movie Star photographs. It came into vogue later.

Fred Sexton circa 1925

(**SKH Note** - Believed to be GHH close friend, Fred Sexton, at age 17. Sexton's daughter in viewing the photo in 2002 said, "it looks like my father, as a young man, but, I can't be sure".)

BCrump: This is a hard-lit photograph from the high, front, top and the single eye makes for a very sinister look. The frown makes it even more annoying. Unsettling look—really creepy.

Untitled

(**SKH Note** - A possible early photo of LA Politico and Crime Boss Kent Kane Parrot. See details in *Black Dahlia Avenger* (Arcade 2003), *Chapter 26, George Hodel: Underworld Roots, The "Hinkies")*

BCrump: This photograph is a grand departure for GH. Here the happy subject is captured leaning back with hands behind his head. Completely different in the way he photographed the others. It is lit nearly straight-on.

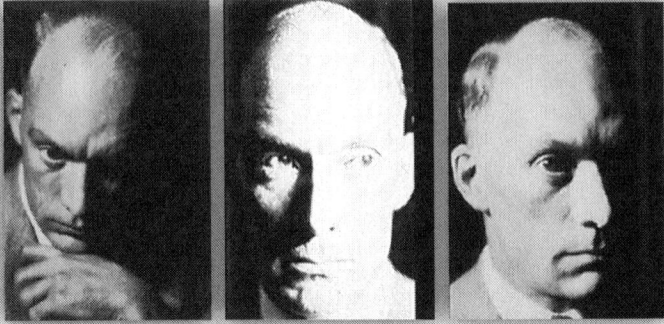

Untitled

BCrump: Another set of unsettling photographs. The first has a Satan-like look. Cross lit to show half of the face. The subject is looking down, which elongates his face and head, and accents the "horn" illusion behind his head. The second, the same person, I suppose, has a more innocent look. Not sure where GH was headed with this one. It is over-exposed giving it a much lighter appearance. And looking away as he is unusual. The third goes back to the catch light in the subject's eye. Same as in the Fred Sexton photograph. Again, a very sinister, frightening look. Glad I didn't know this guy either.

Untitled

BCrump: At first, when this was horizontal, (as shown on previous page - 94), I thought it was a neat exercise in an Art Deco vein. As I looked at it more closely and rotated it to the vertical, I saw the portrait of the guy with the "Boston Blackie" mustache. He is soft-focused and the geometric, Art Deco shapes are superimposed over his face. Not sure how GH did it, but could be a double exposure in the camera, or it could have been done in the printing of the photographs. This is a rather far-fetched experiment for an 18-year-old in the 1920s. It would take a good bit of planning and concentration to do this in the camera. I talked to Robert (Sadler) about this for a while. Still no firm solution. Possibly a plate of glass with the "Deco-esque" shaped printed on the plate of glass. Then had the model-subject behind the glass and GH would focus on the objects on the glass plate, which would be in focus. Then the subject would be somewhat out of focus. It is a strange experiment. I am still trying to understand how it was done.

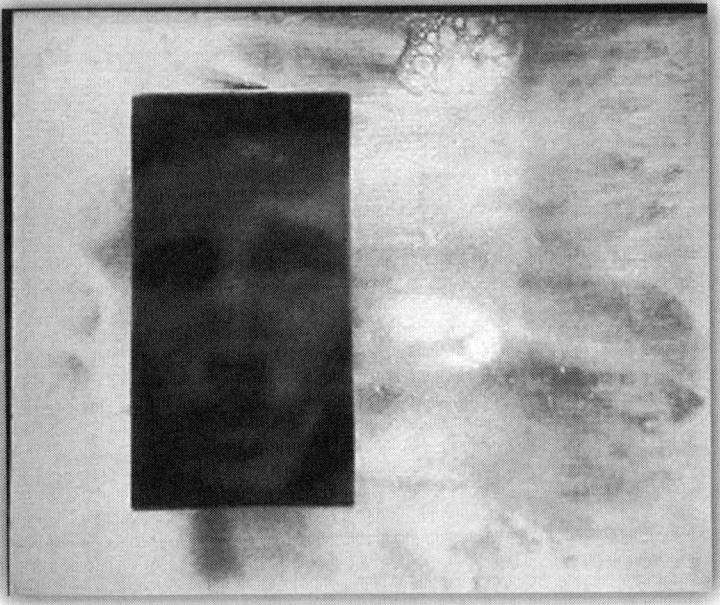

Untitled

BCrump: Another one that is difficult to figure out. The bubbles at the top allude to being in a tray of water or chemicals during the printing process. The modeled tone looks as though the photographic paper was in the print developer in the tray and the print was beginning to develop. It would occur fairly quickly. I certainly am not sure how it was done. The facial image further confuses. I really don't know how this was done. I will continue to look at it and see if I can figure something out.

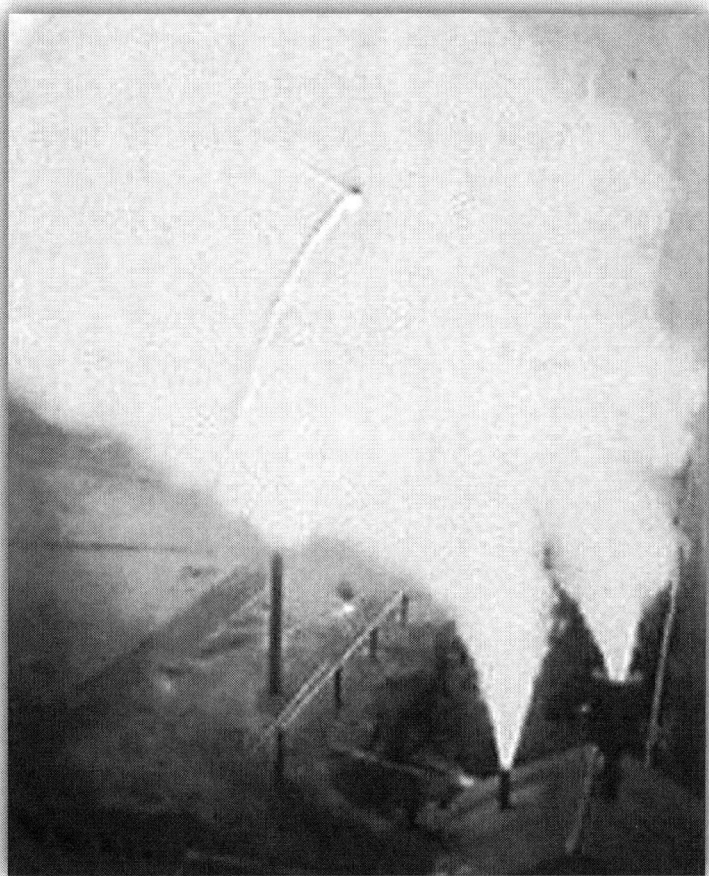

Untitled

BCrump: This one is very nice. The steam coming from, what I assume is a train. GH must have been able to get on top of the engine to make the photograph. Or he was on an upper level with the train below him. That would not have been difficult for the enterprising GH in the 20's. Compositionally it is really strong. The perspective of the rail track and the fence provide a lot of perceived depth. The single pole, left of center, complements the perspective. The steam's travel up and away from the engine on the lower right brings the total composition together. I don't know what the imperfection in the surface is on the steam portion of the print, it might be some damage from age.

Steve Hodel

Untitled

BCrump: As I mentioned before, this one, at first, is a bit confusing. But as I studied it, it is pretty wonderful. Shooting into the strong light was something that GH used to his advantage. The extremely strong light from above and possibly being reflected off the ground, really makes a strong statement. The very strong "X" or crossing lines are amazingly well balanced, with the verticals stabilizing the photograph. A good example of GH's design sense. I don't think these are accidental. I see some really nice design sense in a number of his photographs. Not so much in the portraits, as I believe there was an entirely different intention in making those. Don't know what that is. But they are all "spooky."

~

Untitled

BCrump: This is a deliberate use of perspective. The camera is tilted to intensify the perspective and depth. The low angle makes it much more dramatic. GH's use of the lower portion of the rail car to keep it visually interesting is really great. Had it been shot at waist level, the bland side of the car would dominate. This way the line coming into frame from the lower left then moving on down the photograph to the line moving upward in the right side of the photograph intensifies the perspective. And just to add more to the composition, the telephone pole completes the photograph. Really nicely done. And, again, very deliberate, I believe.

BCrump: At first glance, I didn't think much of this photograph. But after a few seconds of really looking at it, it came together to me. It is a really amazing and very subtle. The shape on the right is a great shape by itself. The lower portion of it and the texture and line of the cast concrete, beneath the finely finished upper portion are really nice. The coarseness of the cast concrete with the cracks and vertical line are in the center of the photograph. The portion, to the right where the texture changed to the horizontal is stabilizing. Then the finished portion on the top with the angles and shadow turn the eye away from the vertical. And then to further make this special is the building behind. The building is out of focus sufficiently to be secondary to the photograph by bringing it all together in the composition. A great contrast from construction or destruction in the foreground to the completed finished building in the background ties it all together. The strong vertical line set by the cast vertical concrete post is in the exact center of the photograph. Then the horizontal texture to the right of that and the finished top pulls that portion away from the symmetric center. Then the finished, "soft" building balances the entire composition. This is something that I would consider inherent understanding of design and composition. Not a photograph that is over-powering but very subtle and well done.

~

Untitled

BCrump: This one is really great. As I mentioned, this is Saul Leitner before Saul Leitner was shooting. The foreground car is moving and the vehicle in the background is still. This really provided motion in the still photograph. And somehow, the tilt of the building in the background intensifies the car's movement as if the car is pulling the building along with it. The stabilizing point is the small portion of the parked car. I put this photograph into Photoshop to try to understand the building being tilted. And I found that the photograph was probably made on a hill with the street headed down to the left. GH either straightened the camera or adjusted its tilt while printing. Still a really nice composition. A favorite.

Untitled

BCrump: I imagine this was a quick study in contrasts of materials and shapes. The wooden pallet leaning on the concrete block are similar but different in materials. Both have three openings in them. Not a lot to argue over here. Again, probably a quick study in contrasts.

Untitled

BCrump: Another very good, yet solid composition. The man in the front left is the main subject, while the lady in the hat is looking out of frame. The vertical pole or tree anchors the design with the background horizontal of the building bringing the composition back to the man in the foreground. GH has no problem shooting into the sun. It might be somewhat filtered, but it looks like the sun is just in front of the man's hat. Very nice. Could be an album cover for a Blues Musician. Contrasts in society and contrasts between light and dark. I really like it.

Untitled

BCrump: A very simple and interesting symmetrical photograph. However, having read your work about GHH, it is possible there might be a face in this photograph. Not sure. The old glass insulator on a pole is simple enough, but for some reason I feel like GH saw more or wanted the illusion to more than the obvious. Just a supposition. Maybe I'm trying to make more of this than there is, but there could be, to some, a human form with the head/face just to the right of center and shoulders just below.

~

Untitled

BCrump:I have no idea what this is. I put it in Photoshop and rotated it and did the perspective readjustment and couldn't get much out of it. Doubt it was frozen, if it was taken in Southern California. Perhaps a gutter drain. Beats me.

Untitled

BCrump: This might be a photograph of GHH's exhibit of his work. Not sure whose work it is, but I believe it is a gallery of artwork or photographs. Shot in the perspective angle to make a composition where content was not important. Maybe just another study or experiment.

Untitled

BCrump: This is my absolute favorite. Great study in black and white, high contrast. Excellent composition. The anchoring tank or object on the left, small building in the background adds interest, the railroad crossing marker in the foreground and incidents on the right. All tied together with the overhead lines.

It is obviously in an industrial area with rail and probably petroleum business going on. Could be down near Long Beach again. I really like this photograph and is solid now as it was then. The modeling in the background sky brings in the age.

The "soft" out of focus verticals near the RR crossing marker might be cables of thin poles. The overhead lines next to the RR crossing marker strengthen the vertical.

I wish I had shot this.

Untitled

BCrump: Another foreboding portrait. Heavily cross-lit with half of the face totally dark. The individual looking right into the camera which makes it more intense. The dark angle from top right to center left really ties the composition together and makes it a fine photograph. I put this one in Photoshop as well to intensify the contrast so the shapes would be more evident.

Great period composition.

Untitled

BCrump: Probably the most comforting portrait of the group. This man may work at the refinery that GH photographs. Obviously, a worker with the overalls. The composition is again strong. GH had no problem shooting directly into strong light, which he used to his advantage. The man could also be a rail worker. The angle of the pole the man has in his hand is a very nice addition to strengthen the photograph.

I hope this does what you need, Steve. I will attach some photographs of cameras that were available at the time.

Possibly something like your father might have used. I assume he did his own film processing and printing. Certainly, his printing.

If I can help further, let me know. This is very interesting. Some of his printing might have been done by others, as I feel like he would have possibly been more attentive to the ultimate quality of the prints.

The photographer, Paul Strand's photographs that are of light and shadow are like your father's work. Saul Leitner's work looks similar to your father's. The one of the moving car particularly.

Ralph Steiner, Ralston Crawford's paintings and Alexander Rodchenko's photographs are in the same vein as GH. I really like his work.

Thanks, Bill

George - Self-Portraits

Also, circa 1924, George took two "self-portraits" that to my mind capture the physical and mental intensity of the young genius. He gave them 'telling' titles.

In the first photograph (page 111) George has taken a picture of himself reading from a book and using his familiar block printing has written on the back:

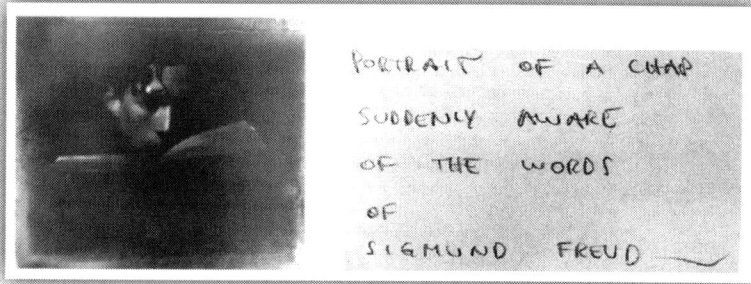

"PORTRAIT OF A CHAP SUDDENLY AWARE OF
THE WORDS OF SIGMUND FREUD."

~

And, on the second (below), staring into the camera,
again on the verso, he writes:

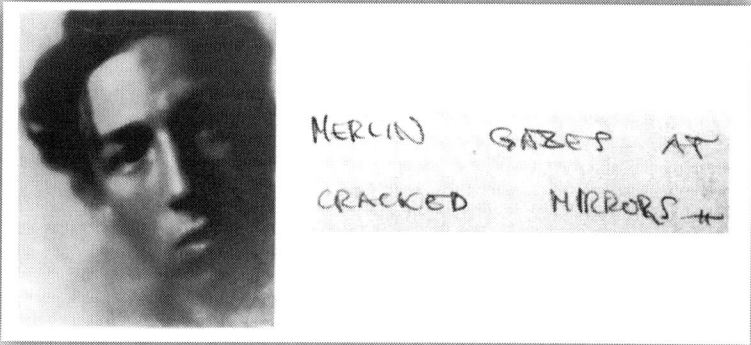

"MERLIN GAZES AT CRACKED MIRRORS."
(see image page 3)

Two Later GHH Photographs

As previously indicated, these early art photographs,
taken by my father circa 1924-1925, were first shown
to me, by June, shortly after my dad's death in May
1999. Before that I had not known of their existence.

However, in the years preceding his death, father had gifted me two separate photographs that he had personally taken—one from his medical school days in 1935 and the second of my mother, shot at the Franklin House in 1946.

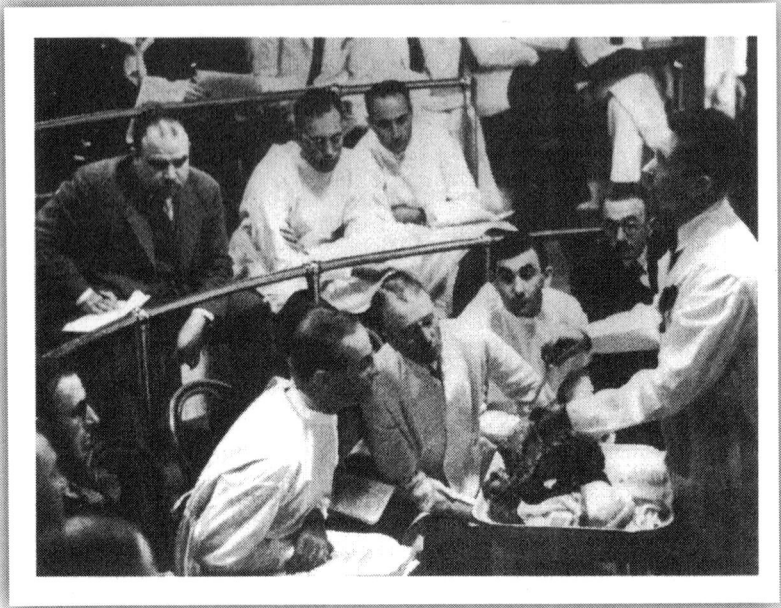

George Hodel took this photograph in 1935. It was enlarged and included as part of a mural at the UCSF Parnassus Cole Hall, Medical School Building. San Francisco Muralist Bernard Zakheim, who had previously created murals for the interior of the Coit Tower, provided large frescoes on the school walls complemented by George Hodel's modern day photographic surgical montage. The Zakheim/Hodel artwork remained on permanent exhibit for many decades. Also, father's photograph was reprinted in the spring edition of the *Bulletin of Alumni-Faculty Association, UCSF School of Medicine* which identified George's classmates (some of whom became world renowned physicians) as follows: (*front row left to right*) Drs. Glaven Rusk, Edwin Bruck, Leroy Briggs, Herbert Moffit, Salvatore Lucia, and Guido Milani. (*back row, left to right*) Urriola Goiota, Clayton Mote, and Walter Port. Lecturer, Dr. Jesse L. Carr.

On February 23, 1936, the *Oakland Tribune* published an article headlined, "FRESCOES BY BERNARD ZAKHEIM COMPLETED FOR MEDICAL SCHOOL: Two Works Depict Ancient and Modern Medical Practice."

The article went on to announce the public opening of the Zakheim/Hodel Exhibit which featured Zakheim's many large frescoes depicting ancient medical practices, juxtaposed and complemented by George Hodel's enlarged photographic montage of modern day physicians performing surgery. Their combined artwork remained on permanent exhibit at Parnassus Cole Hall for many decades.

FRESCOES BY BERNARD ZAKHEIM COMPLETED FOR MEDICAL SCHOOL

Two Works Depict Ancient and Modern Medical Practice; Junior League Members Exhibit in Piedmont

By H. L. DUNGAN

IF we are not mistaken, that wedding of art and science which took place recently at the University of California Medical School, San Francisco, was an unhappy affair.

We have no complaint about the union of art and science, but art should behave itself both before and after the ceremony.

Let us drop the figure of speech and go on about the two frescoes by Bernard Zakheim, San Francisco. They are on the walls of Cole Hall in the medical school. Cole Hall is an amphitheater, where students sit tier above tier and look down at the lecturer who stands below them and behind a large pulpit or desk or table or whatever it is called in a medical college. On the wall back of the lecturer, at his right and left, are the frescoes. One represents ancient medicine and surgery, when incantation and the lash were supposed to drive out disease and demons. The other represents modern medicine and surgery when science stepped in.

All well and good, so far, only Zakheim tried to do too much. You can't put in the whole history of medicine in two frescoes. The frescoes are as complicated as a set of viscera to the lay mind. Perhaps young medical students, who are accustomed to probing into intricate matters, may untangle them, but probably it would be better

...
"When the frescoes were open to public inspection last week, Zakheim exhibited 22 water colors made as preliminary sketches. ...and photographic montages by George Hodel."

OAKLAND TRIBUNE
SUN, FEB 23, 1936

"Primitive Medicine" (1935) One of Bernard Zakheim's
UCSF frescoes

The photograph on the next page (115) is of my mother, Dorothy Huston Hodel. It was taken by my father shortly after we moved into the Sowden/ Franklin House, in Hollywood, California. Probably after his return from China in September 1946.

See Bill Crump's interpretation below the photograph.

Dorothy Hodel photographed & signed by George Hodel 1946

BCrump: This is a photograph of heartbreak, apprehension and maybe fear. A lovely lady carrying a very heavy load in her heart. The way GH lit doesn't soften her anguish. I assume it was daylight as there is no catch light in her eyes. With her eyes looking to the left, it is almost as if she is looking behind, expecting another letdown. I am sure in happier times she was an absolute beauty. Still very attractive, life's burdens have taken a physical toll on her. Not to mention an emotional toll. I don't know if GH spent a great deal of time making this photograph. Having read your first book, I am probably a bit biased in my judgment. It is almost as if this photograph is an illustration of continued torture. And then he autographed it. It is a very sad photograph.

Here resumes my father's biographical chronology where we left off, back in 1925.

George begins double-dating with his friend John Huston and his date Emilia. (Huston, then a sometime amateur boxer and aspiring artist will later gain fame as one of Hollywood's leading film directors). George meets and dates former Los Angeles "Queen of the May" and intellectual Dorothy Harvey. Huston is dating Emilia Lawson, also an intellectual and soon to be a librarian at the L.A. Public Library, which will open in 1926.

At this time, Huston and Hodel make the acquaintance of Fred Sexton, (who was also attending art school with Huston) and the three will remain in close contact for the next twenty-five years.

Still in their teens, John and George will "switch partners." John falls in love with nineteen-year-old Dorothy Harvey and they will marry and run off to New York's Greenwich Village for the next several years, before returning to Hollywood where both become budding screenwriters for the studios.

George and Emilia begin dating and remain in Los Angeles. After my father's passing in 1999, his widow, June, informed me that the two of them, "Opened, or worked at a rare book store in downtown Los Angeles." (No further information?)

In January 1925, GHH as "Publisher and Editor," releases his first edition of his literary magazine, *FANTASIA*. The magazine solicits subscriptions and requests they be mailed to the magazine's publication office, 6512 Monterey Road. (His home residence.)

A Dedication

T O the portrayal of bizarre beauty in the arts, to the delineation of the stranger harmonies and the rarer fragrances, do we dedicate this, our magazine.

S UCH beauty we may find in a poem, a sketch, or a medley of colors; in the music of prayer-bells in some far-off minaret, or the noises of a city street; in a temple or a brothel or a gaol; in prayer or perversity or sin.

A ND ever shall we attempt in our pages the vivid expression of such art, wherever or however we may find it—ever shall we consecrate our magazine to the depiction of beauty anomalous, fantasia!.

January 1925 *Fantasia* cover and GHH dedication "To the portrayal of bizarre beauty in the arts...in a temple or a brothel or a gaol; in prayer or perversity or sin."

GHH, using false ID, claiming he is "twenty-one" (he is seventeen) obtains a Chauffeur's License and becomes a uniformed taxi driver for Yellow Cab. Ironically, he will not only be picking up customers out of Los Angeles's brand new Biltmore Hotel, but one of his driving mates was a young William H. Parker, attending law school and the man who twenty-five years hence, will become legendary as LAPD's greatest police chief.

On &118 is a Xerox copy of GHH's 1925 LA City Chauffeur's License - Chauffeur's Identification Card.

In the 1920s Los Angeles City required taxi drivers to be at least twenty-one.

Seventeen-year-old George's actual height, as listed on the license at 6 feet ¼ inch, likely made it easy for him to fake his age.

1924-1925 George is hired as a crime reporter for the *Los Angeles Record* newspaper. Initially he accompanies LAPD vice squad officers during their Prohibition enforcement raids and writes tabloid-type articles describing the "door kicking busts."

In *BDA*, I reproduced three (3) of my father's 1924 articles. *Life's Café: Where Liquor Is Hard: A Raid on the Humming Bird Café*. In the second, *The Morning After a Party,* he describes the murder scene of Peggy Donavan, a cabaret girl who had been kicked to death. His closing lines on that crime read, "In the GARDEN OF LIFE WOMEN are the FLOWERS, some are gorgeous, gay and yet have NO PERFUME."

Here is an excerpt on the third article reproduced in *BDA*, Chapter 5:

> A few months later, in another crime-scene story in the *Record*, George turns the description into a literary piece by punning in Latin on the last name of victim Teresa Mors. Mors—her name means "death" in Latin—was shot and killed by her jealous lover, the famous welterweight boxing champ Norman "Kid McCoy" Selby, who was immortalized by the sobriquet "the Real McCoy" when he decked with a single punch a drunk who had challenged his identity in a downtown L.A.

bar. Legendary criminal attorney Jerry Giesler would jump-start his career with this famous early Los Angeles murder case by obtaining a manslaughter verdict for his client rather than the death sentence the state wanted.

In his description of the murder scene, the young reporter, George Hodel, writes:

Los Angles Record

Thursday, August 14, 1924.   Two Cents

WORDS OF DEATH

Death.

Mors, mortis, morti—glibly the schoolboy declines it. Thoughtlessly. Like a cage in which the canary has been stifled, this apartment on the second floor of the Nottingham—the tall, expensive building with a front of blazing white tiles.

While the yellow bird was alive—flitting and singing—the cage seemed a pretty thing. Now with the canary dead it is a dirty cage, tawdry and crusted with birdlime.

~ ~ ~

George closes out the article:

Death.
Mors, mortis, morti—what gender is death?
Feminine of course. It is of that declension. Yes, death is feminine.

Again, from Chapter 5 of *Black Dahlia Avenger* (Skyhorse/Arcade 2015 ed.)

By the end of 1925, George had switched his schedule to driving on the night shift while he took jobs as a copywriter, first for a local Army & Navy store and then for the Southern California Gas Company. It was through SoCal Gas that he got his first taste of managing publicity, advertising, and marketing, and landed himself another job as a radio announcer, in which he hosted a live show, introducing the public to classical music during the early evening hours. SoCal Gas sponsored an hour-long program in the early days of radio. Dad, a gas company employee in advertising, possessed the perfect qualities for the job: a musical prodigy with an encyclopedic knowledge of the classics, he also had a beautiful speaking voice. His uniquely meticulous speech patterns, his ability to use just the right words and diction expressed with perfect intonation, rhyme, and meter, would remain his calling card for the rest of his life. George Hodel's voice was as unique and distinct as his fingerprints. However, after shutting off the radio mike for the evening, Dad put on his cab driver's hat and began looking for fares waiting outside the Biltmore.

Though not yet twenty, Father had already accumulated the life experiences of much older men and had led several lives: boy genius, musical prodigy, crime reporter, advertising writer, public relations officer, public radio announcer, editor of a self-published literary magazine, poet, intellectual elitist, and cab driver.

Shortly after my father's passing in 1999, his widow, June informed me that sometime after the birth of "Folly" in the mid-1920s George traveled to the East Coast and "proposed marriage" to the professor's then ex-wife. June said, "He wanted to marry her, be a father and raise his newborn child. She told him, "George get out of my life. You're just a child yourself. Just go away and leave us alone. I don't ever want to see you again."

June added, "Your father got a job at *Boston General*

Hospital as an orderly and stayed and tried to persuade her to marry him, but finally gave up and came back to California."

Birth records show that George's girlfriend, Emilia Lawson, gave birth to a son, in Los Angeles in March, 1928. The birth certificate named the father as "George Hodel currently a resident student in New York City." (I have no further information on this other than what is shown on the birth certificate.)

1929-1936

George, Emilia and Duncan Hodel circa 1930

George, Emilia and their newborn son, Duncan, move north from Los Angeles to Oakland, California, and George enrolls in pre-med school at UC Berkeley.

During these Depression Years, George supplements his income as he had in Los Angeles, by again becoming a taxi driver for the Yellow Cab Company in downtown San Francisco.

While continuing his studies, George and Emilia in 1932 are hired by the *San Francisco Chronicle* newspaper as dual-columnists, and share bylines in a series of fourteen articles, entitled, "*Abroad in San Francisco.*"

Here is how the Editor of the *San Francisco Chronicle* introduced the Hodels to its readers in 1932:

> Editor's Note: This series of articles deals with the foreign colonies of San Francisco. The various foreign quarters— Chinatown, the Latin Quarter, Little Greece and the rest— are veritable cities within a city. There are more than twenty of them, with a combined population of over 190,000. Each Sunday you are to explore one or another of the colonies, with George and Emilia Hodel.

The foreign populations of San Francisco have merged their interests inseparably with those of San Francisco. In many respects life in the "colonies" is indistinguishable from that of the entire American scene. Nevertheless, each group has brought over with it its Old-World heritage— customs, festivals, philosophies, foods. The old ways have in many cases been carefully preserved, and each now lends its special color to the life of San Francisco.

14 SAN FRANCISCO CHRONICLE, SUNDAY, MAY 15, 1932

French Colony Plays Most Important Part In S. F. Development

LANDMARKS OF THE GAUL IN PARIS OF THE WEST

One of fourteen weekly articles written by George and Emilia Hodel that appeared in *SFC* in 1932

George graduates from pre-med in **1932** and he and Emilia and Duncan move across the Bay to San Francisco where he continues his medical studies at the Parnassus campus at the University of California Medical School. (UCSF)

In **1934** George has an affair with a young model, Dorothy Anthony, who becomes pregnant and moves in with George and Emilia.

George and Dorothy's child, Tamar Nais Hodel, is born in San Francisco, late March **1935**.
(Tamar is GHH's 3rd child)
< Tamar Nais Hodel

1936

George completes his medical training at UCSF and after a year of internship at San Francisco General Hospital, receives his MD and graduates in 1936.

Shortly after graduation, the young doctor unexpectedly leaves San Francisco and accepts a position as the sole surgeon at a CCC (*Civilian Conservation Corp*) logging camp near Bisbee, Arizona.

Emilia Hodel and Dorothy Anthony, along with his two children, Duncan and Tamar, remain behind in San Francisco.

1937-1938

After his position as surgeon at the logging camp, George joins the New Mexico State Department of Public Health and is appointed District Health Officer, where he doctors to the Hopi and Navajo Indian reservations near Taos, New Mexico.

In 1937 he is reassigned to a hospital in Santa Fe, New Mexico, where he also serves as the town's Coroner Examiner.

In April 1938 returns to Los Angeles, California, and is hired by the Los Angeles County Health Department as a Social Hygiene physician.

In **1939** he takes a six-month postgraduate course at his old alma mater, UCSF, and obtains a specialty certification in Venereal Disease Control.

While obtaining his certification, George also worked at the San Francisco World Fair at Treasure Island (aka Golden Gate International Exposition) where he served as a staff physician at the Fair's on-site clinic when needed.

George, having maintained a friendship with John and Dorothy Huston since his teens and through the Hustons seven-year marriage (**1926-1933**), resumes dating Dorothy after her divorce from John. (This is the same Dorothy Harvey whom George had initially dated with Huston as teenagers. Dorothy had "switched" from George and had started dating and then married John.)

Dorothy becomes pregnant in mid-October, **1938**, and my older brother Michael is born in Los Angeles in July **1939**.

George opens his private practice in Los Angeles as well as becoming Director and Chief of Staff of the First Street Clinic, located in downtown LA at First Street and Central Avenue.

George and Dorothy marry in Sonora, Mexico, on December 7, **1940,** and I and my twin, John Dion, are born less than a year later, on November 6, **1941**. We are both premature (eighth-month babies) and due to mother's heavy drinking and smoking during pregnancy, we both have exceptionally low birth weights. (Three pounds each at birth, requiring us to remain in incubators.) My twin dies three weeks later due to "failure to thrive."

My younger brother, Kelvin, is born less than a year later, in October **1942**. George receives a commission in late 1942 to the US Public Health Service and is appointed by President Franklin D. Roosevelt as "PA Surgeon" with the effective rank of lieutenant.

(Rear Dr. George Hill Hodel age 36, Duncan Hill Hodel, age 15. Front Left to Right, Steve (author) age 2, Kelvin, age 1, and Michael, age 4.)

This Hodel family photograph was taken in November 1943 by a family friend, Galka Scheyer, a German-American painter, art dealer, collector, famous for being the art agent representing "The Blue Four." (Lyonel Feininger, Wassily Kandinsky, Paul Klee, and Alexej Jawlensky)

George quickly advances his position at the L.A. County Health Department and promotes to become the Chief of Social Hygiene from **1941-1944**. At that time, he was the Venereal Control Officer for all of L.A. County. In a later government application, to join UNRRA, here is how he described his responsibilities as Chief, Division of Social Hygiene:

Duties:

To plan and carry out an extensive public health

program for the control of venereal diseases; to direct and supervise the work of physicians in the treatment of venereal diseases in clinics located throughout the county; to conduct surveys and research studies to obtain information regarding venereal diseases; to correlate the work of private physicians, district health officers, public health nurses, medical social workers and public health education authorities with the venereal disease control program; to give talks to interested groups and organizations; to participate in local professional activities; to promote cooperation between the Health Department, the medical profession and public and private agencies in the field of social hygiene; to keep informed of recent advances in social hygiene and related fields; and to perform such other duties as may be required."

In **1945**, father purchased the Frank Lloyd Wright, Jr. (Lloyd Wright) "Sowden House," a veritable Mayan Temple built in the heart of Hollywood. Dorothy and we three sons move into the residence at 5121 Franklin Avenue.

Unbeknownst to my brothers and me, George and Dorothy were legally divorced in **1944**, (a fact that would remain hidden until my active investigation some fifty-five years later).

That said, we lived together as a "family" until father's sudden departure from the US, in the summer of 1950.

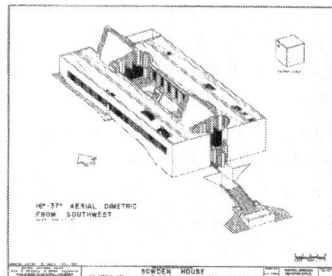

Frank Lloyd Wright, Jr. designed and built this home for John Sowden in 1926. Dr. George Hill Hodel purchased the home in 1945 and we lived there as a family until our father suddenly sold the house and fled the country in 1950.

We three brothers renamed it "The Franklin House."

My investigation and the forensic evidence presented in *Black Dahlia Avenger I and II* revealed this was the original crime scene where Dr. George Hill Hodel slew and surgically bisected Elizabeth "Black Dahlia" Short in the early morning hours of January 15, 1947.

(Secret DA police reports discovered in 2003, revealed that in a transcribed interview with detectives, Dorothy Hodel informed them that, "she and her three sons were not at the residence and were temporarily staying with her brother [our uncle] some three miles away during a three-week period when the crime was committed.")

Dorothy Hodel circa 1946
Steven, Michael, and Kelvin circa 1947
Dorothy and boys in Franklin House center courtyard.

Photo left, believed taken by our father. The photo on

the right was taken by surrealist photographer, Edmund Teske, who was a good friend and along with Man Ray was a regular visitor to the Hodel home. Teske resided just a few blocks away and his fame as a photographer came mostly after his death. Many of his photographs, like Man Ray's, are now on regular display at the Los Angeles Getty Museum. (As a side note, the two black cats pictured in the photograph purportedly died from eating ant or rat poison, that had been placed in the basement. Our father named one of the cats "Satan" and I do not recall the name of the second cat.)

In August of **1945**, George applies to join UNRRA (United Nations Relief and Rehabilitation) requesting a posting overseas. He is accepted and in February **1946** is assigned and sent to Hangkow, China as "Chief Regional Medical Officer" with the honorary rank of Lieutenant General.

After seven months in China, George unexpectedly resigns from UNRRA "for personal reasons." No further explanation is known or given. I suspect multiple reasons accelerated his return. One being from a confidential talk with a co-worker who knew and was stationed with him in China who mentioned George was "having an affair with a Chinese General's wife." A second reason, I detail in BDA, again sourced from DA police reports that indicated his sometime girlfriend, Elizabeth Short, while he was away in China, had taken it upon herself to travel to Chicago, Illinois, and investigate three "Lipstick Murders." The facts suggest Elizabeth may have suspected his involvement in those crimes and inadvertently or naively communicated her suspicions to either George or one of his acquaintances, with the information reaching him in China.

What is known is that George Hodel suddenly and unexpectedly resigns from UNRRA on September 19, **1946**, and immediately returns to Los Angeles. Elizabeth Short, now back from Chicago, begins running and goes into hiding in fear of her life, and within three months becomes the victim of a surgical-torture murder.

Dr. George Hill Hodel is wearing his UNRRA (United Nations Relief and Rehabilitation Agency) top coat. Photo left he is seen embracing a statue of the Tibetan God, *Yamantaka*, "Lord of Death," who is depicted engaged in sexual intercourse with his consort. These photographs were taken by his close friend and our family photographer, surrealist MAN RAY, shortly after George's return to Los Angeles in 1946.

1949-1950

In October 1949 Dr. George Hodel is arrested by LAPD detectives for Incest and Child Molestation. The victim: Tamar, his fourteen-year-old daughter my half-sister.

After running away from home, Tamar is picked up by LAPD and when questioned as to why she ran away, makes the disclosure of having had sex with her father and other adults at the Franklin House. After Tamar becomes pregnant, George sends her to a Beverly Hills physician.

A week following George Hodel's arrest, LAPD arrests Dr. Francis C. Ballard and his associate "Charles Smith." Both men are charged with performing the abortion in September 1949, one month before Tamar runs away from home.

As detailed in **BDA**, a high-profile jury trial was held in December 1949.

Despite multiple adult witnesses confirming being present and witnessing the sex acts, leading criminal defense attorney Jerry "Get Me" Giesler (the Johnny Cochran of his day) and his partner, Robert Neeb, win an acquittal for Dr. Hodel.

The two lawyers paint George's teenage daughter with a "pathological liar" brush claiming she was merely "inventing fantasies."

(**SKH Note** - As alluded to on page 63, my later investigation revealed secret DA Files that included a letter from law enforcement suggesting a $15,000 payoff from George Hodel to the DA's office may have occurred.)

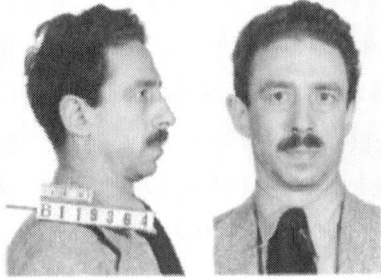

BOOKED—Dr. George Hill Hodel, left, Hollywood physician, with his attorney, Henry C. Rohr. Hodel and 13 boys were arrested as result of reported wild parties.

Tamar Hodel age 15

GHH 1949 LAPD Booking Photo

1950

George Hodel—after being tipped that a joint DA/ LAPD Taskforce of eighteen detectives has been electronically bugging his home 24/7 for six weeks and are about to arrest him as the prime Black Dahlia suspect—flees the country.

1950-53

Relocates to Hawaii (then just a US Territory) and obtains his residency in psychiatry at the Hawaii Territorial Hospital. Served as Director of Rehabilitation Therapies and counseled the criminally insane at the prison. Taught psychology courses at the University of Hawaii.

A daughter, Teresa, is born in Hawaii in 1952. George marries the child's mother, a wealthy Filipina, Hortensia Laguda Lopez, who owns a large sugar plantation in Negroes, Occidental, a province in the Southern Philippines.

George accepts an invitation to become a *Luis Guerrero Memorial Lecturer* at the University of Santo Tomas in Manila, Philippines.

Relocates with his wife and young daughter to Manila. In the next four years, George fathers three more children, Ramon, Diane, and Mark, and in the late Fifties, Hortensia obtains a Papal Dispensation and they separate.

1960-1990

George enters the field of Market Research and over the next three decades becomes one of the leading experts throughout Asia and Europe. Establishes INRA-ASIA with offices in Manila, Tokyo, Hong Kong, Singapore, and Australia.

Conducts major Public Opinion Research for many large companies and governments, and establishes

INTRAMAR Surveys which becomes the leading survey for hotels and airlines worldwide.

In 1969, he hires June Hirano, age 24, to be his Tokyo Office Manager. June then becomes his full-time personal secretary and traveling companion. They marry in Reno, Nevada, in 1982.

As "Director General" of INRA-ASIA, George's business dealings require constant travel throughout Asia to Europe and the US multiple times each year. He is never in any one city more than a few days to a week.

George and June Hodel, Manila, Philippines Office Conference Room circa 1988

1990-1999

After traveling the world and using Manila, Philippines as his "home base" for nearly forty years, George Hodel decides to return to the United States.

In **1990** he and June return to San Francisco and lease a thirty-ninth-floor penthouse suite at 333 Bush Street West, in the heart of San Francisco's downtown Financial District.

On May 16, **1999** at one A.M. I receive a telephone call from June, in San Francisco informing me that the paramedics are at the apartment and they have just pronounced my father dead.

George Hill Hodel's personal physician had been treating him for many years for "congestive heart failure," which was listed as "the cause of death" on his death certificate. No autopsy would be required or performed.

The actual cause of death was "Barbiturate Overdose" (**SKH Note - Seconal**). George, who still kept his MD license active, wrote multiple prescriptions in the name of his wife, June Hodel, over the months preceding his death, and when she had accumulated, enough for a lethal dosage, father committed suicide, taking his own life at age ninety-one.

George's ashes were scattered in San Francisco Bay on the 2nd of June **1999**, a few hundred yards off Point Bonita just outside the Golden Gate Bridge.

June Hodel is seen (montage page 136) holding urn containing George Hodel's ashes as the *Neptune Society's* boat, "Naiad," passes under the Golden Gate Bridge to scatter his ashes off Point Bonita Lighthouse. The two of them were together constantly and rarely out of each other's sight during the previous thirty years.

In yet another example of bizarre synchronicity, June poured my father's ashes from the urn into San Francisco Bay on June 2, **1999**.

That day coincidentally was the birthday of one of George Hodel's greatest heroes—a man whom he strove his entire life to emulate—Donatien Alphonse Francois, Marquis de Sade. The man from whose name we derive the words sadist and sadism.

In actuality, George Hodel far surpassed the horrors of his eighteenth century counterpart. A fellow surrealist, George worshiped de Sade and called him,

"The Divine Marquis."

As kindred spirts, Man Ray and the rest of George's Hollywood inner circle of friends "talked-the-talk" of violent misogyny, sadism and murder, but it was George who, as we now know "walked the walk."

I will close this chapter with this excerpt from an article, *Who Was the Marquis de Sade?* by author, Tony Perrottet, which appeared in the *Smithsonian Magazine,* February 2015.

> While Sade was alive, censors shuddered at his accounts of rape, incest and pedophilia, as well as his vitriolic atheism, and thousands of his books were destroyed. He remained all but unknown in the 19th century beyond a tiny band of cognoscenti, including Flaubert and Baudelaire, who found underground copies of his books or gained access to the forbidden Enfer, or Hell, section of the National Library in Paris.
>
> In the early 1900s, the critic and poet Apollinaire wrote the first unabashed essays in defense of Sade, and by the 1920s his cause was taken up by the Surrealists, including Man Ray, Andre Breton and Dali. They were attracted to Sade's demands for complete sexual freedom and political liberty, as well as the hallucinogenic nature of his imagination.

Chapter 3

George Hill Hodel was a true Renaissance Man. He was child musical prodigy, boy genius, magazine editor, cab driver, crime reporter and newspaper columnist, radio announcer, skilled surgeon and District Health Officer to the Hopi and Navajo tribes. He was Chief Venereal Disease Control Officer, Commissioned Officer in the US Department of Health, Lt. General and Chief Medical Officer for UNRRA China. He was consulting psychiatrist at the Territory of Hawaii Prison System. He was a pioneer and one of the leading Market Research experts throughout Asia and creator of INTRAMAR, the Hotel and Aviation industries most respected international Public Opinion Survey. Those were his "day jobs."

He fathered eleven children with five separate women and lived long and prospered.

George Hill Hodel MD was also one of the world's most prolific serial killers.

In the *Discovery* television series *Most Evil*, (the source of the naming of my follow-up books) Dr. Michael Stone. after reviewing George Hodel's M.O. and crime signatures and devoting a full-hour show to examining his involvement as Chicago's 1945-6 "Lipstick Murderer" along with his 1947 "Black Dahlia" and other "Lone Woman Murders," ranked him on his "Scale of Evil" as a "Category 22," the highest possible depravity attainable, which he defined as:

"Psychopathic torture-murders, where torture is primary motive. In most cases, the crime has a sexual motivating factor."

Other serial killers that Dr. Stone has ranked in this highest Category 22 include: Rodney Alcala, Lawrence Bittaker, John Wayne Gacy, Dennis Rader, Albert Fish, Joseph Mengele, H.H. Holmes, and Jeffrey Dahmer.

Clearly, these psychopaths are the worst of the worst and each—by way of his unique depravity and extreme sadism—has justly earned the title of MOST EVIL.

Dr. Michael Stone's "SCALE OF EVIL"
Discovery Channel, September 2007

22 · GEORGE HODEL
PSYCHOPATHIC/ TORTURE-MURDER /
SERIAL KILLER / SEXUAL HOMICIDE

"George Hodel was a deeply disturbed man, who although brilliant had a twistedly distorted sense of reality. We have every reason to believe George Hodel enjoyed the horrible murder of Elizabeth Short and that he took pleasure in what he had done for the rest of his long life."

...

"I would place George Hodel at the very top of my scale-level 22—psychopathic torture murders, with torture their primary motive."

Dr. Michael H. Stone
Forensic Psychiatrist, Columbia University
Discovery Times Channel
September 2007

George Hill Hodel 5.0

May 16, **2017**, is a dual anniversary for me. It marks the eighteenth anniversary of my father's death, as well as the eighteenth year of my active investigation into his life and crimes.

Nearly one-quarter of my lifetime now has been spent in attempting to uncover "the sins of my father."

That time span has resulted in six books, twenty-five victims, and one suspect.

I fully expect (and hope) that with the completion of this "Early Years" investigation I will literally be able to close the books and finally say, "CASES CLOSED."

Many of my readers are fully "up to speed" on my investigations and a few can even quote chapter and verse on specific evidentiary details that I have forgotten.

For other readers, this book will be their first look. The name Dr. George Hill Hodel will be brand new to them and they will have no knowledge of his "prior rap sheet" so to speak.

As I have said many times before, "The key to understanding Dr. George Hill Hodel and his crimes is revealed in a knowledge of his past."

Consequently, I am going to consider and treat you "new readers" much as I would a new partner, just assigned to work with me back in the 1970s and 1980s at LAPD's Hollywood Homicide Division.

I will do with you now what I did back then—hand

you the large blue three-ringed "Murder Book" and instruct you to: "Read It." "Get up to speed on our suspect." "And familiarize yourself with his prior crime signatures and M.O."

Then we can together begin to look into the new cold case crimes. Those remain as "unsolveds" and possibly connect them to the suspect's "Early Years."

I give you one last admonishment. "Don't get lost in the weeds of each crime. They span nearly thirty years from 1943 to 1969. Mainly, focus on his crime-signatures. George Hodel's are so specific and unique they literally jump off the page. My guess is, these same signatures will be present and help us identify his early crimes. Have at it. We need to get moving on this."

I watch as you carry the big binder over to your desk, pour yourself some coffee, open it and begin to read the summaries on Dr. George Hill Hodel, aka GHH:

GHH CRIMES

(CHRONOLOGICAL 1943-1970)

1. Ora Murray 7/26/43 Los Angeles Murder
2. Georgette Bauerdorf 10/11/44 Hollywood Murder
3. Ruth Spaulding 5/9/45 Los Angeles Murder
4. Josephine Ross 6/6/45 Chicago Murder
5. Frances Brown 12/10/45 Chicago Murder
6. Suzanne Degnan 1/6/46 Chicago Murder
7. Elizabeth Short 1/15/47 Hollywood Murder
8. Jeanne French 2/10/47 Los Angeles Murder
9. Laura Trelstad 5/11/47 Long Beach Murder

10. Marian Newton 7/16/47 San Diego Murder

11. Lillian Dominguez 10/2/47 Santa Monica Murder

12. Gladys Kern 2/17/48 Hollywood Murder

13. Louise Springer 6/13/49 Los Angeles Murder

14. Mimi Boomhower 8/18/49 Los Angeles Murder

15. Jean Spangler 10/7/49 Hollywood Murder

16. Jane Doe 2/18/50 Hollywood Murder

AFTER AN APPARENT 16-YEAR GAP, THE "BLACK DAHLIA AVENGER" REINVENTS HIMSELF AS "ZODIAC"

17. Cheri Jo Bates 10/30/66 Riverside Murder

18. Lucila LaLu 5/28/67 Manila Murder

19. Betty Jensen & David Faraday 12/20/68 Vallejo Murder

20. Darlene Ferrin & Mike Mageau 7/4/69 Vallejo Murder/Att. Murder

21. Cecelia Shepard & Bryan Hartnell 9/27/69 Napa Murder/Att. Murder

22. Paul Stine 10/11/69 San Francisco Murder

22 incidents—25 victims

Crime Victims of Dr. George Hill Hodel MD   1943-1969

As stated in *Most Evil*:

"George Hodel was a prolific serial killer whose signature is visible not in any single method of murder, type of victim, or specific killing ground, but rather as a series of complex arrangements, installations, and obscure references to art, culture, and film that, taken together, reveal a chilling and never-before-documented variety of serial murder: murder as a fine art."

Black Dahlia Avenger/Zodiac MO and Crime Signature Comparisons

The following unique crime signatures and M.O.s were used by George Hodel in his crimes both as the "Black Dahlia Avenger" and "Zodiac":

✓   Serial Killer

✓   Created his own marketing/public relations campaign along with inventing and providing newspapers with a pseudonym for them to use in headlining his crimes and his "reign of terror." (Black Dahlia Avenger and Zodiac.)

✓ Contacted and taunted press by telephone after crimes.

✓ Used press as his instrument to terrorize public, promising, **"There will be more."**

✓ Drew crude picture of a knife dripping blood and mailed the drawing to press.

✓ Brought precut lengths of clothesline and used them to bind and tie victims during crimes.

✓ Mailed more than a dozen notes to press and police feigning illiteracy, using misspelled words and disguised handwriting.

✓ Mailed cut-and-paste notes to press and police.

✓ Mailed typewritten letter describing his actions to police.

✓ Placed excessive postage and multiple stamps on the taunting notes he mailed to press and police.

✓ Addressed press mailings, "To the Editor."

✓ Mailings sent on particular "anniversary dates" related to crimes.

✓ Packaged and mailed personal items belonging to his murdered victims to the press to prove he was the killer.

✓ Told victims and press he was "Going to Mexico."

✓ Used both a knife and a gun(s) in his separate crimes.

✓ Included puns and word games in his mailings.

✓ Continued to send in mailings to press and police months and years after original crimes.

✓ Egomaniacal personality demanded constant media publicity and front-page coverage under threat of additional killings.

✓ Identified himself as an "Avenger," claiming he was wronged by the female victim or that he was getting revenge for being spurned and ignored by the victim.

✓ Informed the public that the crime was "justified" or was "divine retribution."

✓ Stabbed several victims with a long-bladed jungle or bayonet-style knife.

✓ Wrote taunting messages at the scene either on the bedroom wall, a nearby telephone post, a door panel of victim's vehicle, or the victim's body.

✓ Manually ripped away band from a men's wristwatch and left both band and watch at separate crime scenes, on or near the victim's body.

✓ A man's white handkerchief was left at the scene: 1) near the body, 2) or used to wipe away fingerprints from inside the victim's vehicle, or 3) from a knife.

✓ Geographically preselected crime scene locations by plotting coordinates on a map; then randomly murdered victim(s) who by happenstance entered his "killing zone," or

✓ Geographically preselected crime scene locations by plotting coordinates on a map, then had unwitting victim (taxi driver) drive him to that specific location, where victim was then shot and killed, or,

✓ Forcibly kidnapped female victim, strangled her to death, and dismembered the body with surgical skill and precision. Then posed the body parts in public view at a specific location (street name) that provided a taunting clue related to the crime or suspect.

✓ Brutal assault and overkill, particularly savage with his female victims.

✓ Telephoned and/or sent sadistic note to victim's parents after brutal murder of their daughter.

~ ~ ~

I began my murder investigations way before CSI, DNA, and "Criminal Profiling" hit the small screen or were used as a part of forensics or field investigations.

As a rookie detective, responding to my first "call out" I still remember my old-time partner's two admonishments.

He said:

1. "There are only three things you need to bring with you to any crime scene. They are: a blank yellow notebook pad, a pen, and a brain. Use those, use them well, and the rest will all fall into place."

2. "Son, remember this. You and your partner are standing in the shoes of the victim. If you two don't solve it, it likely never will be solved."

So, I say the same to you my reader/partner. Grab a notebook and pen. (And, don't forget to bring your brain.)

Now that you are backgrounded with a knowledge of George Hill Hodel's unique M.O. and varied "crime signatures," we are ready to proceed.

But, first *my* two-cent lecture:

"Partner to partner, just so you know. I'm not real big on what the FBI (In Chief Parker's day we used to call them **F**an **B**elt **I**nspectors) refer to as Criminal Profiling. In our case, there is no need to "call in the experts.""

Fact is, every detective worth their salt automatically "profiles" their own suspect(s) as they move forward in their investigation. And, as the lead detectives, they base it solely on the known facts specific to their crime. There's no need for Wu-Wu speculation or subjective psychological analysis.

Serial killers as advanced as George Hodel, *do it for us.* They profile and introduce themselves to us as the author of their crimes. That's why we call their unique acts, *signatures.* The serial killer generally *signs* his or her work, over and over, usually with only slight variations, as they move from victim to victim.

"O.K. Enuf said.

"Jump into the *Beamback Machine.* Plenty of room for the two of us. You can drive. Reach up there and turn that dial to the year **1921**.

Good, now pull out that black keyboard and type in "Colma, C.O.L.M.A., California" and let's hit the streets."

Chapter 4

On the night of August 2, 1921, at approximately nine PM, the machine stopped in front of the small parish in Colma, California, a small coastal town located some twenty miles south of San Francisco.

A man who was later described by the housekeeper as "small, with a foreign-sounding voice and speaking in broken English" came to the door and asked for the on-duty priest. (No name specified) The housekeeper would later describe the man as "wearing a full-length duster coat with the collar up and driving goggles."

Father Patrick Heslin met with him, and they talked briefly. The small-statured male informed the priest "his friend was on his deathbed, and the priest was needed immediately to perform the last rites."

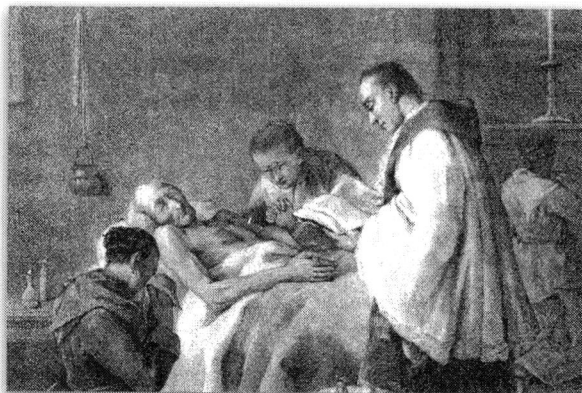

Extreme Unction (Last Rites)
By Marco Pitteri and Pietro Longhi circa 1755

Father Heslin informed his housekeeper that he would be going, and then went next door to his church to obtain the sacraments needed to perform the Extreme Unction (Last Rites) ceremony. The two men then drove off in the suspect's vehicle.

THE REV. PATRICK E.

The home where Rev. Father Patrick E. Heslin lived and the church in which he preached in Colma are shown above. The night that the priest disappeared, he was seen to enter the church, where he remained for several minutes before joining the mysterious visitor.

Suspect described as a "small foreign-looking male appearance disguised by touring goggles and long coat (duster)"

The following day, with Father Heslin failing to return to his parish, church authorities and law enforcement are contacted and begin their search for the missing priest who they now fear has been kidnapped.

San Francisco Chronicle
PRIEST ON DEATH CALL MISSING

August 4, 1921

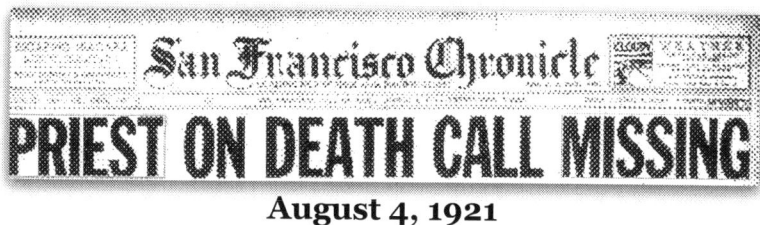

Here is the verbatim article from the *San Francisco Chronicle* of August 4, 1921.

COLMA PASTOR HURRIED OFF IN STRANGER'S CAR

Rev. P.E. Heslin, Lately of Turlock, Gone for More Than 24 Hours

VISITOR SEEN EXCITED

Auto Reported Not Lighted; County-Wide Search to Be Made by Sheriff

Hurriedly summoned on a "death call" by a muffled stranger, who drove up to the parochial residence Tuesday night in an automobile. Rev. Patrick E. Heslin pastor of the Holy Angels' Church in Colma has been strangely missing for more than twenty-four hours, and fears for his safety have aroused many of his parishioners to institute a search of the mountain roads south of Colma.

Father Heslin only recently came to Colma from Turlock, succeeding Father Mathew Concannon as pastor and the fact that he is unfamiliar with the peninsula roads coupled with the fact that he disappeared with a stranger, adds in the uneasiness over his prolonged absence.

Archbishop Acts, Sheriff Forms Posse

Archbishop Edward J. Hanna yesterday detailed two priests to take over the affairs of Father Heslin temporarily and has ordered an investigation into the priest's disappearance.

Sheriff Michael Sheehan of San Marco County arrived at Colma late last night and is organizing a posse for a county-wide search for the missing pastor.

Miss Marie Wendel, who has been his housekeeper for seven years, stated yesterday that never before has the priest been away from his residence on such a religious errand for this length of time.

It was about 9 o'clock Tuesday night that a man drove up to the parochial residence in an automobile. He wore a heavy overcoat and goggles. Met at the door by Miss Wendel, the stranger, who appeared to be considerably excited, said that he wanted to see Father Heslin at once "on a death call."

Car Driven Toward Mountain Road

Called by the housekeeper, Father Heslin listened to the man's story and then walked to the church to obtain the sacraments called for by the mission he was about to undertake. The stranger awaited the priest's return with impatience.

When Father Heslin said he was prepared to accompany the stranger, both entered the touring car, which was driven rapidly toward the Pedro Mountain Road in a generally southerly direction from Colma.

The two were seen to leave in the automobile by the housekeeper and Mrs. Mary Bianchi, living across the street from the church.

The parochial house is a massive two-story structure of concrete and is half again as large as the frame church, which adjoins it.

Woman Describes Mysterious Stranger

"I was standing on the sidewalk in front of my home," said Mrs. Bianchi, "when I saw a light touring car draw up to the church and stop. A man of small stature turned out the lights of the machine, got out, and walked to the pastor's house. He wore a soft hat, which was pulled down over his eyes and goggles. As he approached the house, he drew the collar of his overcoat up about his face.

"He talked excitedly to the priest for a few moments, but I could not hear what he was saying. Father Heslin went back into the house, and the man returned to his automobile, which he turned around. Presently the priest came out of the house and shouted to the man that he was going to the church for a few moments. It was more than fifteen minutes before he came out of the church. The man seemed impatient and called to him in broken English to come and get into the machine. It was about five minutes after nine (9) when they drove off. There were no lights on the machine."

Constable S.A. Landini, nonplussed over the situation, waited late last night for word of a man dying without clerical benefit. That word failing to come, he will leave early this morning with a posse to search ravines and creek bottoms along the mountain road between Colma and Halfmoon Bay on the theory that the priest and the mysterious motorist plunged to injury or death in the thick fog at some treacherous point on the highway.

The Ransom Note

On Aug 5, the *San Francisco Chronicle* confirms that Father Heslin has been kidnapped and is, in fact, being held prisoner. A ransom of $50,000 has been demanded by his kidnapper, but law enforcement is keeping all the details confidential.

San Francisco Chronicle August 5, 1921

Kidnapper's Envelope Containing Ransom Note delivered to St. Mary's Cathedral

Note demanding money for return of Father Patrick E. Heslin of Colma, and the envelope in which it arrived at St. Mary's

Here is the verbatim text of the typewritten note as published in the *San Francisco Chronicle* on Aug 6, 1921:

A U G - 3 RD

"Act with caution, for I have Father *McGinn* in bootleg cellar, where a lighted candle is left burning when I leave, and at the bottom of the candle are all the chemicals necessary to generate enough poison gas to kill a dozen men, and as he is fastened with chains you will see that he is in a very bad way, and if I am arrested, or bothered in any way, I will leave him just where he is and in two hours from the time I leave him he will be dead, for the candle will not burn more than an hour and a half after I leave him, for I cut it at that length.

If door is open to this cellar by anyone except myself it will ignite a bunch of matches and upset a can of gasoline on top of him, and the entire police force and all your damned Knights would not be able to get the chains off of him before he would burn to death, SO THE ONE BEST BET IS FOR YOU TO GET THE SIXTY FIVE HUNDRED DOLLARS IN FIVES, TENS, TWENTIES, FIFTIES AND HUNDREDS, BUT NONE HIGHER THAN HUNDREDS, AND BE SURE THERE IS NO MARKS ON THEM, FOR IF ANYTHING AROUSES MY SUSPICION I WILL LEAVE HIM TO DIE RIGHT WHERE HE IS. I had charge of a machine gun in the Argonne and poured thousands of bullets into struggling men, and killing men is no novelty to me; besides, it will be your own bunch that will kill him if you do not do just as you are told.
GET THE SIXTY-FIVE HUNDRED DOLLARS IN UNMARKED BILLS, WRAP IN PACKAGE AND SEAL IT FOR THE TWO MEN WHO WILL HANDLE IT BEFORE IT GETS TO ME THINK THAT IT IS "DOPE," so don't leave it unsealed or it might not reach me after you send it.
Have car ready with spotlight, and you will get instructions what road to take and you will turn the spotlight upward and drive slowly, until you see a white strip across the road, then stop, get out with the money, leave car, and follow the string that is attached to white strip until you come to end of string, then put down package and go back to town, and remember your brother does not get out until I have the money and am in the clear, besides as

[Unknown word/s], and he is complaining of the pain when he is not gagged so he cannot make a complaint. Better have a doctor ready with you and be at the house where he lived and wait for the messenger with the instructions what road to take. REMEMBER, JUST ONE MAN IN THAT CAR, and he had better be careful, for if he looks suspicious, he will be tagged with a hand grenade, as have six of them ready for treachery, and the waiting man will not be seen at all, and he will not see the man to whom he passes the package, and the second man gives it to me; but remember, if the cops are notified, or any move made that will make it dangerous to me, I will not send you the instructions how to find him and release him, besides, if this becomes public it will be seen how easy it is to trap your bunch of impostors, and others will go and do likewise. "Nuff said."
It's up to you.
You will get the message about nine o'clock at night, perhaps tonight, perhaps tomorrow night."

**Had to hit him four times and he is
unconscious from pressure on the brain so
better hurry and no fooling.
Tonight at 9 clock.**

On August 8, a $10,000 reward was offered for
Information leading to the discovery of Father Heslin
and or the arrest of his kidnappers.

A *Second Note* sent to Archbishop Hanna by the
suspect. Fully handwritten and reproduced below it
read:

**"Archbishop Hanna
Don't Be surprised to get this. It is to tell
you father Heslin is not dead. Neither is he
injured yet. Fate has made me do this.
Sickness & Mizery has compelled my actions.
Must Have Money. Please forgive this act ib.**

Steve Hodel

Handwriting on second note compared to first note printing published in newspaper.

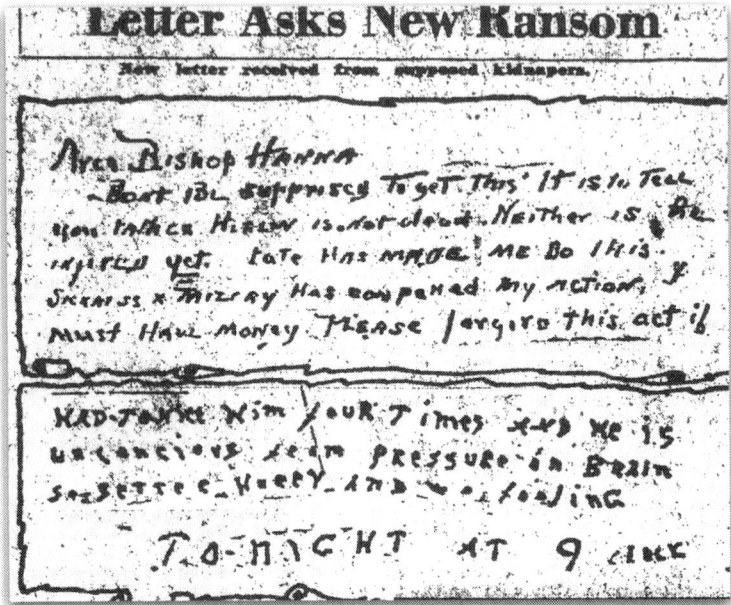

August 11, 1921

Artist's reconstruction of the scene of Father Heslin's murder. It is believed that he was taken over the Ocean Shore highway from Colma to a spot near the big sign that marked the location of his grave, then coaxed or forced over the sand dunes to the edge of the cliff, killed, and dropped down to the place where his grave was found. The dotted line graphically shows the supposed route that the print took to his death.

Witness William Hightower leads authorities to the suspected area where a search revealed the body of Father Patrick Heslin was buried in a shallow grave in a cave near "Pancake sign."

William Hightower Witness or Suspect?

On August 11, William Hightower, an itinerant baker, approached Archbishop Hanna in an effort to secure the reward. Hightower believed if he went to the police first, "They and not he would get the money."

Hightower then went on to relate a bizarre story of having met one "Dolly Mason," an attractive "lady of the night" in Salt Lake City, Utah, and the two of them traveled by train to Sacramento on June 29 then continued on to San Francisco.

The couple went their separate ways but would see each other on occasion in downtown San Francisco.

Hightower went on to relate to authorities that "last Saturday night" (Aug. 6) he reconnected with Dolly

Mason, who informed him that "a drunken foreigner had called upon her who was in possession of a handgun." Dolly went on to tell Hightower that the man told her, "You better be afraid of this gun, it has killed a man. But he is not alone. Beside his grave sits a man also frying pancakes."

Hightower informed authorities that he was familiar with what he suspected might be the location, referred to it as being, "a familiar sign off the highway that pictured a man, an old desert rat frying pancakes over a fire."

Hightower went to the location, searched the area and discovered loose dirt, and what he thought just might be the grave of the missing priest, but claimed he made no further investigation and came to report his discovery to the church and local authorities. He then led police and reporters to the isolated cave, and they together dug in the loose dirt and found the body of Father Heslin.

Photo showing sign of "Pancake Man" (center) off-highway and cave/gravesite below.

Immediately after "Witness" William Hightower led police to the gravesite police took him into custody and arrested him as the probable killer of Father Heslin.

Witnesses Trace Movements of Murder Case Suspect

Scene on Edgmar cliffs, believed to have been the spot where Father Heslin breathed his last. A group of searchers is shown.

Witnesses standing on the cliff above gravesite of Father Heslin

The Crime Scene

The following descriptions were obtained from the 1921 newspaper reportage and the subsequent Coroner's Inquest testimony provided by autopsy surgeon, Dr. John B. Clark.

I quote from the *San Francisco Chronicle* of August 18, 1921: (see top of next page - 162)

MURDEROUS ACT ESTABLISHED AT HESLIN INQUEST

Evidence Confined to Proof of Violent Death and
Finding of Body

Only such facts as were material to establish identity,
cause of death, and connection of William A.
Hightower with the discovery of the body were
brought out yesterday at the Coroner's inquest in
connection with the death of Father Patrick E. Heslin,
murdered Colma priest. District Attorney Franklin K.
Swart of San Mateo County called but two witnesses.
Dr. John R. Clark, autopsy surgeon, testified either
the blows on the head or the bullet wounds in the
body would have been sufficient to have caused death.
Constable S.A. Landini briefly described the case with
which Hightower led the searchers through the
darkness and fog to the obscure grave above Salada
Beach.

...

FOUND SKULL FRACTURED

The inquest, which was attended by some fifty
spectators, was held in the City Hall at Daly City. Dr.
Clark testified to having found the skull fractured in
several places, bits of bone having been driven into
the brain, and two bullet wounds through the
abdominal cavity and through the right lung. There
also was a bullet wound through the arm.

Dr. Clark expressed his belief that Father Heslin was
struck with a weapon and shot almost at the same
instant. While the autopsy surgeon could not
determine whether the priest had been struck first

with the weapon or shot first, he based the theory upon evidence that simultaneous hemorrhage took place from all injured parts of the body.

The verdict of the jury was: "That Father Patrick E. Heslin came to his death by violence consisting of blows on the head that fractured the skull sufficiently to have caused death, or by two gunshot wounds that were sufficient to have caused death, or by both the blows on the head and the gunshot wounds."

Thousands flock to Father Heslin's gravesite to "search for clews" (*SF Examiner* Aug 15, 1921)

The Arrest

Immediately after the discovery and recovery of the priest's body, police detained William Hightower and returned him to police headquarters where an intensive interrogation (think "grilling") was conducted.

Hightower maintained his innocence throughout and stuck to his story of having received the initial information from "Dolly Mason," a "woman of the night" who told him of entertaining "a drunken foreign-looking man (think "trick") who claimed he shot a man with the gun and the man's grave was being guarded by a Man making pancakes."

Police searched Hightower's hotel room and discovered what they termed "an infernal death machine." The San Francisco Chronicle headlines read "DEATH BOMB FOUND IN SUSPECT'S ROOM" —"Planned to Blow Up Pursurers (sp) After Ransom was Paid"

San Francisco Chronicle August 12, 1921

[caption for above *SFC* photo appears on page 165]

William Hightower (lower left), "discoverer" of the body of Father Patrick E. Heslin, being examined by prosecutors and Captain of Police Duncan Matheson. District Attorney Franklin Swart of San Mateo County and Deputy District Attorney I.M. Golden of San Francisco are conducting the examination.

"Prisoner, Religious Fanatic, Tells Police Weak Story; Charged With Crime Today"

The August 12 *SFC* article continues:

The accused man is held in San Francisco to prevent any possible demonstration.

Hightower's explanation of his whereabouts on the day of the abduction and the day following was broken down by police investigation. His story of the alleged conversation with Dolly Mason and the subsequent discovery of the grave is held to be weak.

Infernal Machine Planted On Highway Below Colma

Finding of an infernal machine (in Hightower's hotel room) and Hightower's admission that he had it planted on the Pedro Road a mile beyond Colma, is considered damning evidence against him.

(**SKH Note** - Hightower informed authorities he was an inventor and had taken his invention, which was on the order of a rapid-fire machine gun, out to the isolated highway to test it.)

...

The infernal machine was cunningly contrived with ten shotgun shells loaded with No. 1 buckshot. The shells were encased in short iron pipes firmly set in a base of Plaster of Paris, with nails designed as firing pins controlled by powerful springs. Release of these springs by the mere pulling of a string would have been sufficient to have discharged the shells.

San Francisco Examiner **August 12, 1921 Photo of William Hightower next to his "Infernal Death Machine" Headline shows authorities searching for his accomplice and the actual shooter of Father Heslin. Police were pushing the theory that Hightower is "the brains behind the murder."**

August 14, 1921

Two views of William Hightower, "discoverer" and suspect in the Heslin case.

HIGHTOWER HELD BY 13 LINKS FACES PRIEST MURDER CHARGE

William Hightower Arrested for Murder of Father Patrick Heslin

By mid-August 1921, law enforcement has determined from witness statements that while Hightower was not the actual suspect, "A small dark-complexioned foreign-looking male, possibly Greek" that performed the actual kidnap and murder, still, he must have been "the brains behind the crime" and he was arrested and charged with the murder.

Officers remained confident that, in due time, they would be able to identify and locate Hightower's "accomplice," the small foreign-looking man. Assuring the public they would find the priest's abductor and simultaneous to taking Hightower into custody the newspaper headline read (page 169):

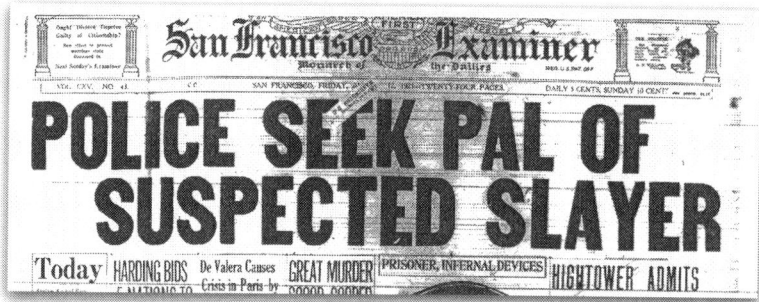

POLICE SEEK PAL OF SUSPECTED SLAYER

In addition to finding "the death machine," a letter, written by Hightower to Miss Dolly Mason, was also found in the suspect's hotel room. It was opened by the police after Hightower's arrest and detention and seemingly supported his initial telling of the facts. The letter read as follows:

"Aug 10—Dear Miss Dolly

I believe there is something to what that drunk told you. I know what he meant by the chap frying hot cakes, and I found two caved-in places, but not caves and something is or has been buried there, for the sand is loose as ashes. If it is a booze cache, we will get it as soon as the hunt for that priest dies down, so it will be safe. I am beginning to think it might have something to do with the priest, anyway. Try to remember all the things he said and watch for him. His talk about killing a man and the big black pistol may not be booze talk at all for I found an empty .45 shell at the place. See me at once as there is a reward offered.

WA HIGHTOWER,
General Delivery

The following article was in the *San Francisco Chronicle* on August 18, 1921, days after Hightower's arrest for murder. I quote from that article in full.

PSYCHOLOGISTS CALLED UPON TO SOLVE MURDER

Scientific Methods Now Being Used to Determine Guilt of William Hightower
NEW DISCOVERIES MADE
Tests Show Suspect Covers Up Important Facts, Says Dr. Larson

Instruments developed in the psychological laboratory were called into play yesterday in an attempt to determine by scientific methods whether or not William A. Hightower is the murderer of Father Patrick Heslin.

The tests were made in the Redwood City jail shortly after midnight Tuesday by J.A. Larson, Ph.D., psychologist of the Berkeley police department; Philips Edson, Dr. Larson's assistant, and District Attorney Franklin K. Swart of San Mateo County.

At the conclusion of the tests, Dr. Larson expressed the opinion that the "suspect was covering up important facts on every crucial question that was asked."

BLOOD PRESSURE TAKEN

The tests were made with instruments which recorded Hightower's blood pressure and respiration during a series of questions.

The instruments were equipped with drums of smoked paper upon which were traced the psychological reflexes of the subject.

There in the line of the curves on these drums every heart beat and every change of blood pressure of Hightower during the course of the experiment was recorded.

In addition, through the use of the pneumograph every respiration was recorded as the subject was being questioned.

NEW LEADS SECURED

"In the present test," said Dr. Larson, "very satisfactory leads were secured." To secure these 'leads' and establish without his knowledge wherein Hightower's deception definitely lay was the purpose of the test." He continued.

"There were marked rises in Hightower's blood pressure, accelerations, and marked irregularities as well, following the vital questions that were asked him."

The experiment was divided into parts. The first test was to determine Hightower's normal blood pressure and respiration. The second test was to determine his reaction to commonplace questions, and the third test was to determine the suspect's reaction when he was asked point-blank important questions bearing on the case.

NET GRADUALLY TIGHTENS

Following the tests, Dr. Larson said the experiment would furnish the authorities many important "leads," which would aid them in building up a case against Hightower.

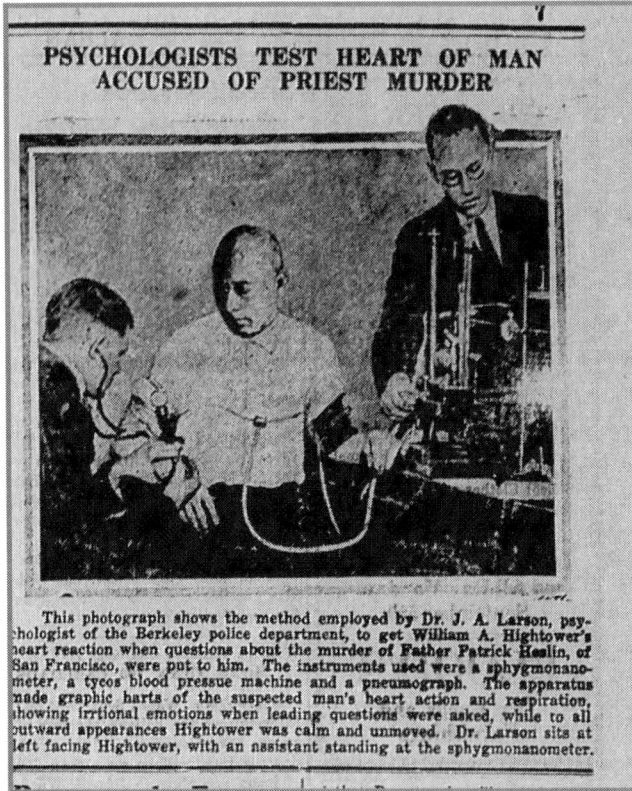

PSYCHOLOGISTS TEST HEART OF MAN ACCUSED OF PRIEST MURDER

This photograph shows the method employed by Dr. J. A. Larson, psychologist of the Berkeley police department, to get William A. Hightower's heart reaction when questions about the murder of Father Patrick Heslin, of San Francisco, were put to him. The instruments used were a sphygmonanometer, a tycos blood pressue machine and a pneumograph. The apparatus made graphic harts of the suspected man's heart action and respiration, showing irrtional emotions when leading questions were asked, while to all outward appearances Hightower was calm and unmoved. Dr. Larson sits at left facing Hightower, with an assistant standing at the sphygmonanometer.

Dr. John Augustus Larson is administering his **"cardio-pneumo-psychogram" machine** to test defendant Hightower's truthfulness.

(Newspapers would later dub it a "lie detector machine.")

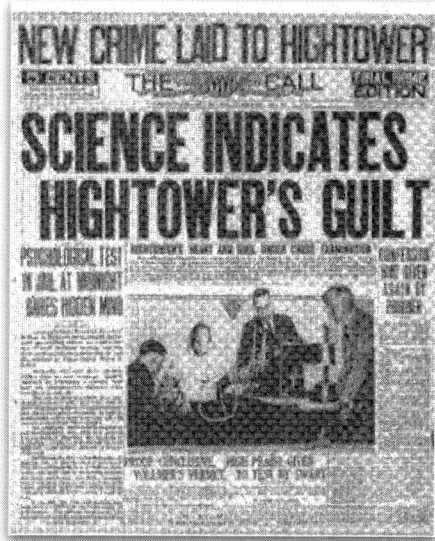

San Francisco Call & Post, August 17, 1921

SKH Note — I came across an additional article in *The Mercury News* published on March 12, **2013**/updated August 12, **2016**, written by Jean Bartlett/Pacific Tribune. The piece, *"Modern-day polygraph dates back to 1921 murder in Pacifica,"* provides interesting historical documentation, which shows that "The Flapjack Murder Trial" of defendant William Hightower, was *the first time the modern-day polygraph was ever used in a criminal proceeding.*

(Sadly, this was prior to later court rulings that the use of its findings, without the consent of all parties involved, would be inadmissible.) Here are some excerpts from Ms. Bartlett's article:

Modern-day polygraph dates back to 1921 murder in Pacifica
By Jean Bartlett

Born in Nova Scotia in 1892, John Augustus Larson became interested in forensic science and went on to receive his Ph.D. in physiology at the University of California, Berkeley around 1919. That same year he also became a Berkeley police officer. A native of County Longford, Ireland, Patrick Heslin was born in 1863. He would go on to become a Catholic priest and eventually serve as pastor of Holy Angels Church in Colma. Born in Texas in 1880, William A. Hightower headed out West and learned to cook at various roadside restaurants. He eventually became an accomplished baker. On Aug 17, 1921, the names of all three men shared in the same "San Francisco Call and Post" front page exclusive, subtitled—"Psychological Test In Jail At Midnight Bares Hidden Mind." Their story began on the evening of Aug 2, 1921, with a knock on the rectory door of Holy Angels in Colma. The air was thick with fog, but still, the housekeeper and a neighbor were able to see clearly enough to later recall that the man knocking was odd, suspicious even, hidden beneath a heavy overcoat, goggles and a pulled up collar which concealed his face. Father Heslin opened the door. He listened while the stranger spoke of an ailing friend in Salada Beach—present-day Pacifica—a man in need of the last rites. The cleric gathered a "red Morocco case containing the bread and wine of the Blessed Sacrament," and hastily climbed into the front seat of the stranger's touring car. Father Heslin never returned.

...

This all happened right during the time that John Augustus Larson had perfected William Moulton Marston's "Detect Deception" apparatus, which monitored an individual's blood pressure as an aid in uncovering the honesty of their statements. Larson's invention additionally monitored respiration, the pulse, and skin conductivity to make the results more reliable. Larson called his machine the "cardio-pneumo psychogram," but it is more commonly known as the polygraph and was immediately christened by the press as the lie detector.

The *San Francisco Call and Post* arranged for Larson to use his invention on Hightower. It would be the lie detector's first case. On the morning of August 17, 1921, the "Call and Post" banner headline read —"Science Indicates Hightower's Guilt."

The Trial

William Hightower's trial for the kidnap and brutal murder of Father Patrick Heslin began on October 3, 1921, and lasted just two weeks.

The hundred-year-old trial was a sham—a jurisdictional circus.

The public, after reading the daily newspaper headlines proclaiming Hightower's guilt along with the "scientific proofs obtained by the lie detector test," had already made up their minds. The public did not need a trial. In their minds, Hightower's guilt was already decided.

In fact, they were ready to lynch the man ahead of any trial.

August 16, 1921 (Seven weeks before the trial)

In this review and summary of the crime, I am not going to present all of the "evidence" used to prosecute William Hightower. But, will show just a few of the "highlights" (think lowlights) of "The Peoples Case."

- Two female witnesses who initially described the suspect as "small, foreign-looking, with a soft cap on his head, a full overcoat with the collar up to disguise himself and wearing automobile goggles to conceal his face." Both positively eliminated William Hightower, but then months later, after being assured by police, "they had the right man in custody," then changed their earlier statements and "identified" Hightower as the suspect. No lineup with other possible suspects, but rather both witnesses were taken downtown and allowed to view defendant alone (in what we used to call a "shotgun show-up"); and then mutually agreed it must be the man they saw.

- Prosecutors introduced the "death machine" as part of Hightower's plan to blow up any police that might try and stop him from collecting the reward money. (Hightower admitted he had invented the machine as a sort of "machine gun" and was planning to test it on an isolated highway in hopes of selling the patent once completed, but stated it had nothing to do with any crime.)

- Forensic handwriting "experts" claimed that the letter "B" written in the ransom note was of the style used by bakers in lettering cakes and that it was identical to the letter "B" written by Hightower, who was by trade "a baker."

Re: *the handwriting*, here are my notes from a book, "San Francisco Murders" (Duell, Sloan& Pearce 1947) from the chapter, *"The Flapjack Murder: The Murder of Father Patrick Heslin"* written by John Bruce.

The referent chapter begins on page 212, with this introduction:

"John Bruce is one of San Francisco's best-known newspapermen and, in the days before he became an editor, was particularly noted as a crime reporter. He did considerable work among criminals when he worked for Fremont Older and claims that his best boyhood friend was a retired but unreformed burglar. Mr. Bruce is at present city editor of the *San Francisco Chronicle.*"

Here, excerpted, are verbatim notes I have taken from the chapter where journalist Bruce writes explicitly about the two handwriting experts hired by the police to examine the Heslin kidnapper notes. Regarding the first, typewritten/handwritten Ransom Note Bruce writes:

> "The note went under the microscopes and power lights of Chauncey McGovern and Carl Eisenschimel, handwriting experts who had fought, bled and almost died at each other's throats in many court battles. This time they were allies against the unknown kidnapper and were being paid from the same source, the police fund. They agreed.
>
> The writer was demented. McGovern came forth with that extra something: a shell-shocked veteran wrote it. This was not the most spectacular deduction in the world since the letter said the writer was a machine-gunner in the Argonne and shell-shock was newspaper language of the day for skiddy nerves There was some block lettering on the envelope and, said McGovern, "The style, of the printed H and A, is that of a deranged person."

Eisenschimel added that the block lettering was "script often used by a demented person."

This was, of course, a lot of pompous chatter, destined it was hoped, for Page One—where it landed. Both handwriting men had long been known in San Francisco court cases for making strange judgments, sometimes very right, sometimes very wrong. Their percentage was about fifty-fifty, and which one outranked the other as an expert was not determined when death interrupted the contest.

The ransom note was fairly clever, well-typed, correctly spelled, almost perfectly punctuated, a well-done job. Yet it was spoiled, apparently at the last minute or by someone who did not write the original, by a few too obviously intended illiteracies added in hand-printing. This block lettering was even in a different mood, a vicious tone suddenly thrust into an otherwise rather sane letter. The hand-printing said:

"Had to hitt him four times and he unconscious from pressure on brain. So better hurray and no fooling. TONIGHT at 9 clock."

The envelope had also been printed in the clumsy style popularly conceived to be that of a kidnapper.

The typewritten part of the note, something over 600 words, was obviously written by a good typist. For the letters had been struck with about equal force as if by one who knew the touch system. In the opening sentence there was a space left for the name of the priest, and in this interval was printed "of Colma" instead of "Heslin." This made it seem rather apparent that the letter was written before the job was undertaken and that the identity of the priest was of small consequence to the kidnapper.

The typewritten note went into considerable detail:
(Here journalist Bruce reproduces the entire First Ransom Note. See my reproduction of it on page 156.)

Page 222: (*San Francisco Murders* from the chapter, *"The Flapjack Murder: The Murder of Father Patrick Heslin"*)

News and the energies of the searchers had, however, been worn threadbare. On August 10, the drooping interest of public and police hardly lifted an eye when a new ransom note was announced. It was full of the usual, unimaginative phrases: "Fate has made me do this. Sickness and misery* has compelled my action. I must have money. Please forgive this act if you can. The father is not dead YET."

(Mr. Bruce has here only partially quoted the second Ransom Note [page 155], and he has spelled the writer's word as "misery," however, I read that word as being misspelled and printed as, "mizery," See my full text of the note on page 156.)

SKH Note - As many of my readers know from my many past comments as relates to handwriting analysis, I remain highly skeptical of its value unless it is strongly corroborated by other evidence. Author Bruce's comment here that both experts were found to be correct "about fifty percent of the time" tells us we might as well flip a coin and save the money paid for their "expertise." In many, most cases, two handwriting experts will be called and testify as to authorship, and one will say, "It's him" and the other, "definitely not him."

That is not science. I pretty much can say the same for polygraph examination results. Just too subjective, and I agree the results should not be allowed in criminal proceedings.

- A "Forensic geologist" who examined sand particles found on clothing at Hightower's hotel room testified that it was consistent with sand particles located near the beach gravesite. (Introduced as "evidence" even though Hightower had admitted to being at the location and finding the grave on the previous day.) Even a hundred years later, our modern forensics would not be able to identify sand with any specificity. For the most part, "sand is sand."

- While authorities never did find the actual "Dolly Mason," they did locate a second "lady of the night" known to have been an occasional hotel paramour of Hightower's who testified to inconsistencies in his statements, which merely added confusion to the case rather than being probative.

- The polygraph evidence indicating that in all probability, he was deceptive (think lying) in his denials of kidnapping and murdering Father Patrick Heslin.

The Verdict

October 14, 1921

Jury Finds Hightower Guilty of Killing Priest

Redwood City, Cal., Oct. 13.—(United News)—William A. Hightower today was found guilty on a charge of having kidnaped and murdered the Rev. Father Patrick Heslin, priest of the parish of Colma, Cal. near San Francisco. Hightower, who was placed on trial Oct. 3, was convicted after the jury had deliberated one hour and fifty minutes.

Hightower showed little emotion when the jury filed into court and read the verdict which found him guilty and recommended that he be sentenced to spend his life in San Quentin state penitentiary.

The verdict was a partial victory for the defense in that the jury saved him from the gallows.

Throughout the trial Hightower had chewed gum industriously. He continued to chew gum while the verdict was read—no more nor no less energetically.

The crowd in the courtroom remained silent for a moment after the decision was announced and then broke into a flutter, which a bailiff soon quieted.

Hightower's lawyer asked that he be sentenced Saturday and the request was granted. Passing of sentence will be merely a formality. Hightower was then led back to jail, chained to the jailer.

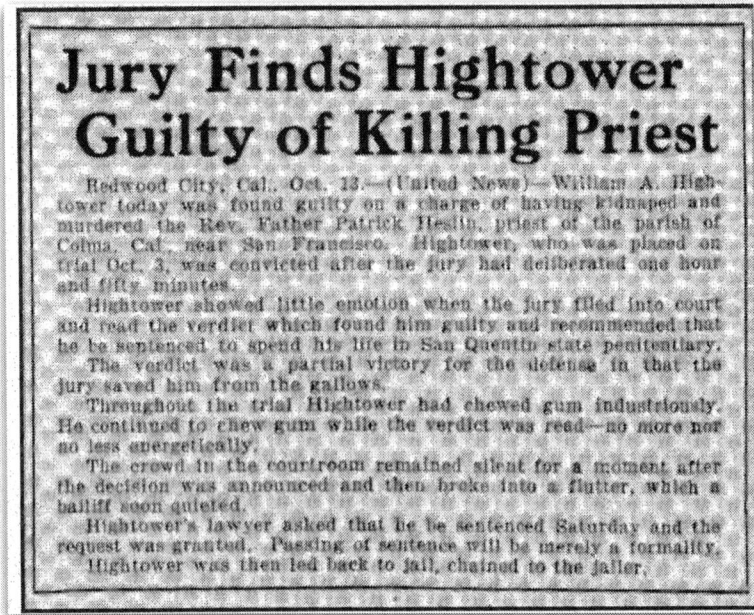

Hightower's defense attorneys considered the verdict somewhat of "a win" in that their client got "Life" rather than a death sentence and execution.

William Hightower served forty-three years in prison at San Quentin and, at the advanced age of eighty-six, was paroled to Los Angeles in 1965 just in time to be a witness to the Watts Riots.

William A. Hightower—A Wrongful Prosecution?

In my examination into "The Flapjack Murder," it is not my desire to attempt to argue for the guilt or innocence of William Hightower.

My impression in reviewing the known facts is that he

may well have been telling the truth, and his desire to collect the reward money after receiving information from "Dolly Mason" could be the truth of it.

Or, to the contrary, he could have been an accomplice and have some connection to the actual killer? We will never know the truth of it, and as far as this summation goes, it does not matter either way.

What is apparent to me, given the original witness statements, is that Hightower WAS NOT THE ABDUCTOR. He was not "the small foreign-looking man who witnesses said drove off with Father Heslin," i.e., kidnapped, bludgeoned and shot the Catholic priest.

Based on my now twenty-one years of ongoing investigations of my father's serial crimes* I believe that this 1921 Father Heslin murder could well have been the young George Hodel's FIRST MURDER.

[*Twenty-five crimes, spanning the years 1938-1969 have so far been presented in my five previous publications.]

I offer here some of the evidence in support of that belief, which I will be adding to in the following crime chapters with additional crime signatures and M.O. (Modus Operandi) linkage.

George Hill Hodel
The actual killer of Father Patrick Heslin?

DATE and LOCATION:
San Francisco Bay Area, Summer (August 1921)

While I have no specific information or knowledge that George Hodel was in San Francisco on that date and time, we do know he would have been out of school and was just seven weeks away from turning fourteen.

Granted, even age fourteen sounds almost inconceivably young to be committing such a horrific crime; however, as we know, *George Hodel was not your average teenager*. In fact in the summer of 1921 he was still thirteen.

Not yet sixteen in the early fall of 1923 this boy-genius entered Pasadena's Caltech with an IQ of 186 and a probable mental age in his thirties.

As far as young George Hodel's ability to drive a car, there is no question about it. In 1925 he would be using false identification, passing himself off as "twenty-one" to obtain a California Chauffeur's License and would be driving a Yellow Cab Taxi in Los Angeles. Prohibition boys grew up fast.

George may have had friends and/or relatives in the San Francisco Bay area at that time?

We know as fact that he would soon be spending the next ten years raising a family and attending premed in Oakland for four years, then move across the bay to San Francisco for another four years and obtain his MD at University of California, San Francisco (Parnassus Campus).

PHYSICAL DESCRIPTION

The original description provided by the two witnesses that observed the kidnapper at the front door of Father Heslin's residence (his housekeeper and the next-door neighbor) described the suspect as:

Male, small in stature, spoke with broken English and was foreign-sounding. Possibly Greek? Unable to recognize his face as he wore a long overcoat (driving duster) collar turned up to disguise himself and wore driving goggles, which hid his features and wore a soft cap, covering his head.

Young George Hodel was just weeks away from his fourteenth birthday, October 10th 1921. Here are some photographs that were taken in his teen years.

GHH teen (unknown year)

George Hodel
Adj.—Intelligent
By-word—Myself
Activities—Honor Society
1-2-3
Activities—Latin Club 1-2-3-4
Assembly
Class Programs 1-2
Debating 2-3-4
Short Story Contest 2-3
Spelling Contest 3
Economics Club 4
Senior Play 4
Tiger Staff 4
Jumbles 4

GHH South Pasadena Yearbook 1922

Re-creation of clothing similar in style to that worn to disguise kidnapper's appearance.

GHH Identification Card 1925

CITY OF LOS ANGELES
CHAUFFEUR'S IDENTIFICATION CARD
Name Geo. H. Hodel
Age 21   Height 5 ft. 7 in.
Weight 148 lbs.   Color Hair Black
Race White   Color Eyes DK. Brown

6512 Monterey Rd
So. Pasadena, Address
City   State
Badge No. 1976 Badge No. 34879

This image (a poor Xerox copy of a photo no longer in my possession) is probative in that it is a copy of GHH's original 1925 "Los Angeles City Chauffeur's Identification Card." The license was required and issued to uniformed cab drivers within the city limits showing their home address, age, height, weight, and City and State badge numbers.

Here is an enhanced version. Note the flowing signature of the young GHHodel with ending flourish.

George has falsified his real age and listed himself as age "21" (His actual age was 17 or 18 depending on the month) with a height of 6'-1/4" and weight, a skinny "148 pounds." This Chauffeur's license ID listed his home address as 6512 Monterey Road, in South Pasadena. (In 1925, he was still living at that address with his parents, albeit in a separate home on their property, which they had built for him as a fifteenth birthday present.)

Young George had a dark complexion and appeared to be of Middle East, Greek, or Turkish heritage. As we know, his parents were both born in Russia and came through Ellis Island circa 1901.

My guesstimate of my father's height four years earlier in the summer of 1921 would be (much smaller than recorded on his 1925 ID) perhaps 5'-7."

Dressed in the duster, goggles, and cap (described by witnesses) and possessed of the skill to drive at that young age, George could easily "fit the description" of Father Heslin's kidnapper.

Identical Crime Signatures/M.O.s

In earlier publications, I have posted a list of thirty-two distinct crime signatures used by my father in varying degrees in his twenty-five serial crimes from 1938-1969. I draw from that list to show how many of those (Identical Crime Signatures/M.O.s) are specifically included in Father Heslin's murder which—as I have indicated—I suspect was his "*first*" murder.

Here is the list of nine of George Hodel's thirty-two known crime signatures that were found to be present in the murder of Father Patrick Heslin in 1921. Note the last two (2) crime signatures are new to GHH's Early Year's crimes and are shown in italics.

- Handwrites and types ransom note/delivers threat to do harm to victim's person
- Kidnap abduction of the victim using a vehicle
- Used tire iron or unknown weapon to inflict blunt force trauma to victim's head

- Wore gloves
- Uses handgun
- Leaves behind the victim's valuables and cash, robbery not the motive
- Serial Killer
- *Handwrites threatening note to harm witness if they agree to testify in court*
- *Uses explicitly the term "Fate" as part of the reason/excuse for his crime.*

Father Heslin murder forerunner to George Hodel's later "Zodiac" Crimes

I believe that this 1921 murder of Father Heslin was at least in part, the "inspiration" for George Hodel's "Zodiac" crimes committed nearly fifty years later.

Why?

- The *San Francisco Chronicle* newspaper led all the other papers in 1921 reportage of the crime. It was above the fold headlines from day one of the murder and its reportage literally convicted Hightower on the front pages a month in advance of his "fair trial." The pretrial "nail in the coffin" was when they printed the "scientific results of the polygraph examination as proof Hightower was lying about not committing the murder."

- The *Chronicle* provided photographs and was the first to refer to Hightower's "Infernal Death Machine" found in his hotel room. The paper informed its subscribers of the police theory that the killer was planning to place his "death machine" on the highway and explode it and kill any officers who attempted to arrest him.

- I believe this sensational coverage was the very "food for thought" that inspired George Hodel as "Zodiac" to "write back" to the *San Francisco Chronicle* using their own original 1921 "copy."

~ ~ ~

Reproduced in part are two excerpts from Zodiac's 1969 handwritten "Bomb/Death Machine Letter" in which Zodiac threatened to plant his 'death machine' on a roadside and detonate it when little children get off a school bus."

Images as printed in *San Francisco Chronicle* November 9, 1969 and retyped below for clarity.

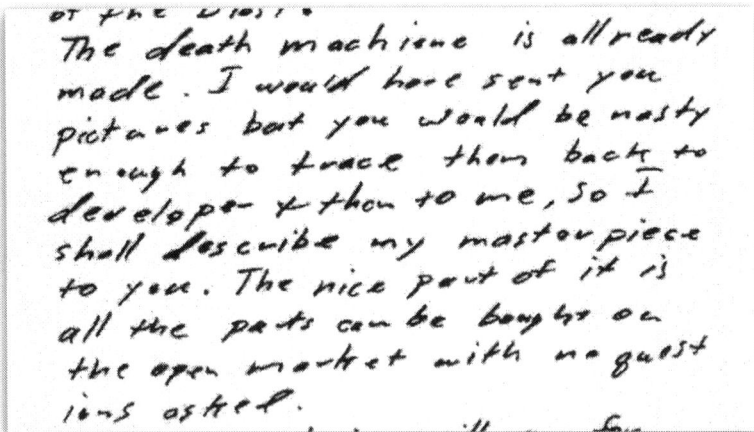

"The death machine is all ready made. I would have sent you pictures but you would be nasty enough to trace them back to developer & then to me, so I shall describe my masterpiece to you. The nice part of it is

all the parts can be bought on the open market with no questions asked."

"the system checks out from one end to the other in my tests. What you do not know is whether the death machine is at the sight or whether it is being stored in my basement for future use. I think you do not have the manpower to stop this one by continually searching the road sides looking for this thing."

I am confident that the source (*San Francisco Chronicle*) of the term "death machine" and the idea of planting it on a highway to blow up innocent people was copied and used by GHH in his Bomb Threat Letter in 1969—five decades after the idea's original publication in the 1921 reporting of Father Heslin's murder.

Below: November **1969** *San Francisco Chronicle* published Zodiac's handwritten diagram of his roadside "death machine."

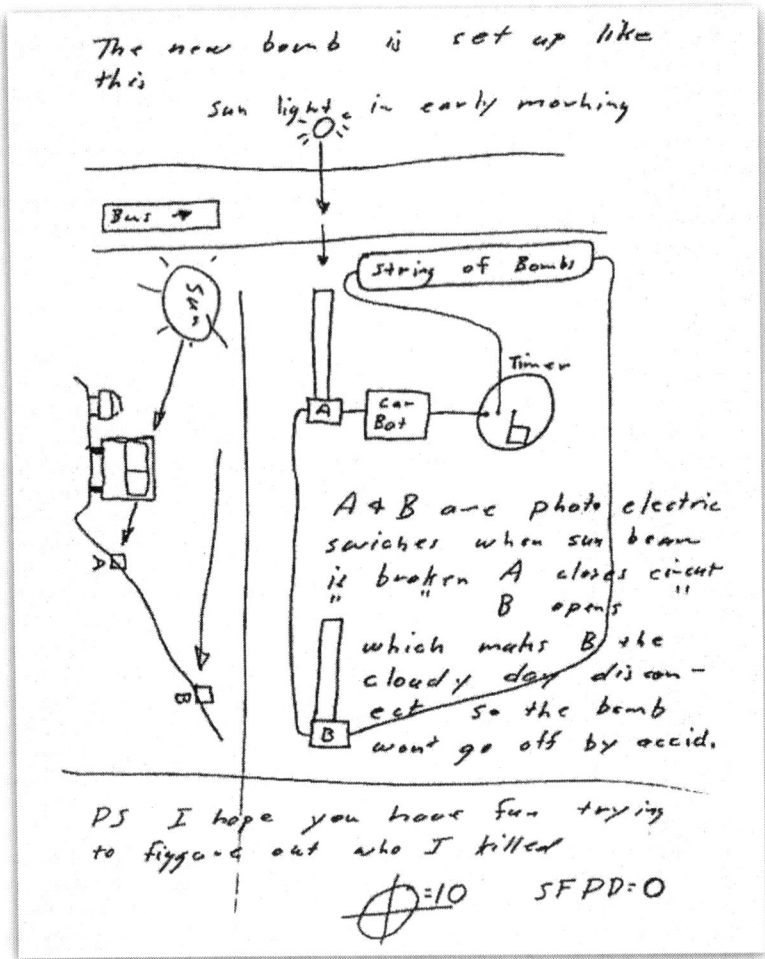

Also, as mentioned in my earlier books, keep in mind that GHH was hired and worked as a reporter/columnist for the *San Francisco Chronicle* newspaper in 1932, some eleven years after the sensational murder while attending premed at Berkeley and UCSF San Francisco. George's lengthy articles *"Abroad in San Francisco"* featured extensive coverage of the various ethnic communities within the city. There are no coincidences!

~ ~ ~

The Second Note - 1921 Ransom Demand

As they would some twenty-six-years later, in the 1947 Elizabeth Short "Black Dahlia" mailings to the police and press, the 1921 law enforcement and newspaper reporters also theorized the second Ransom Note to "likely be the work of a publicity-seeking crank."

In my opinion, it was not.

Not only is the handprinted/handwritten style consistent with George Hodel's, but in examining the note, I believe I have found what I have termed in previous writings, A THOUGHTPRINT.

In my first book, *Black Dahlia Avenger: A Genius for Murder* (*Arcade* 2003 updated by *SkyHorse* 2015) I coined the term "Thoughtprint" and defined it in the introduction.

Beginning on page (5) five of that book, I wrote the following:

"Most murders are not solved by brilliant deduction, *a la* Sherlock Holmes. The vast majority are solved by basic 'gumshoeing,' walking the streets, knocking on doors, locating and interviewing witnesses, friends, and business associates of the victim. In most cases, one of these sources will come up with a piece of information that will point to a possible suspect with a potential motive: a jealous ex-lover, financial gain, revenge for a real or imagined wrong. There are as many motives for the crime of murder as there are thoughts to think them.

"Our thoughts connect us to one another and to our actions. Our thought patterns determine what we do each day, each hour, each minute. While our actions may appear simple, routine, and automatic, they really are not. Behind and within each of our thoughts is an aim, an intent, a motive.

"The motive within each thought is unique. In all of our actions, each of us leaves behind traces of our self. Like our fingerprints, these traces are identifiable. I call them *thoughtprints*. They are the ridges, loops, and whorls of our mind. Like the individual 'points' that a criminalist examines in a fingerprint, they mean little by themselves, and remain meaningless, unconnected shapes in a jigsaw puzzle until they are pieced together to reveal a clear picture.

"Most people have no reason to conceal their thoughtprints. We are, most if not all the time, open and honest in our acts: our motives are clear, we have nothing to hide. There are other times, however, when we become covert, closeted in our actions: a secret love affair, a shady business deal, a hidden bank account, or the commission of a crime. If we are careful and clever in committing our crime, we may remember to wear gloves and not leave any fingerprints behind. But, rarely are we clever enough to mask our motives, and we will almost certainly leave behind our thoughtprints. A collective of our motives, a paradigm constructed from our individual thoughts, these illusive prints construct the signature that will connect or link us to a specific time, place, crime, or victim.

"Solving Los Angeles's most notorious homicide of the twentieth century, the murder of a young woman known to the world as the Black Dahlia, as well as the other sadistic murders discussed in this book, is the result of finding and piecing together hundreds of separate thoughtprints. Together with the traditional evidence, these thoughtprints make our case more than fifty years after the event and establish beyond a reasonable doubt the identity of her killer, the man who called himself the 'Black Dahlia Avenger.'"

~ ~ ~

How many "thoughtprints" does it require to "make your case and identify your suspect?" Who can say?

Typically, a criminalist/fingerprint examiner will require eight to twelve "points" to make an identification of any individual to a fingerprint "lift."

Perhaps one might need twenty or thirty "thoughtprint points" to be confident in his positive ID on a given person.

Let's play a game. Below is a reproduction of the second ransom note delivered to Archbishop Hanna at his San Francisco church. It followed shortly after the first lengthy typewritten and handprinted note confirming the kidnap of Father Patrick Heslin.

Take a look and see if you can see what I am seeing—a "thoughtprint"—just one single "point" in the building of our ultimate positive identification of the perpetrator/writer/thinker. It has been overlooked for one hundred years and only now has surfaced.

Take your time and study this second note. Like Poe's purloined letter, the "clew" is there in plain sight. I will present my answer on page 197. No peeking.

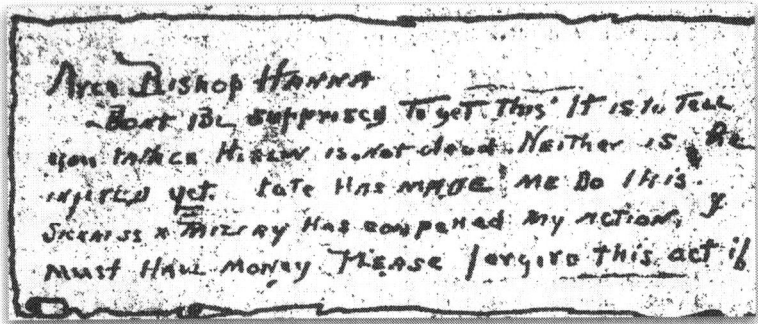

Second Ransom Note—from 1921 Kidnapper of Father Patrick Heslin delivered to Archbishop Hanna

Find the thoughtprint? Congrats if you found it and if not well, take heart, others have missed it for the last 99 years. It involves three 'very George' traits: Subtle, Sneaky and Snobbish—the essence of George Hodel the adolescent "Boy Genius."

Give up?

Here it is, hiding in plain sight and revealed for the first time in nearly 100 years.

The note writer reveals himself in the coda to his ransom demand that closes with the sentence:

"Please forgive this act ib."

ib? Yes, as in "ibid."

Let me repeat that definition: "... to refer to the source *cited in the preceding note* or list item."

To my mind, the young genius/scholar George Hodel is showing off his erudite knowledge and schooling in Latin.

His "ib" clearly is referencing "the preceding note," which was his first demand note to the Archbishop delivered just two days prior. A subtle "thoughtprint" not written by an "itinerant baker" but rather by a young intellectual confident that he can easily outwit the keystone cops with his superior mind as an up and coming "master criminal."

And what of the penultimate word "act" in this thoughtprint? Is he referring to the act (or acts) of kidnap, extortion, and murder? Or is he referring to his actions and activities as an 'act,' like a stage or movie portrayal, for the benefit of observers? Was it all a diabolical theatrical 'act' with intended fatal results?

On the following page (199) is his "ib"— his "preceding note," his "quoted work previously mentioned" delivered just days prior.

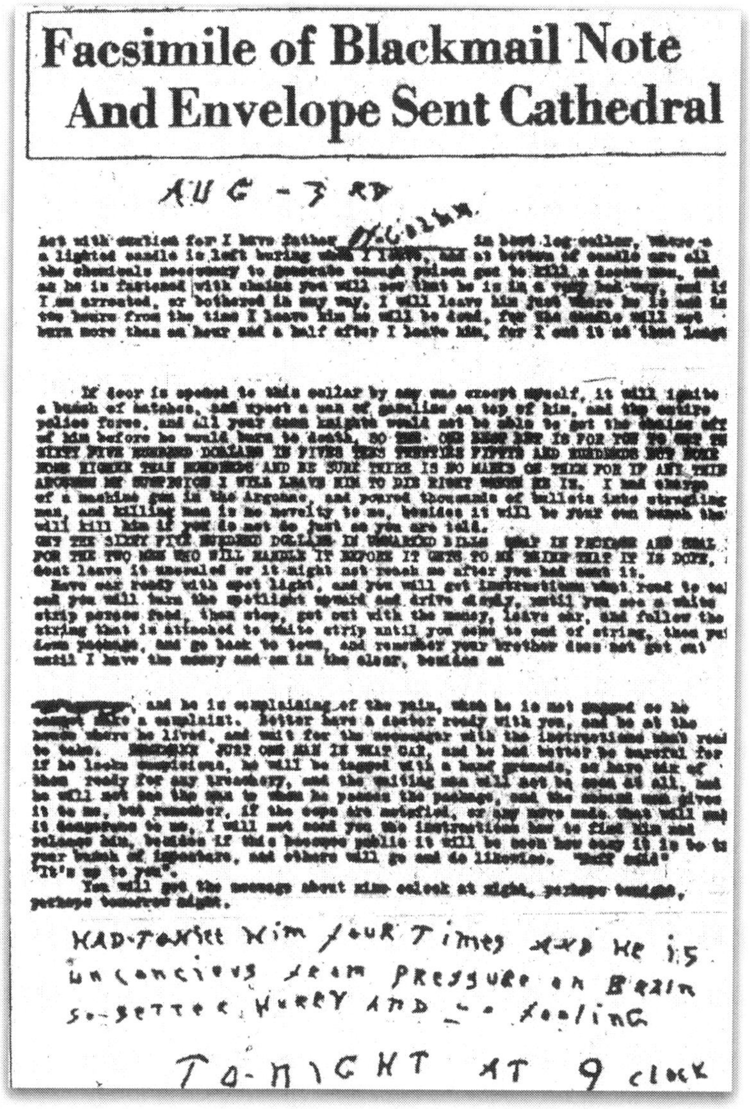

Facsimile of Blackmail Note And Envelope Sent Cathedral

AUG - 3 RD

[typewritten note text largely illegible]

HAD TAKEN HIM FOUR TIMES AND HE IS UNCONCIOUS FROM PRESSURE ON BRAIN SO BETTER HURRY AND -- FEELING

TO-NIGHT AT 9 CLOK

There are many more examples of George Hodel's similar crime signatures and MO.

Such as the 1944 Georgette Bauerdorf murder where George Hodel sends the taunting typewritten note to the police and press after smearing Mercurochrome on it to simulate blood, promising "the killer will be at the Hollywood Canteen" on a certain date and time.

Below is the retyped text from the "message" that appeared in the paper's article (see page 201) below the photo of Georgette behind the wheel of a car.

```
To the Los Angeles police—
Almost a year ago Georgette
Bauerdorf, age 20, Hollywood
Canteen hostess was murdered
In her apartment in West Holly-
Wood—
Between now and Oct. 11-a year
after her death—the one who
murdered her will appear at the
Hollywood Canteen. The murderer
will be in uniform. He has since
he committed the murder been in
action in Okinawa. The murder
of Georgette Bauerdorf was Divine
Retribution—

Let the Los Angeles police arrest
the murderer if they can--
```

NB: that in this wartime message (WW2 - 1944) the writer claims her killer was a soldier who "*has been in action in Okinawa.*" And attributes the murder to "**Divine Retribution.**"

Similarly in the 1921 Father Heslin note, from twenty-three years earlier, the writer/killer also indicates he saw wartime action in WW1 (1914-1918) and "*had charge of a machine gun in the Argonne, and poured thousands of bullets into struggling men, and killing men is no novelty to me...*" Also, similar to the Bauerdorf note where the writer attributes her murder to "**Divine Retribution,**" in his 1921 note of the killing of Father Heslin he writes, "Fate has made me do this."

On the original Typed Bauerdorf Note 1944 as it appeared in the paper (copy above), Dr. George Hodel used red Mercurochrome (spots on paper) to simulate blood. GHH's training as a crime reporter is showing as he writes the "Who, What, When, Where and Why" in his note.

Similarly a later message also is mailed to the paper to acquire the attention of the public.

Below is the 1947 undisguised handprinted note where George Hodel claims he will be: "Turning in Wed Jan 29, 10 AM Had my fun at police" and signing it, "Black Dahlia Avenger":

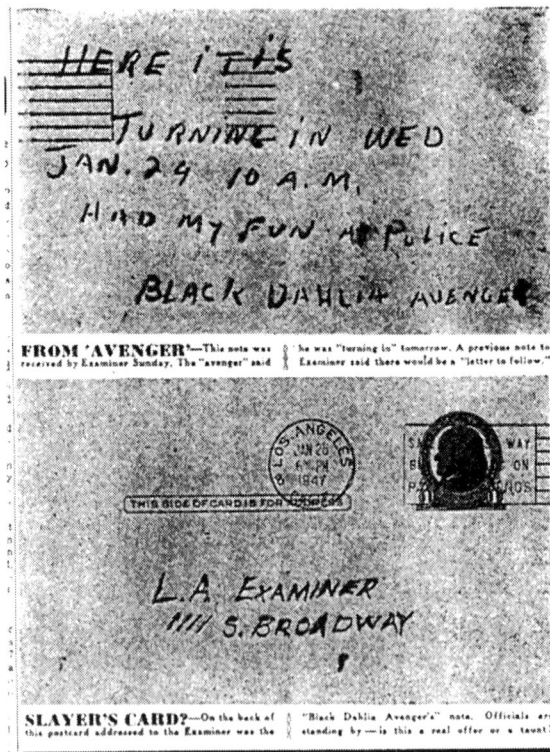

GHH handprinted Black Dahlia Avenger note on the back of postcard sent to *LA Examiner* and postmarked January 26, 1947

Reasonably, this is a lot of information to assimilate, particularly as it relates to the following crimes. For the moment, then, let me close this chapter, this "first murder" investigation and move on to what I believe was his next victim.

~ ~ ~

Summer 1921 in San Francisco is over. The three previous months of sensational crime headlines in the daily papers of William Hightower's arrest, trial, and conviction ("Guilty As Charged") now subsiding, the dailies replaced them with articles on corrupt local officials and the occasional "Dog Bites Man" piece.

Time to move south, back to more familiar territory. The trail returns me to my and my father's hometown, *El Pueblo de Nuestra Senora la Reina de Los Angeles.*

It is just four months later.

Young George Hodel is back in his parents' home in South Pasadena. School has resumed. It is February 1922.

Chapter 5

1922 - The William Desmond Taylor Murder

On the night of February 1, 1922, at approximately 7:50 PM, a loud "bang" was heard in the area of the Alvarado Court Apartments, 404 South Alvarado Street.

The group of bungalows was located in the upscale Los Angeles neighborhood of Westlake, which is located between Hollywood and downtown Los Angeles. Neighbors assumed the noise came from a possible car backfiring.

The following morning, at approximately 7:30 AM, witness Henry Peavey, William Taylor's valet, entered Bungalow B, and found his employer lying dead on the floor.

Initially, Taylor's death was thought to have been by natural causes, but when his body was turned over it was immediately determined that it was in fact, a homicide, as he had suffered a gunshot wound to the back.

Due to the victim's high-profile celebrity status the word of his death spread like wildfire. First call went to the film studio heads who arrived at the residence ahead of the police, then came the LAPD detectives and the local press, who arrived shortly afterwards and within an hour the word was on the street that, "William Desmond Taylor's dead. He was murdered. Shot in the back."

That same afternoon, the *Los Angeles Evening Herald* led with the headline:

MYSTERY GUNMAN KILLS
FILM DIRECTOR TAYLOR

Los Angeles Evening Herald 2/2/22

The Victim

William Desmond Taylor
Taylor in 1917

William Desmond Taylor was born in County Carlow,
Ireland, in 1872. William Cunningham Deane-Tanner
was his birth name. He was one of five children born

to Major Kearns Deane-Tanner (retired British Army officer) and the major's wife, Jane.

William Deane-Tanner, at age eighteen, moved to the United States in 1890.

In New York City young William met and married an actress, Ethel May Hamilton, in 1901 and they had a daughter, Ethel Daisy, the following year.

Here is an excerpt from Wikipedia that discusses his abandonment of his family:

(https://en.wikipedia.org/wiki/William_Desmond_Taylor)

Taylor and his family were well known in New York society and were members of several clubs. He was also a heavy drinker, possibly suffered from depression, and was known to carry on affairs with women. Taylor suddenly disappeared on October 23, 1908, deserting his wife and daughter. After his disappearance, friends said he had previously suffered "mental lapses," and his family thought initially he had wandered off during an episode of amnesia. Taylor's wife obtained a state decree of divorce in 1912.

Little is known of the years immediately following Taylor's disappearance. He traveled through Canada, Alaska and the northwestern US, mining gold and working with various acting troupes. Eventually, he switched from acting to producing. By the time he arrived in San Francisco around 1912, he had changed his name to William Desmond Taylor; in San Francisco, some New York acquaintances met him, and provided him with some money to re-establish himself in Los Angeles.

In Los Angeles, at age forty, recently divorced and having assumed the new name, William Desmond Taylor, his career skyrocketed. Below is a list of his remarkable accomplishments as a filmmaker in the newly formed and still "silent screened" Hollywood.

During WW I, Taylor interrupted his Hollywood film career to enlist and serve in the Canadian Expeditionary Force in 1918, and then after being sent overseas, was reassigned to the Royal Army Service Corps where he served as a temporary grade lieutenant and discharged in 1919 when he returned to Hollywood and resumed his civilian career as a film director.

IMDB credits as William Desmond Taylor:

Director (60 film credits from 1914 to 1922), one of his most famous films was the 1919 production, "Anne of Green Gables" starring Mary Miles Minter. Miss Minter would figure prominently as a witness in his murder just three years later.

To name a few of his most notable films: "The Green Temptation" (1922), "Tom Sawyer" (1917), "The American Beauty" (1916), "Davy Crockett" (1916). Taylor directed film legend Mary Pickford ("America's Sweetheart") in "How Could You, Jean?" in 1918. Always in high demand in Hollywood, Taylor eventually became the leading director of Famous Players-Lasky Studios.

Taylor's acting credits total 27 from 1913-1922.

Print Biographies (5)

Robert Giroux. *A Deed of Death.* New York: Alfred A. Knopf, 1990.

Bruce Long. *William Desmond Taylor: A Dossier.* Metuchen, NJ: Scarecrow Press, 1991.

Sidney Kirkpatrick. *A Cast of Killers.* New York: E.P. Dutton, 1986.

William J. Mann. *Tinseltown: Murder, Morphine, and Madness at the Dawn of Hollywood.* New York: Harper, 2014.

Michael B. Druxman. *Murder in Babylon.* BearManor Media, 2014.

Film poster for *Anne of Green Gables* 1919 starring Mary Miles Minter, who was William Desmond Taylor's protégée.

The Investigation

I can say with confidence that the William Desmond Taylor murder is one of the most "overly investigated" crimes in the past century.

It even exceeds the "Black Dahlia Murder" both in the number of headlines across the nation and the number of journalists and writers who have come up with their multiple theories on "whodunit."

At least a dozen suspects have been offered up to the public through the decades. "The butler did it." "The ex-chauffeur did it." "His lovelorn actress/ingenue did it." "No, it was her mother, the overprotective 'Movie Mom' that shot him to protect her daughter's innocence." "It was the other young actress's drug dealing friends who killed him."

As the days and months passed with no solution, facts were replaced with speculation, which rapidly became **The Myth**.

On the next page (210) is an image of one of the best early articles that dealt with what was known in the hours immediately following the discovery of his body, the February after the August 1921 murder of the priest. It presents a Joe Friday: "Just the Facts" type documentation of the primary witnesses and what they saw before any speculation and "whispered rumors" had a chance to take hold.

I here reproduce it as initially reported in the *Los Angeles Times* on February 3, 1922, the day following the discovery of the body.

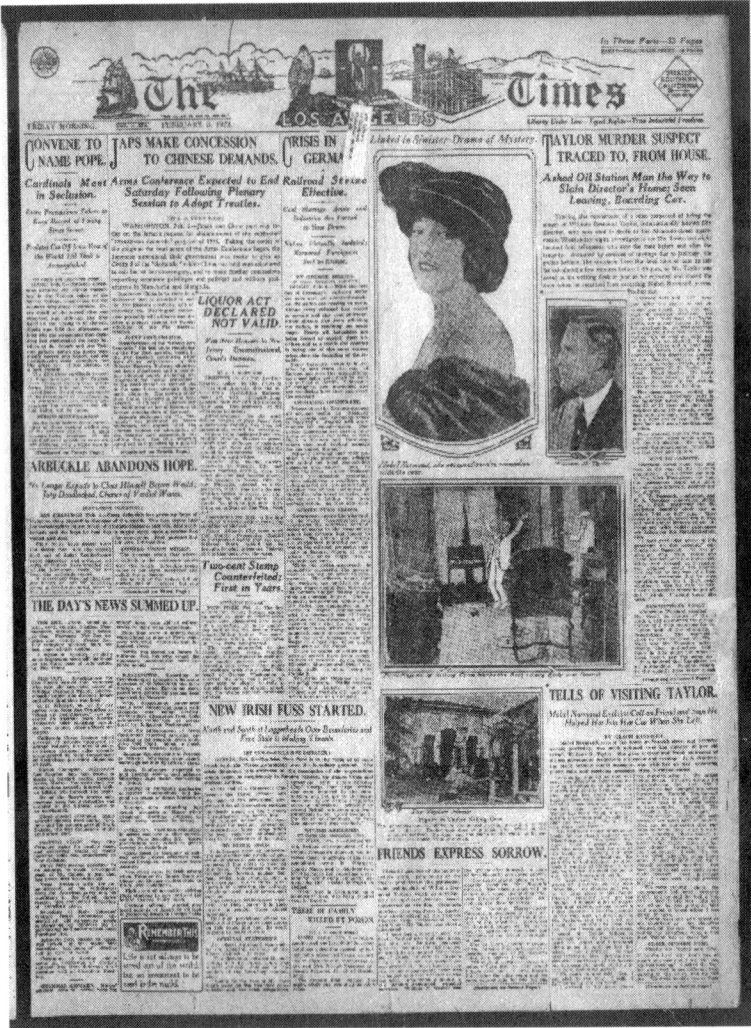

***Los Angeles Times*, February 3, 1922 Front Page
and continued on subsequent pages**

The complete text (210-216) of the above article reads:

Tracing the movements of a man suspected of being the slayer of William Desmond Taylor, internationally known film director, who was shot to death in his Alvarado-street apartments Wednesday night, investigators for *The Times* last night located four witnesses who saw the man before and after the tragedy. Actuated by motives of revenge due to jealousy, the police believe, the murderer fired the fatal shot as near as can be calculated a few minutes before 7:45 PM, as Mr. Taylor was seated at his writing desk or just as he returned and closed the door when he returned from escorting Mabel Normand, actress, to her car.

Between 7:45 and 7:50 PM, just after the report of the revolver was heard, Mrs. Maclean, wife of Douglas Maclean, the actor, who lives near the Taylor home, saw a man leaving the Taylor apartments. He was described as being about five feet nine-or ten-inches tall, of medium build and roughly, but not shabbily dressed in dark clothes and a plaid cap.

Shortly before 6 o'clock a man answering this description stopped at the Hartley service station, Sixth and Alvarado streets, and inquired where W. D. Taylor resided. Floyd Hartley, 231 South Bonnie Brae Street, and L. A. Grant, in charge of the station, were in the place at the time.

The circumstances recited by both of these witnesses tally to the minutest detail. The inquirer was 26 or 27 years old, they said, weighed about 165 pounds, wore a dark suit, probably of blue serge, and a light hat or cap. He had dark hair and was of medium complexion.

They directed him to the Alvarado Terrace Apartments, and he left the oil station. He walked toward the apartments. That was the last they saw of him.

Maryland Street runs east and west at the rear of Mr. Taylor's apartment. It is a street car stop on the West First-street car line, but passengers board cars there at only rare intervals, possibly not for months.

E. W. Dascomb, conductor, and R. S. Woodard, motorman, stated that a man answering the description boarded their car at either 7:54 or 8:27 PM. They were not certain which stop it was but took notice because of the infrequency with which passengers are taken on the Maryland-street stop.

"I took particular notice of this passenger on that account," said Conductor Dascomb. It was an inbound trip. This fellow was about five feet and ten inches tall, fairly well dressed, as I remember, weighed about 155 pounds, and his hat or cap was of a lights color. I remember that he wore something tan, but I don't recall whether it was his coat or vest. I can't remember where he got off, but I think I would know him again."

Motorman Woodard recalled that Mr. Grant, in charge of the oil station, had mentioned the circumstances of a man inquiring for Mr. Taylor, and of the similarity in descriptions. The descriptions given by Mrs. Maclean, Mr. Woodward, and Mr. Dascomb tally so closely that authorities believe there is littIe doubt but what that three people saw the same man.

It is believed that the slayer had no automobile. Persons residing in the vicinity have taken special notice of machines parked there because the noise kept them awake and they do not recall having seen any cars parked on Maryland Street that night. This lends confirmation to the theory that the killer boarded a West First streetcar.

Mrs. J. H. Tander and her three sons reside directly across from Mr. Taylor's apartment at 350 South Alvarado Street. The occupants of the house were awake until after 9:30 PM and observed no automobile nor saw anyone loitering in the vicinity.

Persons residing at 401 Westlake Avenue, the house adjacent from Mr. Taylor's apartments, gave similar information.

Several hours were devoted yesterday to questioning Mabel Normand, well-known motion-picture actress and asserted fiancée of Mr. Taylor. Miss Normand is the last person thus far found who saw him alive. Her chauffeur, William Davis, also was questioned.

Their stories were that Miss Normand left the Taylor apartments, 404-B South Alvarado Street, at 7:45 p.m. Wednesday. Mr. Taylor accompanied her to the automobile.

Immediately after checking up on this phase of the case the police started a search for the man Mrs. Maclean saw leaving the apartments between 7:45 and 7:50 PM soon after the report of a pistol shot was heard.

While a search was under way for this man, the police also were making energetic efforts to find E. F. Sands, former secretary of Mr. Taylor, who was accused several months ago of forgery by the latter. Since a warrant was issued for the arrest of Sands on the asserted forgeries no trace of his whereabouts has been found.

The tremendous resources of the Famous Players-Lasky organization were offered the police yesterday by Jesse L. Lasky, first vice-president, of the company, for the capture of the assassin of the film director. Unlimited supply of money, time and effort was promised to the detectives, and every possible assistance will be given them by Mr. Taylor's friends and former associates, the officers were told.

News of the murder stirred the motion-picture colony. Several intimate friends rushed to the home, among them being Mary Miles Minter, who became almost hysterical.

The revenge and jealousy motive as a theory was strengthened by the fact that none of the valuables in the apartments or in Mr. Taylor's clothing was disturbed. About $78 in money was in his pocketbook, a two-carat diamond ring was not taken, and his platinum watch also was left.

Detective Sergeants Herman Cline, Murphy, Cato, Cahill, Zeigler, and Wallace checked many clews. Among one of the leads furnished the police was a report that a man, eager to see Mr. Taylor, had inquired two days before at the Morosco Theater for his residence address, and insisted on getting it at once. The actions of this man aroused suspicion.

An autopsy performed at the Ivy Overholtzer undertaking establishment showed that Mr. Taylor had been shot from the back with a .38-caliber revolver. Only one bullet was found. It entered on the left side toward the back about six inches under the arm pit. The course of the bullet indicated it had gone upwards and it was extracted in the fleshy part of the neck on the right side just below the ear. Both lobes of the left lung had been punctured.

The nearest approach to an eyewitness account of the crime was furnished by Mrs. Maclean. About 7:45 p.m. she heard the shot and when she looked out the window, she saw a man she described as roughly dressed, wearing a plaid cap, open the door of the Taylor apartment. The porch light was turned on, as were the lights in the rest of the house, she stated.

This man paused as he came out of the door, looked around as if talking to someone inside and then left. He walked to an alley that leads to Maryland Street, passing between Mr. Taylor's house and that of Mrs. Maclean.

The murderer, it is believed, lurked in the shadows back to the Taylor flat and in the narrow alley between it and the garage, waiting for his opportunity.

This theory of the police was reinforced last night by the discovery of six cigarette stubs in the immediate vicinity of the back door of the Taylor flat and in the alley facing the east windows of the murdered man's apartment. A maid at the Maclean home also said she heard someone lurking in the alley about 7:15 PM and heard the fatal shot about thirty minutes later.

The man who smoked the cigarettes was very nervous. The half-smoked cigarettes show that. They were scattered around. One was barely touched. Evidently this one was the last one smoked by the man while waiting. It was found in the alley, leading the detectives to believe that the man threw it away almost immediately after lighting it, and that he watched Mr. Taylor leave the house.

The back door of the Taylor flat opens on the sidewalk of the south side of Maryland Street, just east of Alvarado. Between the east side of the structure where the Taylor flat is located and the garage used by occupants of the flats in the court is a narrow, cement-paved alley. This alley, too, leads into Maryland Street. A large tree affords ample protection from the light on Alvarado Street at night, blocks the view of the house. It is in the shadow of this tree, the officers believe, that the murderer lay in wait, smoking his cigarettes. More than half a dozen of matches were found on the lawn between the curb of Maryland Street and the back window of the Taylor flat.

The opportunity for him to enter the house came, the police believe, when Mr. Taylor escorted Miss Normand to her automobile. During the few minutes required for this, the murderer slipped into the open door and waited behind it for the return of Mr. Taylor, the officers think.

Mrs. Maclean, who knows Sands, stated the man who left the Taylor apartment did not look familiar to her. The investigators, however, have not relaxed their efforts to find Sands in order to question him in the hope he may be able to aid them in solving the mystery.

Mr. Taylor left the Famous Players-Lasky studio, where he was a director, at 4:30 PM, Wednesday, according to Barrett Keisling, publicity man.

From the story related by Henry Peavey, negro, houseman, who found the body, Mr. Taylor came immediately home, ate dinner, and was visited by Miss Normand.

Los Angeles and New York film colonies were deeply affected by the news of the murder. Roscoe (Fatty) Arbuckle, awaiting the verdict in his manslaughter trial in San Francisco, said: "Mr. Taylor's death comes as a great shock to me. We were good friends and never a whisper of scandal arouse about him. He was one of the finest fellows on the 'lot'."

Detective Sergeants Cline, Wynn and Murphy questioned several friends of Mr. Taylor late last night in an effort to obtain any information that may aid in solving the mystery.

Detective Sergeants Cato and Cahill, both personal friends of Mr. Taylor, left the police station late last night to question a former sweetheart of Mr. Taylor. They declined to divulge her name.

Mary Miles Minter, who was directed in several plays by Mr. Taylor and who holds high regard for him, declared yesterday she could think of no enemies or persons who would have a motive in killing him.

She denied reports she had ever been engaged to marry him, saying she was extremely sorry she never had been, because she admired him greatly as a man.

The following three images are enlargements of photographs contained in the article (page 210).

The Taylor Home

Figure in Taylor Killing Case.

The photodiagram reconstructs the actual slaying, according to the police theory. Taylor was shot by a man, who lurked in the shadows between the door and the piano at the right, as he re-entered the house from the curb.

The Taylor Home, Alvarado Street Apartments
404 South Alvarado, West Lake Park

Photodiagram of Killing. Cross Marks the Spot where Body was Found

Artist rendition of suspect and victim just before the shooting inside Taylor apartment

Photo of Mabel Normand, actress/friend of Taylor, and last to speak with him just minutes before he was shot.

The Los Angeles Times reporters, in this article, as they would be for decades to come, were way ahead of the LAPD and from the get-go were out there knocking on doors and scouring the neighborhood for witnesses and potential leads. Their "johnny on the spot" sleuthing was immediately rewarded with a handful of essential eyewitnesses to the crime.

In truth, this LAT article, from Day One, *has nailed just about everything we KNOW about the shooter.* And nearly one hundred years later, despite the massive amount of SPECULATION and Hollywood Spin and myth-making, we know little else.

What followed in the pulp magazines and the hundreds of chapters in "true crime books" is the Hollywood Dream Factory hard at work.

Below is a sketch of the Alvarado Street Apartment complex, 404 S. Alvarado Street, as it appeared at the time of the murder. (The units were torn down in the 1950s to make way for business development.)

As we review a summary and timeline of what we know from the primary witnesses' statements, we can use the diagrams to help us picture the sequence of events as the suspect approached Taylor's apartment, entered, and then left the premises.

Timeline per Witness Statements:

February 1, 1922 6:00 PM Witnesses Floyd Hartley and L.A. Grant spoke with the Suspect, who stopped at Mr. Hartley's gas station at the corner of 6th Street and Alvarado and asked, "Can you tell me where Mr. W.D. Taylor lives?" Both men directed him to the Alvarado Terrace Apartments and described him as Male, 26-27 years, 165 pounds, dark hair, medium complexion, dark clothing, light cap. They directed him, and he was last seen heading in the direction of the Taylor apartment.

February 1, 1922 7:50 PM Witness Mrs. Douglas Maclean hears what sounded like a gunshot coming from Taylor's apartment and sees suspect, exit Taylor Apt. B, turn as if he was talking to Taylor, then exit and walk to the alley. She described him as "Male, 5-9, dark clothing, plaid cap."

February 1, 1922 7:54 or 8:27 PM Streetcar conductor, E.W. Dascomb and motorman R.S. Woodard saw the suspect board their streetcar at the Maryland Street stop which is located behind the Taylor apartment. It was the West First Street inbound stop that runs East and West, and the suspect was headed towards downtown Los Angeles. These two witnesses confirmed that the description was "A male, 5-10, 165, fairly well dressed, wearing a light-colored hat or cap."

LAPD, after obtaining statements from these five separate witnesses, believed that all sightings were of the same individual, the man that shot and killed William Desmond Taylor.

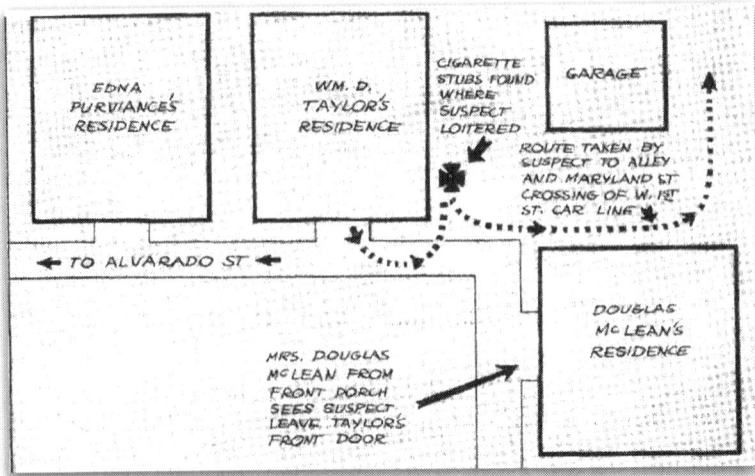

Crime scene sketch showing route of killer from WDT apartment to alley to streetcar line

Los Angeles Electric Red Car of type suspect boarded to make his getaway in 1922

"The Cast of Characters"

As referenced earlier, the pulps and press, after the initial few days of legitimate investigation died down, with no leads or identification of the actual shooter, then turned to tabloid journalism to ensure the story remained as headlines, "above the fold" for months.

Sampling of early headlines, "The Myth" begins

The Victim - Witzel Portraits

**Portrait of William Desmond Taylor
taken and signed by WITZEL**

**William Desmond Taylor
(true name William Deane Tanner)
This portrait also taken and signed by WITZEL
a Los Angeles-based top
"Hollywood photographer to the stars."**

The Victim and his Friends

Most of the "close acquaintances" of William Desmond Taylor, thanks to the tabloids and later "true crime books," transitioned from "friends" to "witnesses" then some of them to "suspects."

While dozens of persons were at one time or another suspected of being involved in the murder, here is a list of some of his close friends.

Actress Mabel Normand, a good friend of Taylor's and was the last person to see him alive at his Alvarado Street bungalow. Taylor walked Ms. Normand to her chauffeur-driven car in front of the complex, said "Goodbye," and returned to his apartment where the suspect lay in wait after entering the open door.

Mabel Normand was reportedly addicted to drugs, and it was said that Taylor took an active role in attempting to help her rid herself of the addiction. (This led to speculation that "it was Mabel's drug suppliers who 'took him out'.")

This photo was also **taken and signed by Hollywood photographer WITZEL**.

Actress Mary Miles Minter, good friend of Taylor's and rumored to be romantically involved with him at

the time of his murder. Photo of Ms. Minter also
taken and signed by photographer, WITZEL.

Actress Olive Thomas was a friend of Taylor's, but not
a witness or suspect as she died September 10, 1920
while in Paris, France, nearly 17 months before his
February 1, 1922 murder. Her death under suspicious
circumstances was reportedly due to an "accidental
overdose," wherein she mistakenly took the wrong
medication. William Desmond Taylor gave the oration

at her funeral. At the time of her death, Olive Thomas was married to actor Jack Pickford (brother of Mary Pickford). Jack had starred in several of Taylor's films, which included the lead role as Huckleberry Finn. Thomas's photograph (page 226) was **taken and signed by WITZEL** circa 1920.

George Hill Hodel as the possible suspect

Location:

Fourteen, at the time of the murder, George Hodel was living with his parents at their home, 6512 Monterey Road, in Northeast Los Angeles.

In the fall of 1923, at the age of fifteen, George began college as a freshman at the prestigious California Institute of Technology (Caltech) in South Pasadena.

He did not own a car at that time and would have had to rely on rides with friends or the public electric "Red Car" to travel any distances. At that time, the electric car route from George's home in the Northeast to get to West Lake Park would require he board and travel through downtown Los Angeles then west towards Hollywood. The shooter after the murder was observed boarding the Eastbound streetcar, which would return him to downtown Los Angeles and out to Northeast Los Angeles.

Physical Description:

George Hodel, though still a teenager, could have passed for a young man in his mid-twenties. His height would have been about five nine, weight likely a little less at around 150, but if he were wearing dark clothes, he could appear heavier than his actual weight and appear to be the stated, "165 pounds." He, like the Suspect, had dark hair and had medium to dark complexion. He certainly would and did own a cap as described by the witnesses.

Here is a photo of young George Hill Hodel, believed taken in his late teens circa 1925 and showing him wearing a cap similarly described as the one worn by the shooter of William Desmond Taylor.

Weapon:

Ballistic analysis of the spent slug removed from the victim's body revealed the gun used was a .38 caliber.

(**Note** - This would have been identical to the type and caliber of handgun used to kill Father Patrick Heslin some six months prior in the San Francisco Bay Area. That weapon used by a similar described Suspect was never recovered.)

Numerous references indicated that "all the physical evidence including the bullets have disappeared from police custody," so no ballistic comparison to Father Heslin or any other possible related crime can be conducted now, one hundred years later.

WORLD'S
LARGEST-SELLING
QUALITY REVOLVER

The Smith & Wesson 38 Military & Police

Advertisement for a .38 caliber handgun of the type used to kill Taylor

Motive:

LAPD established the motive was NOT robbery as numerous items of value, and $85.00 in cash was found on Taylor's person. (Eighty-five dollars in 1920 is the equivalent today [2020] of having $1,262.00 on your person.)

Initial speculation by LAPD was "jealousy" perhaps because William Taylor was dating or affectionate with one of several young famous actresses/film stars, including Mary Miles Minter and Norma Desmond.

Recall that GHH, as the Black Dahlia Avenger and later as Zodiac, claimed that the killing of the young woman was "Divine Retribution" and, in a separate murder, claimed it was "payback for his being scorned by a young brownett girl in high school."

So, it is possible that authorities were correct in the "jealousy" motive and that the killer of William Desmond Taylor was "in love with" one of the young screen stars. That he either knew and had met her or more probably, he "fantasized the love affair" and took vengeance on Taylor as his "competition."

Another crime signature/M.O. that stands out to my mind is the "high profile notoriety" of the crime. The selection of a crime victim that the killer knew would make sensational headlines and be sure to secure his status as a "master criminal" which was and will remain a significant motivating factor in George Hodel's future serial crimes.

This concludes the summary on what I believe may have possibly been my father's second crime.

Granted the evidence in this murder, standing alone and by itself, is thin, but it should be viewed *holistically*, as there is much more to come.

There exists more linkage, specifically to this crime, which I will be presenting in a future homicide.

However, that evidence must remain moot for now and be offered at the right time in its proper chronology, which is for now about a decade away.

So, stay tuned, we have barely begun our sleuthing.

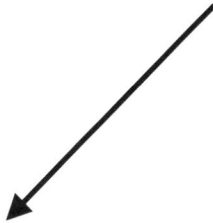

Oh, I almost forgot, there is one additional interesting piece of potential evidence I would like to present as relates to the unsolved murder of William Desmond Taylor.

Here it is. (see next page 232)

Here is a *never before shown* or published photograph of then fifteen-year-old George Hodel. The picture was **taken and signed by** famed Hollywood photographer to the stars, **WITZEL**.

The date "October 6, 1923" is written in pencil on the bottom, which I can only assume, is the date it was taken. (Four days before his sixteenth birthday.) George had entered college at Caltech and is living in his separate private residence on his parents' property, built for him as a fifteenth birthday present.

Ironically, this, his one-bedroom house at the rear of the main house, has a street address of 6511 *Short Way*, the name of his most infamous future victim, Elizabeth *Short*, known to the world as "The Black Dahlia."

Most, or all of the **WITZEL** photographs shown previously as the "Cast of Characters" were printed in many newspapers across the nation in 1922 and 1923.

Did young George Hodel select **WITZEL**, the "photographer to the stars" as a post-mortem taunt to twist a knife in the back of his now yearlong dead "rival" as if to say, "Hey, look, Taylor, I'm as good as you." And, also, perhaps to put himself on an equal stance with his imagined "love fantasy," be it Norma Desmond or Mary Miles Minter, both subjects of the **WITZEL** camera?

Or was it mere coincidence? (As many of you know, I do not believe in coincidences.)

You decide.

Or, better yet, reserve judgment for now, as there is much more to come.

Chapter 6

1924- The Martin Sisters

On August 23, 1924, two young girls, Nina Martin, age eight, and her sister, May Martin, age twelve, both living in Los Angeles, were abducted from the sidewalk of their residential neighborhood by two males in an automobile.

Los Angeles newspapers ran the story of their kidnapping for weeks, and massive searches were conducted by police and civilians, to no avail.

FEARS FOR GIRL TOTS GROW

Relatives Failing in Search Express Belief Two Martin Sisters Are Dead or Prisoners

Los Angeles Times, Friday, August 29, 1924

A belief that May and Nina Martin, pretty sisters of twelve and eight years of age, who have been missing since last Saturday, have been slain or are being held prisoners by fiends, was expressed last night by the girl's stepfather, Paul Buus.

...

Many are the reports that find their way to the home of the missing children. One concerned screams heard shortly after their disappearance emanating from the direction of a slough near their home. The slough was thoroughly searched yesterday, but no trace of the girls was found.

Another concerned a tale told by a playmate of May and Nina Buus. The playmate declared she had seen the two girls as they were being lured into an automobile by a man.

Still another concerned a mysterious automobile which was believed to have stopped in front of the Buus home about nine PM. Saturday and then continued in the direction of the slough.

~ ~ ~

In the meantime, the search of the slough and the Baldwin Hills district will be resumed today. A corps of 100 Boy Scouts under Scoutmaster Hoffman has volunteered to participate in the hunt that will be launched at dawn today.

Note Gives First 'Clew' to Martins

On September 20, 1924, an anonymous note was mailed to the grieving parents of the Martin sisters instructing the stepfather, Mr. Paul Buus, to go to a specific street corner in Venice at 10 a.m. and the children would be returned to him.

The stepfather followed instructions and waited two hours, but the note writer failed to comply and deliver the children as promised.

Venice police officers, observing Buus's loitering at the intersection, became suspicious and approached him, and he was taken to the police station where he reluctantly informed officers of the kidnappers' demand and showed them the note.

The handwritten note, written in the upper margins of a newspaper, was taken into evidence by LAPD detectives, but not published in the newspapers.

I quote an excerpt from the *Los Angeles Times* article of Saturday, September 20, 1924:

NOTE GIVES FIRST CLEW TO MARTINS
Stepfather Keeps Futile Vigil After
Anonymous Note Promises Return

•••

Chief of Detectives Home immediately dispatched every available officer and detective to the beach city. There they were joined by Nick Harris detectives who had been notified by Mrs. Buus, and Venice police and a cordon were thrown around an area of four blocks. At a late hour last night, no trace of the girls had been found. The step-father, however, refused to leave Venice, believing the girls are hidden there somewhere.

The letter to Buus was written on the upper margin of a newspaper and in a clear handwriting. An effort is being made to trace the letter. Aid of Federal authorities will be asked.

Escorted by a police detail Aimee Semple McPherson, pastor of the Angelus Temple, and several hundred members of her party, visited Chinatown last night in search of the missing girls. This was done after Mrs. McPherson and her party conferred with Lieut. Hollowell, head of the vice squad. Led by Detective Lieutenant Davis, Sergeants Simpson and Sweetnam, Mrs. McPherson, was unable to find any trace of the girls.

Six months later, in February 1925, the sisters' bodies would be found in a culvert.

As in the 1921 Father Heslin "Flapjack Murder," sheriff's detectives, despite evidence to the contrary, arrested an elderly night watchman, S.C. Stone, for the crimes. Stone was nearly lynched by a mob outside the jail, and after being severely assaulted is tried, speedily convicted, and given a life sentence.

Prior to Stone's arrest, local authorities hired a world-renowned Russian criminologist, Dr. Elias Feodorovitch Morgenstiern, known as "the Ferret of Europe," to assist in the investigation.

Dr. Morgenstiern used the opulent and newly built downtown Biltmore Hotel as his headquarters, and after weeks of interviews and investigation, provided authorities with *both the motive and names of two young men who he believed committed the kidnap murders of the Martin sisters.*

**Dr. Morgenstiern "The Ferret of Europe"
May 1925**

The names of the two youths named by Dr. Morgenstiern were never made public; however, it is my belief that further investigation may well prove that they were, in fact, George Hodel and Fred Sexton. (Sexton has been identified as Hodel's killing partner in some of the later crimes presented in my first book, *Black Dahlia Avenger*, as well as new crimes, which are forthcoming.)

(**SKH Note** - Also, as documented in my earlier publications, Fred Sexton would be identified and arrested along with Dr. George Hodel for having sex with my half-sister, Tamar Hodel, age fourteen, in the 1949 Hollywood sex scandal. Separately, on his own, Sexton would commit incest with his own teenage daughter and later repeat the child molestation acts with a second adolescent stepdaughter from his second marriage and then flee to Mexico to avoid prosecution.)

It is known that the Martin Sisters' neighborhood witnesses initially provided Dr. Morgenstiern with the information linking a "highly intellectual Los Angeles youth" to the crime.

Indications are that one of the suspects was a young newspaper reporter who was in the neighborhood "asking questions." (It is known and documented that George Hodel was employed in 1924 as a crime reporter for a local newspaper *Los Angeles Record* and would have likely covered the story.)

Despite Dr. Morgenstiern's information, and disregarding witnesses' statements that the girls were seen getting into a car driven by two younger males, authorities ignored the evidence and arrested the elderly night watchman, S.C. Stone.

It is the author's opinion that not only did Dr. Morgenstiern identify and name George Hodel and possibly Fred Sexton as the killers but also provided a "copycat crime" as the motive.

At the exact time the Martin sisters were kidnapped and slain, the world was glued to the reporting of the "Crime of the Century," the Leopold & Loeb kidnap murder of fourteen year old Bobby Franks in Chicago.

Bobby Franks, age fourteen, was kidnapped and murdered in Chicago on May 21, 1924.

Victim Bobby Franks

Young Bobby Franks was walking home when he was offered a ride in the kidnapper's rented automobile. He was then gagged and beaten to death, and his body placed in a culvert south of Chicago.

The two young killers then returned to the city and telephoned the victim's mother and informed her a ransom demand would be forthcoming.

A typewritten demand was mailed to the Franks home shown below:

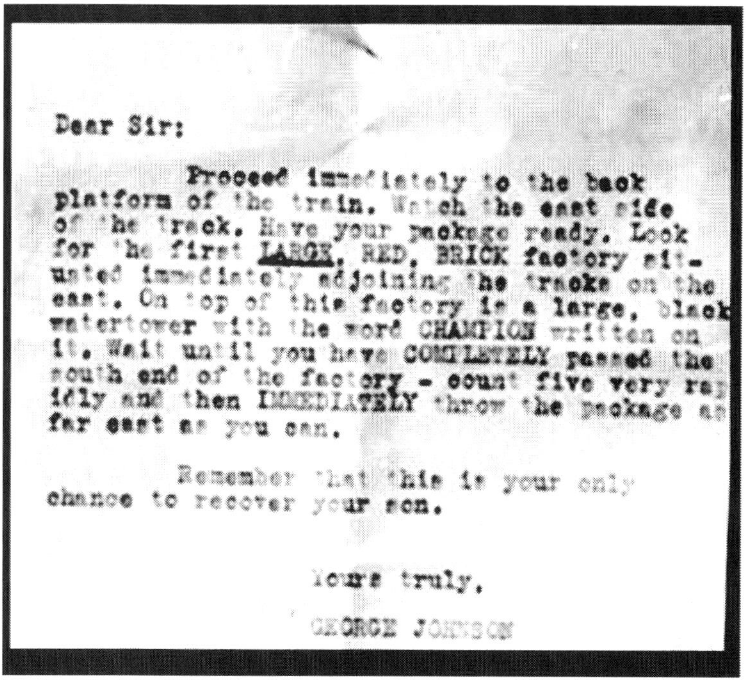

Dear Sir:

Proceed immediately to the back platform of the train. Watch the east side of the track. Have your package ready. Look for the first LARGE, RED, BRICK factory situated immediately adjoining the tracks on the east. On top of this factory is a large, black watertower with the word CHAMPION written on it. Wait until you have COMPLETELY passed the south end of the factory - count five very rapidly and then IMMEDIATELY throw the package as far east as you can.

Remember that this is your only chance to recover your son.

Yours truly,

GEORGE JOHNSON

At the same time the note was read by the grief-stricken family; their son's body was found in the culvert.

Bobby Franks' body found in a culvert near Wolf Lake, some twenty-five miles south of Chicago in Hammond, Indiana. A pair of eyeglasses were found near the body, which were later identified as belonging to Nathan

Leopold, which he suggested: "may have been dropped by him during a bird watch excursion."

Nathan Leopold and Richard Loeb

Due to its relevance to our own Martin investigation it is worth noting the following reference from Wikipedia:

"Chicago police launched an intensive investigation; rewards were offered for information. While Loeb went about his daily routine quietly, Leopold spoke freely to police and reporters, offering theories to any who would listen. He even told one detective, 'If I were to murder anybody, it would be just such a cocky little son of a bitch as Bobby Franks'."

Wikipedia and The Sunday Morning Star
July 27, 1924

Nathan Leopold [born 1904] and George Hodel [born in 1907] were clones, born with genius IQs. Both considered themselves to be "master criminals" and "untouchable."

If Dr. Morgenstiern's original reports and documentation can be found, it is likely he offered this scenario. It is also probable that George Hodel decided, through these killings, that he would prove to the world that while Leopold and Loeb in their "Crime of the Century" failed as Nietzschean "Supermen" in their effort to outwit the police and commit "The Perfect Crime," George would not.

Nevertheless, he, George Hodel, with his superior intellect, who had already "been there, done that" would at the same time, while Leopold and Loeb remained atop national newspaper headlines, commit a kidnap and murderous act and succeed where they failed.

Three months after Leopold and Loeb's failed attempt in Chicago, George, along with his ride-along Loeb counterpart (who I believe was Fred Sexton), successfully executed their copycat crime.

On August 23, 1924, the two men would use a car to kidnap the Martin children as they walked on the sidewalk. They would brutally strangle both girls and bury their bodies in a shallow culvert and follow up the crime with a taunting handwritten letter to the parents promising to return the children if the parents would go to a specific street corner in nearby Venice Beach and wait.

Again, this MO: child abduction, personal calls, and notes sent to the parents will be used in George Hodel's later child kidnap/murders, some of which I have identified in previous publications (Suzanne Degnan, "Lipstick Murders") and others yet to be presented in my "Early Years" summaries.

George Hodel
Los Angeles Record Crime Reporter

Let us first review and expand upon young George Hodel's connections to the *Los Angeles Record* in the 1920s.

Excerpted here is what I initially presented in my first publication of *Black Dahlia Avenger: A Genius for Murder* (Arcade 2003 Hardback ed.)

(Excerpts referenced above *BDA Pages 59-68* begin here on next page 247 and conclude on page 256.)

completing only one year, for reasons that still remain unclear. There [...] lege because he had a sexual liaison with a faculty member's wife, who became p[...] by her husband. In the second version, he was kicked out for playing poker, because gambling was prohibit[...] y event, by the time he was seventeen he had left [...] and was working at a variety of jobs.

In 1924, mostly as [...] formance on IQ tests required by the Californi[...] em during his early teens, the noted Stanford psy[...] s Terman selected him to become a member of a [...] n as "Terman's Termites." This was one of the firs[...] eriments in developmental psychology, in which P[...] edited with originating the terms "IQ" and "gifted[...] vey of more than a thousand intellectually en[...] eginning in 1924 with a group of specially selec[...] n's study began to collect data and follow them as [...] see how their intellectual gifts manifested thems[...] and careers. In the seven decades since Dr. Term[...] studies began, five books have been published an[...] vided from these original students.

Over the years, Fat[...] urn the extensive research questionnaires; clearly [...] by Dr. Terman as a validation of his own belie[...] His scrupulous return of the qu[...] uired of him doubt[...] ted in him by his parents. I als[...] placed him in Terman's highest catego[...] to be studied was a vital component of his extraor[...] eem that stood him in good stead during his toughest times, [...] into his final years.

From 1924 through 1928, my father worked in various professions in the Los Angeles area normally reserved for much older and more experienced people. In his first job, he worked as a crime reporter at the *Los Angeles Record* during the most violent years of Prohibition. His particular beat was the LAPD Vice Squad, where he rode shotgun on their raids of downtown nightclubs and local speakeasies. Extracts from an article he wrote on August 20, 1924, when he was only sixteen, provide insight not only into what was happening in L.A. during Prohibition but also into my father's thoughts and activities.

LIFE CAFÉ

WHERE LIQUOR IS HARD

A Raid on the Humming Bird Café

Outside the brilliantly lit Humming Bird café, 1243 East 12th street, officers are waiting, watch in hand, ready to swoop down on the place, on the stroke of 12 Saturday night.

All possible exits are guarded, all avenues of escape are watched. They are determined that this raid should not fail — that they should clean up the wettest hole on Central Avenue.

It lacks five minutes of midnight.

Inside, a motley crowd is reveling unaware of what developments are about to take place.

The atmosphere is saturated with the odor of intoxicants. The spirit of the men and women inside is changing from one of tipsy fun to that of licentious debauchery. Strong liquor is doing its work . . .

Three minutes of midnight.

The Negro orchestra strikes up a tune, assertively synchopative. The players sway their bodies in rhythm with the music, deftly juggling their instruments . . .

Abandonment, unreserved and unblushing, is permeating the café. A loud knock at the door. Four men stride in, officers of the prohibition enforcement and vice squads.

They walk rapidly about from table to table, seizing bottles and collaring men. The proprietor calls excitedly to waiters, who dash about warning the men and women. Dozens of glasses are overturned, dozens of bottles are emptied or smashed.

The noise of broken glass fills the room.

The floor is soaked with alcohol.

The four officers have taken five men, sixteen officers could have arrested four times that number.

The siren of the police patrol dies off in the distance.

The music starts up lurchingly.

Bottles are lifted from the floor. Glasses are refilled.

A woman looks sorrowfully at the broken neck of a smashed whisky flask. She breaks out into a loud high-pitched sob, gasping drunkenly . . .

Arrest Men for Booze

While white women careened drunkenly in the Arms of Negro escorts, in the Humming Bird café, 1243 East Twelfth street, early Wednesday morning, vice squad officers swooped down on the place and arrested several prominent citizens for illegal possession of liquor, marking the third raid carried out on the café in as many days . . .

According to the officers the Hummingbird has been a nightlife rendezvous, where whites dine, dance and drink with members of the city's Negro colony. A bevy of showgirls from a downtown burlesque theater were on the scene, enjoying the festivities.

Many complaints have been received by police authorities against the Hummingbird and it is said that the wildest sort of orgies are carried on there nightly. White women of the underworld make the place a headquarters, according to the officers, and ply their vocation there.

George isn't just reporting on the raid; he is describing a lifestyle and sexual fantasies that had fully engaged him even as a teenager. He actually recreates an atmosphere of forbidden sexual promiscuity that violates even the taboos of the 1920s. Father's writing was so colorful that he was quickly promoted from cub reporter to his own crime beat. Now he was working with the city's top cops on the LAPD's homicide squad. In a front-page *Record* story from 1924 about a murder scene he covered with homicide detectives, where the victim, Peggy Donovan, had been kicked to death, he wrote:

Los Angeles Record

June 3, 1924   Two Cents

THE MORNING AFTER A PARTY

The splashes of red about the rooms are beginning to change into brown . . .

Lying in the dust of the floor and bestrewn with the fallen ashes and stubs of innumerable cigarettes are scraps, scraps of paper — rubbish. There are letters — diaries of forgotten years — prayer books — playing cards — . . .

Lying face up on the floor is a card — the ace of diamonds. Over it has fallen a large drop of blood that converts the printed figure of the red diamond to a shapeless and blurred blotch of red.

Sheets Bloody

Blood-smeared sheets lie crumpled and torn on the littered floor of the bungalow.

A pair of dice have fallen from the smashed dressing table. One of the cubes has on it a splashed red stain.

Rising above the unmistakable odor of spilled and drying blood are mingling those of liquor, of Jamaica gin, of tobacco.

Forgotten Advice

"Give up every friend that is sinful and learn the 'Truth that makes . . .'"

Hopeful, pathetically hopeful, words written last December, one day before Christmas, to Margaret Donovan — cabaret girl who was killed in a drunken brawl . . .

"Give up every friend that is sinful . . ."

"Find the Truth."

"I confess to Thee, O Lord Jesus Christ, all the sins that I have committed even unto this hour. May the Almighty Lord grant to me pardon, absolution and remission of all my sins. Amen."

These words are underlined in a little blue book of "Prayers for

250

Steve Hodel

DR. GEORGE HILL HODEL JR., 1907–1999   63

Daily Use" "Read this some time for Mother's sake," is inscribed on the title page . . .

Wisps of dark brown hair — long and silken — are strewn about the floor. They are blood-clotted, torn.

Torn stockings of sheer silk.

Detectives Aghast

In the adjoining room detectives are muttering. "Good God, Archie, those ——— kicked her to death about three in the morning and then went and slept till nine!"

Between the pillow and pillow-slip of the overturned cot in which Peggy Donovan was found dead was an age-yellowed newspaper clipping, its sentences underlined:

"In the GARDEN OF LIFE WOMEN are the FLOWERS, some are gorgeous, gay and yet Have NO PERFUME."

A few months later, in another crime-scene story in the *Record*, George turns the description into a literary piece by punning in Latin on the last name of victim Teresa Mors. Mors — her name means "death" in Latin — was shot and killed by her jealous lover, the famous welterweight boxing champ Norman "Kid McCoy" Selby, who was immortalized by the sobriquet "the Real McCoy" when he decked with a single punch a drunk who had challenged his identity in a downtown L.A. bar. Legendary criminal attorney Jerry Giesler would jump-start his career with this famous early Los Angeles murder case by obtaining a manslaughter verdict for his client rather than the death sentence the state wanted.

In his description of the murder scene George Hodel writes:

Los Angeles Record
Thursday, August 14, 1924   Two Cents

WORDS OF DEATH

Death.

Mors, mortis, morti — glibly the schoolboy declines it. Thoughtlessly.

Like a cage in which the canary has been stifled, this apartment on the second floor of the Nottingham — the tall, expensive building with a front of blazing white tiles.

While the yellow bird was alive — flitting and singing —

The cage seemed a pretty thing. Now with the canary dead it is a dirty cage, tawdry and crusted with birdlime.

The canary is dead on the floor of this soft room that seems so close — impinging with walls and ceiling — close like a cage . . .

She lies dead in an unpleasant disarray that is not art but death. And the two batiks of Larry Darwin, monsters of the new niode, *bulge with immensity just as the ordered vision of* Rubens shrinks into insignificance before the monstrosity on the floor. Larry Darwin's nudes are phantasms — succubi. One smokes a cigarette, perched cross-legged on the devil's head. The other, with stuffed limbs, prances through a garden of exotic lotus flowers. Both leer at *the figure on the floor.*

The figure on the floor. Hair waved and hennaed, perhaps. Redly, dankly — plume for a face disfigured by a bullet hole. Eyes purpled. Blood on the bare white arms. And this photograph — of "the Kid." Clasped like a rosary to the breast, flat now, and hard; retreated as a woman's breast retreats when she is on her back.

The Kid placed the photograph in the white hand.

A gesture of drama, a futile touch of the romantic school that heightens the grotesquerie; that causes the naked batik succubi to leer the more it seems.

Pull it away — the picture. The newspapermen would photograph it, too. Yes, it's a picture of the kid.

Bloodstains on the glass. The Kid stands up young and proud.

The clutching fingernails scratch and rattle across the back. Ugh! Put it back in the hand. Let her hold it . . .

On their pedestal the nymph and satyr of Perl's have never eased the tension of their eternal embrace . . .

Death.

Mors, mortis, morti — what gender is death?

Feminine of course. It is of that declension. Yes, death is feminine.

Later in 1924, George decided to give up reporting and become a publisher. The following month, he and a friend decided to create a literary magazine. Now living in his own detached studio on his parents' South Pasadena property, he published a magazine with his own printing press and named it *Fantasia*. In his January 1925 introduction to the first issue, he made the following editorial statement:

A Dedication

To the portrayal of bizarre beauty in the arts, to the delineation of the stranger harmonies and the rarer fragrances, do we dedicate this, our magazine.

Such beauty we may find in a poem, a sketch, or a medley of colors; in the music of prayer-bells in some far-off minaret, or the noises of a city street; in a temple or a brothel or a gaol; in prayer or perversity or sin.

And ever shall we attempt in our pages the vivid expression of such art, wherever or however we may find it — ever shall we consecrate our magazine to the depiction of beauty anomalous, fantasial.

George Hodel wanted to explore bizarre, off-the-edge fantasies, mostly having to do with forbidden sex and violence. His magazine survived two issues; its only notable piece was my father's review of the newly published book by the then relatively unknown author Ben Hecht, entitled *The Kingdom of Evil*. This was a sequel to Hecht's first book, *Fantazius Mallare: A Mysterious Oath*, a journal narrated by the fictional reclusive artist-genius Mallare, which describes the author's visions of decadence, insanity, and, ultimately, murder. Mallare creates a beautiful mistress, Rita, who becomes his phantom or hallucinatory lover. In this twisted story delusion becomes reality and reality dissolves to dreams until, at the story's end, Mallare has transformed himself into an insanely jealous avenger who beats Rita to death because of her flagrant, wanton seduction, in Mallare's own presence, of his Caliban-like manservant, Goliath. The reader never really knows whether Rita is real or a twisted fantasy spun out of Mallare's psychotic torment.

The novel's highly erotic pen-and-ink drawings were created by Wallace Smith, who like Hecht had been a journalist, artist, and author in Chicago. Smith was arrested and prosecuted for what the government considered pornography, and because the book was judged obscene, was jailed for a brief period. Both authors would later come to Hollywood to write screenplays, where Hecht would eventually become one of the highest-paid screenwriters in the industry.

My father's review of *The Kingdom of Evil*, in which he's completely absorbed into Hecht's belief system, is the most accurate picture of his psychology. He writes, in part, "Macabre forms, more dank and putrescently phantasmal than any of Hecht's former imagining, grope blindly and crazedly in the poisonous fog out of which loom the rotting fancies that people his 'Kingdom of Evil.'"

My father's magazine went out of existence in the spring of 1925. A few months later he applied for a job as a cab driver. Lying about his age, which was seventeen, he managed to pass himself off as twenty-one in order to obtain his chauffeur's license (City badge no. 1976, State badge no. 34879) from the city's Board of Public Utilities, permitting him to drive a taxi within the city limits. That he was just over six feet and a solid 148 pounds, with black hair and dark brown eyes, made him look older than he was. Dad's route took him mostly downtown, where he shuttled fares among the various hotels, including the Biltmore, and out to Hollywood. Ironically, one of Father's fellow cab drivers out of the same station, and likely his early acquaintance, was a young man studying for his law degree, who twenty-five years later was destined to become LAPD's most famous chief of police, William H. Parker.

Toward the end of 1925, another story about Father appeared in print, this time by Ted Le Berthon, the drama critic for the *Los Angeles Evening Herald*, who wrote the following unusual and highly illuminating article about Father. In it, Le Berthon changes Dad's last name from Hodel to "Morel" and the name of his magazine from *Fantasia* to *Whirlpools*.

This article reveals another side to my father. Besides being a pampered mama's boy, intellectual elitist, poet, and pianist, he was also a fighter who at the slightest provocation would be eager and ready to trade punches.

Los Angeles Evening Herald   December 9, 1925

THE MERRY-GO-ROUND

By TED LE BERTHON

The Clouded Past of a Poet

GEORGE MOREL is tall, olive-skinned with wavy black hair and a strong bold nose. His eyes are large, brown, somnolent. A romantic, hawklike fellow, a pianist, a poet, and editor of Whirlpools, a bizarre, darkly poetical quarterly.

"George is a nice boy but —"

How often did one hear that!

What his friends hinted was that George, being young, was inclined to write of melancholy things.

Of course, George could have pointed to Keats, Rupert Brooke or Stephen Crane for precedent, but — "It's not George's gloom, his preference for Huysmanns, De Gourmont, Poe, Baudelaire, Verlaine and Hecht that pains us," these "friends" would parry, "but his stilted elegance, his meticulous speech!"

George drowned himself at times in an ocean of deep dreams. Only part of him seemed present.

He would muse standing before one in a black, flowered dressing gown lined with scarlet silk, oblivious to one's presence.

Suddenly, though, his eyes would flare up like signal lights and he would say, "The formless fastidiousness of perfumes in a seventeenth century boudoir is comparable to my mind in the presence of twilight."

One might have answered "What of it?" — but one just didn't.

As one of George's "friends" put it: "He's young. He'll get over it. What he needs is contact with harsh realities. At present his writing is tenuous, dreamy, monotonous — and he is like his writing."

A Future Realistic Novelist

I HADN'T seen George for about a year —

And last night, strolling up Spring street in a sort of Morelian reverie myself, I was startled by hearing a familiar voice. The next moment I saw a tall young fellow in a taxi driver's uniform seize a burly, argumentative man by the coat lapels and growl menacingly:

"Come across with that taxi fare or I'll smack you in the nose, right here and now!"

The speaker was GEORGE MOREL.

By the end of 1925, George had switched his schedule to driving *on the night shift while he took jobs as a copywriter, first for a local Army & Navy store and then for the Southern California Gas Com*-pany. It was through SoCal Gas that he got his first taste of managing publicity, advertising, and marketing, and landed himself another job as a radio announcer, in which he hosted a live show, introducing the public to classical music during the early-evening hours. SoCal Gas sponsored an hour-long program in the early days of radio. Dad, a gas company employee in advertising, possessed the perfect qualities for the job: a musical prodigy with an encyclopedic knowledge of the classics, he also had a beautiful speaking voice. His uniquely meticulous speech patterns, his ability to use just the right words and diction expressed with perfect intonation, rhyme, and meter, would remain his calling card for the rest of his life. George Hodel's voice was as unique and distinct as his fingerprints. However, after shutting off the radio mike for the evening, Dad put on his cab driver's hat and began looking for fares waiting outside the Biltmore.

Though not yet twenty, Father had already accumulated the life experiences of much older men and had led several lives: boy genius, musical prodigy, crime reporter, advertising writer, public relations officer, public radio announcer, editor of a self-published literary magazine, poet, intellectual elitist, and cab driver.

In addition to George Hill Hodel being one of the **Los Angeles Record's crime reporters**, he was also that newspaper's Georgie-on-the-spot literary critic.

The actor Sadakichi Hartmann had a bit part as the Mongol Prince's Court Magician (see below) in the silent swashbuckler film *The Thief of Baghdad* (1924), which starred the great Douglas Fairbanks.

Sadakichi appeared before a small intimate gathering where the "poet, critic and artist" talked on French Poetry.

On the following page (257) is an article and review George Hodel wrote about the event for **The Record** in 1924.

LOS ANGELES RECORD 1924

ORIENTAL HARMONIES

*** *** *** *** ***

Sadakichi Hartmann Talks on French Poetry

By GEORGE HILL HODEL

In a small room, filled with tobacco smoke, fantastically decorated, redolent of boldly assertive Bohemianism, he is talking- Sadakichi Hartmann, poet, critic and artist.

A small group of Los Angels "intelligentsia" are listening to him, absorbed, fascinated by the exotic spell he is creating.

The man harmonizes perfectly with the mad splashes of color in the room—the zinzoline draperies, the weirdly decorated hangings.

His face has the seeming of an oriental mask; his expression is imperturbable and wearily calm. Hartmann is half German, half Japanese, and the mixture in his blood produces a strange blend that is weirdly harmonious.

Tangled Hair

His sunken eyes have a strongly Asiatic slant. Over his pale and sallow face, of a dull Mongolian saffron color, falls a heavy mass of tangled grey hair.

Sadakichi Hartmann is a disciple of Edgar Allan Poe, and like Poe, he has a keen understanding of the shades and colorings and variegated nuances of poetry.

Hartmann is a literary aristocrat.

"Art must be by the few and for the few," he is saying. "Poetry can only be the religion of the aristocratic minority."

Talk Indistinct

He talks indistinctly and gutturally, due to a defect in his speech. And yet his voice is low, and musical and strangely sonorous.

He waves his long bony hands in fanciful gestures, as if in magic incantation.

One closes one's eyes and one is in some dark Confucian temple, with the incense curling, languorously, fantastically.

It appears young George Hodel worked as a crime reporter for *The Record* for about a year in 1924 and left towards the end of that year and decided to publish FANTASIA magazine and "move on."

We do not know why he left the newspaper, but I do have a copy of a letter of recommendation for George Hodel from *The Los Angeles Record's* Editor, Burton Knisely. Here is the Editor's glowing recommendation for "this most brilliant young man" written just days before Christmas, on December 19, 1924.

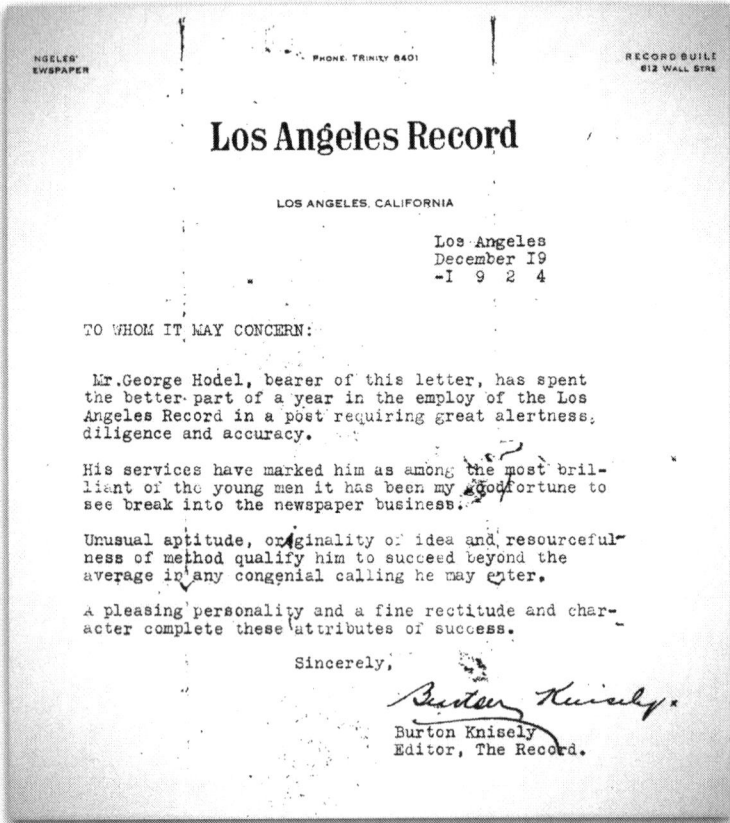

In his excellent book, *Red Ink White Lies: The Rise and Fall of Los Angeles Newspapers 1920-1962* (Dragonflyer Press 2000) author Rob Leicester Wagner, has this to say about *The Record* newspaper and its Editor, Burton Knisely:

Page 10:

THE EVENING RECORD It was founded in
1895 by E.W. Scripps. By the end of World War I,
it shifted toward advocating Social causes under
Editor Henry B.R. Brigs and Burton Knisely. The
newspaper tucked away on Wall Street near Skid
Row; was unabashed in its advocacy journalism
and encouraged a literary approach to writing.
Leroy Sanders and Zack Farmer assumed
ownership in 1933. It was renamed the *Post-
Record*. In 1935, a controlling interest in the
newspaper was purchased by *Daily News*
publisher E. Manchester Boddy. It eventually
merged with the *Daily News* to become the
Evening News. By 1940, the old *Record* had
been completely absorbed by the *Daily News*.

And this on Burton Knisely from page 304:

KNISELY, BURTON – A committed Socialist
whose early career included stints on the
Cleveland newspapers. Knisely was the
managing Editor of the *Evening Record*. Under
Knisely and Henry B.R. Briggs, the newspaper
did its best crusading journalism. Knisely
founded the Pomegranates and Pemmican Club,
an informal group of a half-dozen reporters who
discussed and practiced literary journalism.

On next page 260 is the obituary of Burton Knisely
appearing in the *Los Angeles Times* January 29, 1930:

Times

END COMES TO KNISELY IN HOSPITAL

Former Editor of 'Record' Expires After Five Years of Poor Health

Willis Burton Knisely, Los Angeles newspaper man and formerly editor of the Los Angeles Record, died yesterday morning at the Good Samaritan Hospital. Although Mr. Knisely had been in poor health he was not thought to be dangerously ill and was taken to the hospital only a few days ago for an examination.

Mr. Knisely retired from active newspaper work five years ago on account of poor health and has been living in Eagle Rock. He was born in Canton, O., and after graduating from the Western Reserve University joined the staff of the Canton News. Later he served as Pacific Coast representative of the Newspaper Enterprise Association and was sent to China and Russia as a special correspondent in 1918 and 1919. During 1919 he came to Los Angeles as the editor of the Record, and held that post until five years ago.

He leaves his widow, Mrs. Bertha McCord Knisely, who is a member of the staff of the Saturday Night. Funeral services will be conducted Thursday at 3 p.m. in the Wee Kirk of the Heather Forest Lawn Memorial Park.

With this additional background information on young George Hodel's activities in the early and mid-Twenties, let us now return to the Martin Sisters investigation.

Jailhouse Snitch Used to Convict Elderly Night Watchman

Though vigorously denied by the sixty-year-old defendant, S.C. Stone, the testimony of a jailhouse prisoner was received and presented to the jury at Stone's trial.

I quote in full from the *Oxnard Press-Courier* newspaper article of November 21, 1925:

ADMITS KILLING MARTIN
SISTERS
CLEARS MYSTERY

S.C. Stone, Night Watchman,
Stepfather of Jack Hoxie,
Makes Confession
TELLS HIS CELL MATE

Lured Girls to His Room
With Candy
Kept Bodies Month
Hundreds Search

LOS ANGELES, NOV 21

S.C. Stone, 60-year-old stepfather of Jack Hoxie film star, has confessed the brutal murder of the two Martin girls, May, 12, and Nina, 8, whose tragic disappearance and death mystified Southern California for more than a year, the district attorney's office claimed this afternoon.

Stone, a Los Angeles night watchman, long under suspicion of the crime and now facing trial on a grand jury indictment charging him with the murder, made the purported confession to a cell mate in the county jail, A.H. Floyd, Culver City police judge recently convicted on charges of misappropriation of public funds.

In his alleged confession to Floyd, who turned it over to the district attorney's office, Stone was said to have confessed that he lured the Martin sisters to a room with candy, bound and gagged them and kept them, prisoners, for three days and then strangled them to death.

The purported confession also stated that Stone kept the bodies of the little girls in his room for more than a month while hundreds of police and citizens were searching for the missing children.

This statement, according to the district attorney's office, clears up the mystery of why the bodies were not found until February 18, 1925, six months after the girls disappeared, although the district where they were discovered had been thoroughly searched.

The bodies of the two girls were found in a shallow grave in the hills. Officers said that the girls' clothing had been partially torn from their bodies.

In checking for information on "The Police Judge A.H. Floyd" turned jailhouse snitch and who was one of the prosecution's chief witness, who literally put the nail in night watchman Stone's coffin, I discovered that just months before his testimony Floyd was sentenced to prison for a term of from three to thirty-four years.

Former Judge Gets Term as Embezzler
Santa Ana Register 20 May 1925

Los Angeles, May 20th—A. H. Floyd, former police judge at Culver City, was sentenced to a term of three to thirty-four years in prison today when Superior Court Judge Charles S. Crail overruled his motion for a new trial. Floyd was found guilty by a jury on 13 counts of embezzlement and falsification of public records. He was accused of pocketing the money received from heavy fines imposed on auto speeders.

Talk about your motivation for a jailhouse snitch to **'testilie.'**

I haven't been able to locate documentation on the judge's actual time served. But, I will bet you two tickets to the police ball that he was given a "get out of jail free card" at about the same time defendant Stone was convicted and sent to prison six months later, in December 1925.

For the moment, let us disregard the defense testimony that Nightwatchman Stone had a slam dunk alibi and, at the time of the kidnapping, was nowhere near the abduction location.

That two adult witnesses testified before the jury that Stone was with them, showing the couple a house at the time of the abduction far from the kidnap location.

Also, let us disregard the Martin sister's neighborhood committee, who came to Stone's defense and attempted to present evidence pointing the finger to the two young men that Dr. Morganstiern had investigated and named in his formal written summary.

Dr. Morganstiern informed police that these two men had motive, opportunity, and means to commit the copycat crime similar to the Leopold and Loeb "Crime of the Century." Readers of the daily papers saw headlines for both the Leopold and Loeb and the Stone trials simultaneously.

Convicted felon A.H. Floyd's testimony standing by itself is factually absurd.

It is inconceivable that S.C. Stone could keep the two dead girls' bodies in his house "for months." The decay and stench would have been unbearable, and there would have been signs and forensic proof and decay.

STONE ORDERED TO GALLOWS FOR MURDERING GIRLS

Aged Los Angeles Man Must Pay For Brooding Crime Against Two Children

On December 22, 1925, S.C. Stone was found guilty of the Martin Sisters double homicide and sentenced to death. After the judge ordered that the defendant be executed within ninety days, Stone declared to the court:

> "I am not guilty. Before God, I am not guilty.
>
> I am innocent of this crime. There is a God in heaven, and He will not let an innocent man hang for this terrible murder. If He believes this murder must be avenged by more deaths, He will bring the guilty persons to light."

On the following day, December 23, 1925, this *Los Angeles Evening Express* headline appeared:

HUNT FOR EVIDENCE TO BRING SMITH TO TRIAL ON CHARGE OF BEING STONE ACCOMPLICE

EVERY EFFORT BEING MADE TO BREAK 'SHORTY'
Denies He was Instrumental In Disappearance, Murder Of Martin Girls

Stone's Execution Temporarily Delayed Pending Perusal By Appellate Court

...

With the execution of S.C. Stone, Glen Airy night watchman, for the murders of Nina and May Martin, temporarily delayed pending perusal of the case by the appellate court, the district attorney's office today busied itself with the acquisition of evidence on which it hopes to hang Arthur "Short" Smith for the crime.

Deputy District attorney E.J. Dennison, who led Stone's prosecution, announced that every effort is being made to "break" Smith, or otherwise obtain sufficient evidence to bring him to trial on a charge of being Stone's accomplice in the murder.

ARRESTED DURING TRIAL

Smith was arrested during Stone's trial, admitted knowing Stone, but denied he was instrumental in the disappearance and murder of the little Glen Airy school children.

This article clearly establishes that the prosecution was convinced *that an unknown accomplice(s) remained at large,* and while not about to concede that they may have convicted the wrong man, nevertheless, they did believe one or more additional suspects were involved.

Nothing came of the prosecution's attempts to link "Shorty" Smith to the crimes, but California Governor C.C. Young did commute S.C. Stone's death sentence on March 10, 1927, to "life imprisonment."

On August 1, 1941, just ninety-five days before my birth in Los Angeles, the *Los Angeles Times* published the following article:

OLSON FREES CONVICTED MURDERER OF TWO GIRLS

Stone, 75, Originally Given Death Penalty For Double Slaying Here in 1925, Released

From the Governor's mansion in Sacramento yesterday came an order signed by Governor Olson granting executive clemency and freedom to Scott C. Stone, 75, lame Glen Alry night watchman convicted in 1925 of the murders of May Martin, 12, and her sister Nina, 9.

Governor Olson commuted Stone's sentence to time served with the statement that a study of the records convinced him Stone was falsely convicted on testimony, which Olson said has since been repudiated.

REASONABLE DOUBT

In granting the commutation, the Governor said:

"The crime committed is deserving of the highest form of punishment provided for under the laws of State, but to my mind, the evidence that has been offered in support of this application raises more than a reasonable doubt that the applicant was the perpetrator thereof."

"However, I cannot say that there is proof beyond a reasonable doubt that the defendant is innocent and that that proof, I believe, should be required before a full pardon is granted."

HOME PROVIDED

Governor Olson also stated that Stone now is aged and infirm and that Dr. L.L. Stanley, chief surgeon at San Quentin, reported the prisoner will not be able to take care of himself.

However, Olson said, Salvation Army officials in Los Angeles are not only willing but eager to provide a home for Stone.

The slaying, known as the "Red Ridinghood" murder because of the red cloaks worn by the girls, is believed to have occurred on the night of August 23, 1924, when the little girls disappeared after they had left their parents' home to visit their grandmother.

Their bodies, partially covered by the red cloaks, were found February 5, 1925, in a ditch near the Baldwin Hills.

SUSPECTED LATER

Stone, a nightwatchman in the district, was not suspected of the crime until October of 1924 when he was arrested charged with mistreating a 13-year-old girl whom he had induced to enter his automobile for a ride.

Deputy sheriffs conducting the investigation immediately became suspicious and questioned Stone concerning the Martin sisters whom he admitted knowing but denied having seen on the night of their disappearance.

Witnesses during the trial told of seeing a man, whom they identified as Stone, in the vicinity of where the girls' bodies were found carrying a bundle out into the weeds. Not only identifying Stone, the witnesses said the man walked with a limp.

Another witness was found who told of seeing the Martin sisters riding with Stone in his car on the evening of their disappearance, both of them eating candy.

Officers found a tiny vanity case underneath Stone's bed in his bungalow, which a neighbor of the Martin girls identified as one she had given to them.

SENTENCE COMMUTED

All these things, and many more details, added up in the mind of a jury in Superior Court to a verdict of guilty of first-degree murder with no recommendation for life imprisonment, which meant death.

For years Stone fought the death penalty through appeals until March 10, 1927, Governor C.C. Young, questioning the man's guilt, commuted the death sentence to life imprisonment.

Continuing his fight for freedom, Stone kept pressing his pleas for freedom contending that he is innocent of the crime until Governor Olson finally granted him freedom.

~ ~ ~

Though these victims are the first (earliest chronologically) "child murders" connected to George Hodel, sadly, they will not be the last.

The M.O. in these two crimes will fit a pattern that continues into the 1930s... and beyond.

SKH Author's Note:

In June 2020, several months before writing this chapter, I came across a book on Amazon, entitled, *UNCIVIL TWILIGHT: The 1920s Death Sentence That Left a Serial Killer Free to Talk and Kill Children in 1937 (CreateSpace Independent Publishing, May 8, 2015)* by author George Sherwood.

Discovering it was written about The 1924 Martin Sisters Murders, I deliberately held off reading it until completing this chapter.

In the last few days (August 2020), I have now read Mr. Sherwood's book, and for those wanting more information, I do recommend it with a personal caveat.

In my opinion, the book is challenging to read mainly because most of the chapter contents are verbatim court transcripts and documents, which by definition, are dry and due to the nearly hundred-year-old vernacular rather dull and stale.

That said, **Mr. Stewart's findings and the information revealed in his research material ARE NOT.**

He clearly makes the case for a wrongful conviction, and for me, the highlight of his book was Chapter 8, "Preventing a Wrongful Execution."

The author provides verbatim quotes from letters sent to the governor just days before Stone's scheduled execution. These included pleas for leniency on the death sentence from almost all the involved prosecutors, a lead detective, and numerous public witnesses, and *even the murdered children's mother, Mrs. Paul Buus.*

The Martin girls' mother wrote a heart-wrenching letter to the California governor pleading for Stone's life, "that he not be executed" and expressing her doubts as to several prime witnesses' testimony as possibly being perjured.

For those wanting a deeper dive detailing many of the facts as presented in actual court documents and testimony, I do recommend reading Mr. Stewart's book.

Chapter 7

AIMEE SEMPLE MCPHERSON

Sister Aimee circa 1926

For more than two decades (1924-1944), "Sister Aimee" was *the* powerhouse in Los Angeles's religious community

Tens of thousands of Angelenos flocked to Angelus Temple, Sister Aimee's International Church of the Foursquare Gospel, which she had built in 1923, from the grateful donations of her true believers.

Angelus Temple, on Glendale Blvd., in Echo Park, and is a few miles west of downtown Los Angeles and was named a National Historic Landmark in 1992. At the time it was constructed, it was considered the largest religious "temple" in America and seated some 4,300 souls.

Sister Aimee preaching inside Angelus Temple circa 1930

I just entered a name search for Aimee Semple McPherson in Google and received almost half a million responses.

There have been dozens of books written about her life and ministry, as well as numerous documentaries and several full-length feature films.

For this chapter, I am going to focus mainly on the five weeks of her life and ministry in 1926; then, we will fast forward to the last days of her life in 1944.

However, to fully understand the magnitude of Sister Aimee's life and influence on the world, it is necessary to present an abbreviated biography on this amazing woman.

A Short Biography

Aimee Elizabeth Kennedy was born on October 9, 1890 in Salford, Ontario, Canada. (Coincidentally, one day and seventeen years later George Hodel was born on October 10, 1907.)

Aimee's parents were James Morgan and Mildred Ona (Pearce) Kennedy.

Aimee was married three times.

Her first husband, Robert James Semple, was a Pentecostal missionary she met at a revival meeting and married at the young age of seventeen.

Robert and Aimee Semple circa 1910

Newly married Robert and Aimee Semple embarked on a missionary tour to China, where both contracted malaria. Robert died from dysentery in Hong Kong. Aimee recovered and gave birth to her first child, Roberta Star Semple.

Upon returning to the United States, Aimee joined her mother in New York and then, in 1912, met and married Harold McPherson, an accountant.

The following year, in 1913, she gave birth to a second child, Rolf Potter Kennedy McPherson.

Aimee and Harold McPherson

Her second husband >

Aimee divorced Harold in 1918, stating her preference to be on the "Sawdust Trail" over a life of ordinary domesticity. Their marriage was officially over when a final divorce was granted to her in 1921.

(**Author Note** - The term "Sawdust Trail" was a term used to designate tents and temporary buildings constructed and utilized by itinerant ministers for revival meetings. The floors were covered with sawdust to hold down the dust. It also served to soften the noise as well as provide a pleasant odor to the gatherings. Source-*Wikipedia*)

Her third husband.

David L. Hutton and Aimee on their honeymoon.

Aimee met and married her third husband, David Hutton, an actor, singer, and musician, in 1931, the marriage was short-lived, they separated two years later and divorced in 1934.

"Go West Young Woman"

Aimee Visits Dayton, Ohio in 1919 on her way west in her "Gospel Auto" (A seven-seater Oldsmobile)

My first thought was to provide my readers with a very condensed biography of Sister Aimee's life. However, having just read California author/historian Kevin's Starr synopsis of her life and influence on Los Angeles, I feel it best to include his remarkable observations on the life and times of Sister Aimee.

The *Los Angeles Times* had this to say about Starr's *MATERIAL DREAMS*:

> "Indispensable...Starr's book does for California what Henry Nash Smith's *Virgin Land* did for the opening of the West: it demonstrates how idea, myth, misconception, and hope shaped and often distorted a developing society."

Here below are a few pages from Starr's book, *MATERIAL DREAMS: Southern California Through the 1920s (Oxford University Press 1990) - 452pgs.*

Excerpts from MATERIAL DREAMS, pages 140-144:

> Aimee Semple McPherson, as she now styled herself, loved automobiles as well as Jesus Christ—big, open touring cars which she could emblazon with evangelistic slogans and take to the road, preaching an amalgam of Pentecostalism, Holy Rollerism (with its emphasis upon popular music, theatrics, and audience participation), and the Foursquare Gospel she herself devised. Appropriately, she drove to Los Angeles in 1918 with her mother and two children after her divorce from McPherson, already a preacher of some reputation, stopping en route to preach to subscribers to her *Foursquare Monthly* but looking for a new life as well along with thousands of others similarly motivated, heading west in flivvers. Before setting out on her trek, McPherson promised her two children a bungalow and a pet canary when they reached Southern California. When the children grew tired or cranky on the long journey, she comforted them with stories of the bungalows, canaries, gardens, and rosebushes of Los

Angeles, of the happiness they would all enjoy together in that magical little house. In later years she remembered this automotive hegira (she claimed she put four thousand miles on the speedometer) as a Biblical journey, a spiritual quest for the promised City of the Angels.

...

The words of Joshua 6:16 came to her: "Shout, for the Lord hath given you the city," which the Lord seemed very much willing to do. As in the case of Jericho, the walls of Los Angeles all but tumbled down as she drove into the city with her mother and two children, $100 to her name and a tambourine with "Jesus Is Coming Soon —Get Ready" emblazoned across the side of her touring car. Two nights later, she preached in a rented upper room. Shortly thereafter, she signed a lease on a small church. She was soon preaching to standing-room crowds in the Philharmonic Auditorium, the largest assembly space in the city, with ushers struggling to keep the aisles free in conformity to fire laws. When she shared her bungalow story with her audience, men stood up volunteering land, lumber, and labor and built her a bungalow near Culver City.

Los Angeles, however, was a material city. Or was it that America, as well as possessing a strong evangelistic strain, was also a material place? In any event, Aimee Semple McPherson soon became a very material woman. She wanted her own temple, not a rented hall, and by January 1923, she had one—the $1.5 million Angelus Temple at the northwest edge of Echo Park. Seating 4300, Angelus Temple was claimed as the largest class A church building in the United States. McPherson had herself raised most of the money for it through revival tours throughout California, the Midwest, and Australia. She and her mother, and not the congregation, held the deed to the property. Adjacent to the Temple, she built a Bible school and administration building from which she administered the Foursquare Gospel program, which eventually enrolled some 240 affiliated churches throughout Southern California and the Southwest. Skilled as a preacher, McPherson was a gifted organizer as well, among the first to establish a ministry of affiliated individuals and congregation brought together through the written word and through the power of Angelus Temple radio station KFSG (Kall Four Square Gospel), the third radio station to be established in Los Angeles. Flamboyant on the stage as a preacher, McPherson—Sister Aimee to her congregation— nevertheless ran an organizationally sophisticated ministry, complete with choir and orchestra, rescue mission, home visitors' organization, and publishing house. From her Salvation Army background, she promoted the use of uniforms for herself and for a phalanx of female attendants who escorted her to the stage and stood guard as she preached. With success came money ("Sister has a headache tonight," she would say at collection time, "just quiet money please") and a mansion to replace the bungalow near Culver City, a shiny new car, expensive coiffures, and elegant clothes. Now when she preached on the road, she traveled by train and stayed at first-class hotels.

Today, Aimee Semple **McPherson is remembered**, if at all, for her eccentric, histrionic preaching and **for the faked kidnapping and sex scandal of 1926**.*

Each of these tend to be recounted from a comic point of view, as if she were of no other significance. The comedy, however, is understandable. It derives easily from the material. Take her preaching, for example. Knowing her audience, their limited background, their credulity, their love of movies, and make-believe. McPherson evolved a technique of costumed sermonizing linked to a theme. Dressed as a USC football player, she preached on carrying the ball for Christ. Entering the Temple on a motorcycle in a policeman's uniform, she placed sin under arrest and urged her audience not to speed to ruin. Prodding with a pitchfork, she chased the devil from the stage. Dressed as a nurse, she prayed over the sick. Other appearances included one as an Admiral in the Salvation Navy or as George Washington at Valley Forge. When she travelled, she collected costumes, which she added to her already impressive dressing-room press for later pulpit appearances. As Sister Aimee acted, preached, and prayed, the mighty Temple organ thundered in accompaniment, joined by a brass band, and a well-rehearsed female choir in the Salvation Army-like uniforms. In architecture and usage, the Angelus

Temple was more motion-picture theatre than church. It even had an electric marquee over the entrance, announcing Sister Aimee's latest sermon.

Once widowed, once divorced, Sister Aimee was in her mid-thirties, vital in every aspect of life, at the height of her fame. The object of one aspect of her vitality was Kenneth G. Ormiston, employed at the Temple as station engineer for KFSG, but unfortunately, a married man. The ensuing farce survives today as Aimee Semple McPherson's enduring claim to notoriety. On the afternoon of May 18, 1926, McPherson was last seen at Ocean Park, a swimming area near Venice. She was presumed to have drowned, but a massive search by police and Temple members failed to discover any body. In the search, two people, a diver and a Temple member, were themselves drowned. A little more than a month later, three days after an all-day memorial service at Angeles Temple, McPherson resurfaced on June 23 in the small Sonoran town of Agua Prieta, claiming to have been kidnapped and to have escaped from a shack in the Sonoran desert where she was being held captive. Researchers with a taste for American-style *Grande Guignol* have patiently unraveled the entire episode. It is all but certain that Sister Aimee took a month's vacation in the company of Kenneth Ormiston, spending part of this time in a honeymoon cottage in Carmel. District Attorney Asa Keyes produced a grocery list from the Carmel cottage in what was unmistakably McPherson's handwriting. For nearly half a year, Keyes gathered evidence preparatory to taking McPherson to trial on charges of conspiracy to produce false testimony. The embattled minister defended herself vociferously all the while against the storm of scandal and innuendo that swept Los Angeles.

...

McPherson escaped going to trial when the District Attorney, fearing that his case fell short of the total conclusiveness needed to convict a person of McPherson's popularity, withdrew charges at the last possible moment. Her disappearance and feigned kidnapping, however, spiced by the motive of sexual adventure, rendered her a laughingstock. After a year and more of press scrutiny and legal investigation, Aimee Semple McPherson became that from which no public figure can ever recover momentum—an object of public ridicule. The faithful held on, joyously mobbing her in a Temple celebration on the evening charges were dropped; but any larger influence she might have once possessed disappeared.

* (**Ed. Note** - Bold emphasis mine)

My sincere thanks to historian and former California State Librarian Kevin Starr for that excellent biographical summary on Sister Aimee's life and ministry.

Starr's remarkable multi-volume series on California history is known as *Americans and the California Dream,* which I highly recommend reading.

Kevin Starr was unquestionably a large nugget of California Gold. Born in San Francisco (not far from Sutter's Mill) on September 3, 1940. He died, at the age of seventy-six, in that same city on January 14, 2017.

(Astonishingly, his death came *on the very day, the 70th anniversary of one* of California's most infamous crimes, one which Starr had extensively chronicled as an important part of California history—the murder of Elizabeth "Black Dahlia" Short.)

To underscore Mr. Starr's historical importance as relates to Sister Aimee, I would like to introduce some additional excerpts from the *Harvard University Press* blog of September 28, 2011—*The Resurrections of Aimee Semple MacPherson.*

The blog introduces us to Matthew Avery Sutton, an associate professor of history at Washington State

University, and the author of *Aimee Semple McPherson and the Resurrection of Christian America* (Harvard University Press 2009) and goes on to state:

...

"With the revival of Kathie Lee Gifford's musical *Saving Aimee* scheduled to premier in just a few days, we invited Sutton to explain why McPherson is such an appealing character to fictionalize."

You can read his take below.

Excerpts
from Author Matthew Sutton's blog response:

There is perhaps no religious leader in American history who has been resurrected in American popular culture as often as Aimee Semple McPherson. The subject of numerous films, novels, poems, and songs, McPherson has certainly captured the imaginations of Americans. Most recently, she served as the basis for the musical *Saving Aimee*, which opens this month in Seattle.

...

She eventually settled in Los Angeles, where she built the spectacular Angelus Temple, a five-thousand seat megachurch that opened in 1923. The next year, she launched her own powerful radio station, Kall Four Square Gospel (KFSG). But she is most famous for a 1926 scandal. At the peak of her fame, she mysteriously vanished. She reappeared over a month later, claiming to have been kidnapped, although she was more likely shacked up with a lover.

The mystery of her whereabouts during those five weeks in 1926 has never been solved. Instead, it continues to be replayed in American culture. The first writer to transform McPherson's story into fiction was Upton Sinclair. Having watched the kidnapping unfold from his Los Angeles home, he wove McPherson's story into his novel *Oil!* (1927), a muckraking critique of Southern California. Sinclair Lewis's masterpiece *Elmer Gantry* followed closely on the heels of *Oil!* Although Lewis had begun work on the project before McPherson disappeared, she served as a model for Sister Sharon Falconer. A few years later, Frank Capra's film *The Miracle Woman* (1931) explored faith, sexuality, and scandal. The film was based on the play *God Bless You Sister*, which in turn was based on McPherson's life. In this film, the young Barbara Stanwyck plays a McPherson character, Florence Fallon.

A decade and a half after Aimee's death, Richard Brooks resurrected *Elmer Gantry*, transforming Sinclair Lewis's novel into an Academy Award-winning motion picture. The film captures some of the issues that McPherson's popularity illuminated, including the controversies ravaging Protestantism and the tensions surrounding the redefinition of gender roles in the interwar era. Folk singer Pete Seeger's "Aimee McPherson" (1961) retells the story of the infamous kidnapping in song, mixing fact with fiction. "Did you ever hear the story of Aimee McPherson," it begins, who "preached a wicked sermon, so the papers said." The same themes emerge in this song, performed thirty-five years after the events of 1926, which have characterized so much of the art depicting McPherson. She appears as a sexual vixen, an alluring siren, a religious hypocrite, and the darling of newspapers. But not everyone has viewed this song as a work of criticism. It found its way into the *Liberated Women's Songbook* (1971). The most recent literary work seeking to conjure the evangelist's legacy is Mick Farren's *Jim Morrison's Adventures in the Afterlife* (1999). His work presents McPherson as a complex, sex-crazed woman. His Aimee finds true happiness not in religious devotion but in a hyper-sexual relationship with Jim Morrison of the Doors.

But what has all or any of this have to do with George Hodel, you ask?

Let's take a look.

The Chronology of the "Kidnapping" of Aimee Semple McPherson

The Sister Aimee disappearance and subsequent reported kidnapping and all that followed became "breaking news" and were above-the-fold headlines for the following three months. The scandal that followed remained front-page news through October 1926.

The following chronology will hit the "highlights" that are pertinent to presenting my investigation and suspected linkage of George Hodel to the kidnapping.

May 18, 1926

Sister Aimee travels from her home to nearby Venice Beach for a swim in the Pacific Ocean and simply "disappears." A massive search is conducted, and while no body is found, she is "presumed drowned." Sadly, two searchers are drowned during the search and rescue efforts at Venice Beach.

In the days and weeks following Sister Aimee's disappearance, "sightings" of her are reported across the nation from San Francisco to New York. Still, by month's end, her mother, Mrs. Kennedy, and her children have given up hope and prepare for a transition of power to name a church successor.

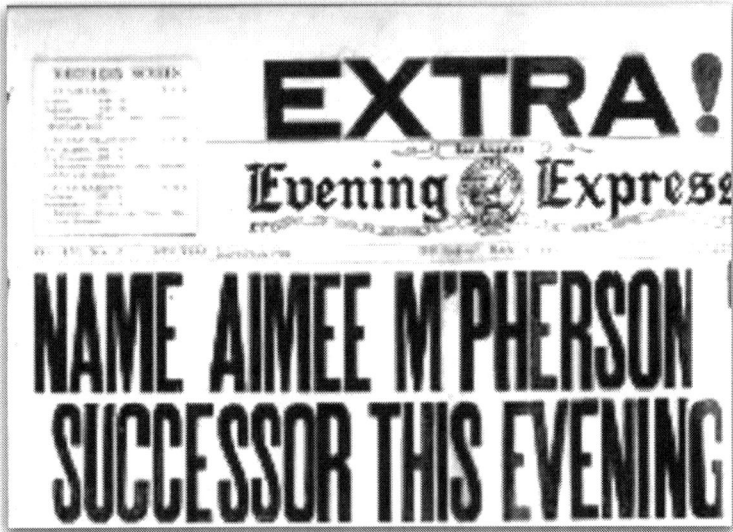

June 18, 1926 "Avengers Note"

(see next page - 287)

Mrs. Minnie Kennedy,
Angelus Temple,
Los Angeles, Cal.

Dear Madam:-

Exactly one month has elapsed since we grabbed Aimee McPherson and now is the time for action. We nearly bungled it once, but we've moved her to a safe place now and have doped out a plan of ransom payment that is absolutely safe to us. You wont be able to trap us if you do act in bad faith. We doubt if you will attempt any funny business though when you are convinced this is no hoax or Sunday school picnic and that we really have your daughter. Do what you like with this letter (we realize you got to use it to raise the dough) but the next one must be kept absolutely to yourself and its instructions followed exactly or there will grave consequences to your daughter.

First, in order that you may know without any doubt that Aimee is alive and in our hands, we are enclosing a lock of her hair. We tried to get answers to your silly questions but because she knows about the half million ransom she wont answer them. Says she would rather die than cripple the church to such an extent. But before she knew what it was all about we tricked her into a couple fool answers something like "A woven wire one between two apple trees" and the hound was black and named Gyp. She shut up then realizing what we were after but if you insist a lighted cigar against a bare foot often gets results. Her middle right hand finger has a scar on it you ought to recognize, suppose we chop it off and sent it along to kill your doubts? Weve got her alright and trust by now youll believe it and know that we mean business. She has been taken good care of by a woman who has been with her constantly, an ex-nurse who knows her business. She is suffering with hysteria and the heat and is pretty weak but physically and mentally theres nothing wrong with her that wont mend soon once shes home. But though we've treated her respectfully in fairness to her position and value to us, what the future holds for her is entirely up to you. Our alternative is to sell her to old Felipe of Mexico City. We are sick and tired of her infernal preaching, she spouts scripture in answer to everything.

We took her for two reasons-:First To wreck that damned Temple and second: to collect a tidy half million. We have held her for a month during which time her name and standing have been just about ruined. We had to fight hard to kill that "drowning" idea of yours but a little palm-oil brought plenty reports of her being seen all over the place and the newspaper hounds were only too anxious to play it up. They seemed to have an axe to grind too and sure helped us grand. You've taken some of our girls Damn you, and given us many a jolt, but guess we are square now eh?

Now as to the ransom. We've been stumped for a method of collecting which would be safe, because you spilled it to the police before. Its plain no ordinary methods will work with you, so weve sure doped out a corker, and while it has taken time and delayed things a bit it is apple pie for us. You got a week to raise the money, and on June 25th you will get the final letter with the instructions how to proceed to get the money into our hands and how to get your darling daughter into your hands.

It might interest you to know just what happened on the beach a month ago today. Well we had inside workers who kept us informed as to her whereabouts, and that day she went to the beach looked like our chance. We watched until she was alone, then a man and

woman stepped up to her with a heart-breaking tale of a deathly sick baby in a car across the street, and that Mother Kennedy had sent then down to beach to find Aimee and ask her to pray for the kid. She kicked and insisted on going to hotel to dress first but the argument of dying kid together with the use of a long coat the woman carried persuaded her to come as she was. When she got into the car to pray for the imaginary kid, a quick shove, a gag with some dope on it and a couple of blankets thrown over her, and away we went. Simple, wasnt it?

Now get busy. Have the $500,000 ready in big bills. Watch for the final letter of instructions which will reach you next Friday. That letter you must keep absolutely confidential but you will alright when you read it. Follow the instructions exactly and on that same night you will have your Aimee back and we'll have the dough. If anything slips Felipe gets her.

Till Friday,

THE AVENGERS.

Below is the verbatim "Avengers Note" as typed and delivered to Sister Aimee's mother, Minnie Kennedy, at Angelus Temple, written precisely one month to the day after her daughter's "kidnapping."

Editor's Note - The ransom note here is typed and punctuated as the suspect/s originally wrote it and is rendered here in a smaller font so that the lineation remains as close as possible to the original.

Mrs. Minnie Kennedy,
Angelus Temple,
Los Angeles, Cal.

Dear Madam: -

Exactly one month has elapsed since we grabbed Aimee McPherson and now is the time for action. We nearly bungled it once, But we've moved her to a safe place now and have doped out a plan of Ransom payment that is absolutely safe to us. You won't be able to trap us if you do act in bad faith. We doubt if you will attempt any funny business though when you are convinced this is no hoax or Sunday school picnic and that we really have your daughter. Do what you like with this letter (we realize you got to use it to raise the dough) but the next one must be kept absolutely to yourself and its instructions followed exactly or there will grave consequences to your daughter.
First, in order that you may know without any doubt that Aimee is alive and, in our hands, we are enclosing a lock of her hair. We tried to get answers to your silly questions but because she knows about the half million ransom she won't answer them. Says she would rather die than cripple the church to such an extent. But before she knew what it was all about we tricked her into a couple fool answers something like "A woven wire one between two apple trees" and the hound was black and named Gyp. She shut up then realizing what we were after but if you insist a lighted cigar against a bare foot often gets results. Her middle right hand finger has a scar on it you ought to recognize, suppose we chop it off and sent it along to kill your doubts? We've got her alright and trust by now youll believe it and know that we mean business. She has been taken good care of by a woman who has been with her constantly, an ex-nurse who knows her business. She is suffering with hysteria and the heat and is pretty weak but physucally [sic] and mentally theres nothing wrong with her that wont mend soon once shes home. But though we've treated her respect-fully in fairness to her position and value to us, what the future holds for her is entirely up to you. Our alternative is to sell her to old Felipe of Mexico City. We are sick and tired of her infernal preaching, she spouts scripture in answer to everything.
We took her for two reasons-:First To wreck that damned Temple and second: to collect a tidy half million. We have held her

for a month during which time her name and standing have been just about ruined. We had to fight hard to kill that "drowning" idea of yours but a little palm-oil brought forth plenty reports of her anxious to play it up. They seemed to have an axe to grind too and sure helped us grand. You've taken some of our girls Damn you, and given us many a jolt, but guess we are square now eh?

Now as the ransom. We've been stumped for a method of collecting which would be safe, because you spilled it to the police before. Its plain no ordinary methods will work with you, so weve sure doped out a corker, and while it has taken time and delayed things a bit it is apple pie for us. You got a week to raise the money, and on June 25 you will get the final letter with the instructions how to proceed to get the money into our hands and how to get your darling daughter into your hands.

It might interest you to know just what happened on the beach a month ago today. Well we had inside workers who kept us informed as to her whereabouts, and that day she went to the beach looked like our chance. We watched until she was alone, then a man and woman stepped up to her with a heart-breaking tale of a deathly sick baby in a car across the street, and that Mother Kennedy had sent then [sic]down to beach to find Aimee and ask her to pray for the kid. She kicked and insisted on going to hotel to dress first but the argument of dying kid together with the use of a long coat the woman carried persuaded her to come as she was. When she got into the car to pray for the imaginary kid, a quick shove, a gag with some dope on it and a couple of blankets thrown over her, and away we went. Simple, wasn't it?

Now get busy. Have the $500,000 ready in big bills. Watch for the final letter of instructions which will reach you next Friday. That letter you must keep absolutely confidential but you will alright when you read it. Follow the instructions exactly and on that same night you will have your Aimee back and we'll have the dough. If anything slips Felipe gets her.

Till Friday,

THE AVENGERS.

~ ~ ~

Five days after the "Avengers Note" *was received, Sister Aimee* **miraculously** "**escaped**" *from her* kidnappers *and was* "**found**" to be in a Douglas, Arizona, hospital.

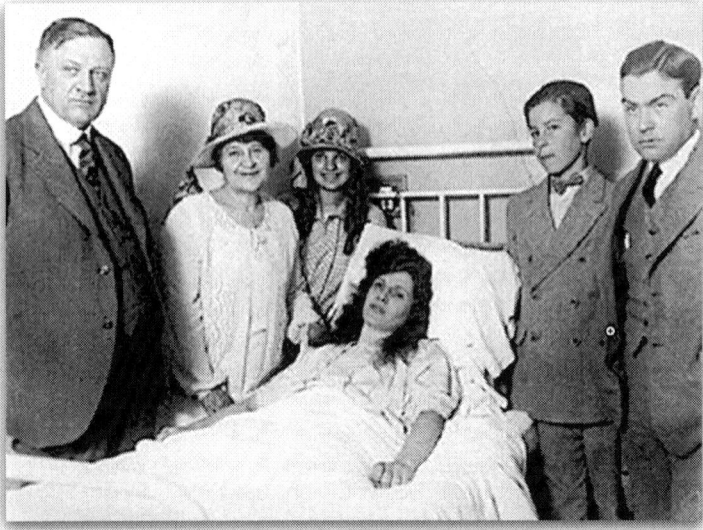

Sister Aimee recovering in Douglas, Arizona, hospital bed.
(Lt to Rt) LA DA Asa Keyes, Mildred Kennedy (Aimee's mother)
Roberta Star Semple (Aimee's daughter), Rolf McPherson
(Aimee's son), and DDA Joseph Ryan.
Pasadena Evening Post - June 23, 1926

Here, as reported by the *Pasadena Evening Post,* is
HER STORY detailing her "abduction and escape."

SKH Note - Major excerpts from that article are in Sister's Aimee's own words.

Pasadena Evening Post
June 23, 1926

FIND AIMEE SEMPLE MCPHERSON IN ARIZONA

Mother of Evangelist Talks With Daughter Over Telephone

EVANGELIST TELLS STORY OF ABDUCTION AND ESCAPE WITH THRILLING DETAILS

Thrust Into Sedan Where Woman Throws Coat Over Her and Sweet Sticky Odor Assails Nostrils, and She Is Spirited Across Border Into Mexico

DOUGLAS, Ariz. June 23—Positive identification of a woman in a hospital here as Aimee Semple McPherson, Los Angeles evangelist, who was reported drowned there May 18, was made today over the telephone by Mrs. Minnie Kennedy, the evangelist's mother, in conversation with William F. McCafferty, editor of the Dispatch, this morning. Identification was established through a long white scar on the second finger of the woman's hand, and also by her giving the name of a pet pigeon.

The woman said the scar was the result of being accidentally cut by a sickle years ago. She also gave the name of a cousin, Mrs. Emma Nickerson, now dead, and described the birthmarks on her babies for McCafferty.

The former evangelist from her cot in the hospital told a story of abduction from Ocean Park, Calif., a trip across the border to Mexico, and of how she escaped about noon yesterday and ran until she fell with exhaustion. Finally, sighting a mountain, which has been identified by officers here as the famous "Nigger Head" mountain, 15 miles south in Sonora, Mexico, she headed for it.

Reaching the mountain about dusk, she found a road and struggled along, falling from time to time with fatigue. She said she sighted the glare from the slag dumps of the copper smelters in this city as the night wore on.

She finally reached the outskirts of Agua Prieta, and approaching a house occupied by Mexicans, called for help, and asked that the police be notified. The Mexicans, she said, offered no assistance, and she went on, falling unconscious before another house.

An American, whose name was not learned, and who was in Agua Prieta, brought her to a hospital here. When she told police who she was, a guard was established about the building.

McCafferty, who had known Mrs. McPherson in Denver, where he had covered her meetings for a newspaper, was recognized. She greeted him with a smile, and asked him to notify Los Angeles at once, and to ask Los Angeles police to protect her daughter Roberta, who she feared the abductors would attempt to kidnap.

While she talked, the woman lapsed many times into a semi-conscious state, due to her exhaustion.

The story of her abduction as she related it to McCafferty was:

"I went to Ocean Park with my secretary, Miss Schaeffer. There I changed into my bathing suit and slipped on a dress over it. We went to the beach where we rented a little beach tent. I went in swimming. I sent Miss Schaeffer to get the names of some soloists and some music. Before she returned, I came back out on the beach. There were life savers drilling there. I went back into the water a short distance, and while I was watching the guards, I heard someone calling: "Mrs. McPherson."

"I turned to face a woman who explained her baby was dying, and that she wanted me to pray for it. She said her husband had the baby in a car nearby. She had a coat over her arm. I accompanied her to the car, in which there was another woman with a bundle in her arms, which I thought was the baby.

"The next thing I knew, I was pushed into the car on the floor. The woman threw the coat over me, and a sweet, sticky odor assailed my nostrils and filled the automobile, which was a sedan.

"That was the last I knew until I came to on a bed, like a hospital cot. It was in a room with a window almost completely closed. I was violently ill. The woman who was called 'Rose' was with me. It was dawn. I did not know whether or not it was the next day, but she told me it was the morning following.

"The other woman came in, and I asked them what they wanted with me. They said they were holding me for a half million dollars' ransom. I told them they were foolish, that I did not have that much money, nor did the church have it, but they replied that they knew better, and I was kept there day after day.

"Later they told me they had made plans to get the ransom. Then, from the remarks I overheard later, I learned that they had almost been captured in San Francisco when trying to make arrangements to get the money.

"A few days ago, I was moved. We were in two automobiles and traveled long distances. We came to another house and remained there two days.

"The men were not there. Previously they had burned me with a cigar on the finger to make me answer the questions they said my mother had asked to prove I was alive. They threatened to cut off this finger (the one with the long white scar) so that my mother would know when she received it that they did have me captive.

"I refused to talk, and while I did answer one question, I would not answer the rest, because I knew my mother, friends, and members of the church would extend every effort to raise and pay the sum of half a million dollars which my captors demanded for my release."

...

After completing the details of her abduction, Mrs. McPherson expressed the belief that her captors had planned to do away with her, or her daughter Roberta.

"From what I understood of their conversation, they had planned to make away with either myself, my daughter Roberta or Mary Pickford," Mrs. McPherson said.

"They also planned to kidnap another motion picture actress whose name I will not mention. My abductors threatened to give me or sell me to a Mexican called Felipe. One day after one of the men called Steve had burned me with cigars in an attempt to force me to answer their questions, they brought a great hulking man whom they said was Felipe. I think it was a bluff.

"They told me Felipe was from Mexico City. I had never seen any of my abductors before.

"I believe that they got the dress that the woman called Rose gave me to wear a day or so ago from some part of the country near here."

The mud-stained garment worn by Mrs. McPherson was a plain gingham, the same material, nurses recalled, that had been seen here a day or two ago.

"How did I escape?" she remarked in answer to a question. "I had been in the last place where they took me for about four days. I was hysterical, frantic. I could not remember days. I do not know what day it was.

"After they got me in the last house, I understood that the two men were going to make their final attempt to collect the ransom. They were to get the money Friday, I understood."

"The woman called Rose said she was going to go for provisions. I begged her not to gag me any more. They had gagged me when they captured me. She promised. With the aid of the men, I was tied up with a sort of flat rope.

"When they tied me, they had used little round ropes, like telephone wires. They cut into my flesh and hurt terribly. The flat rope did not hurt so much.

"After they were all gone, I was left locked in the room. There was a syrup can there. I crawled, bound as I was, to that can. I sawed and sawed on the edge until my arms were tired, so sore and weak, but God gave me strength. I breathed a prayer of thanksgiving to God.

"I sawed on the can until the rope that bound my arms was cut, and then I released myself from the ropes that bound me. I got the window open and knocked off the board. I ran. I ran. God gave me strength. He answered my prayers.

"I believed from what I overheard my abductors say that I was being held at some place near Mexicali if there is such a place by that name. That was as near as I could understand it.

"The woman, Rose, treated me very nicely. She was always with me, and the men did not molest me."

San Francisco Examiner's Storyboard telling of the "kidnap and escape" in their June 24, 1926 article.

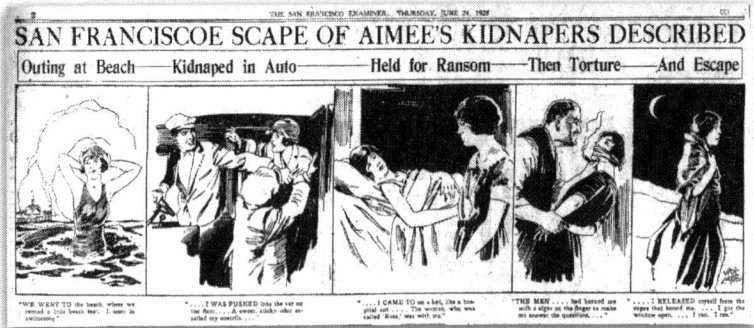

RANSOM NOTE No. 1

The *San Francisco Examiner's* June 24 article also included new details of an earlier ransom note demand sent to Sister Aimee's mother, Mrs. Minnie Kennedy. The handwritten note, mailed from San Francisco to Los Angeles, on May 24, just six days after the initial "kidnapping" named a date, time, and location for the delivery of the ransom money.

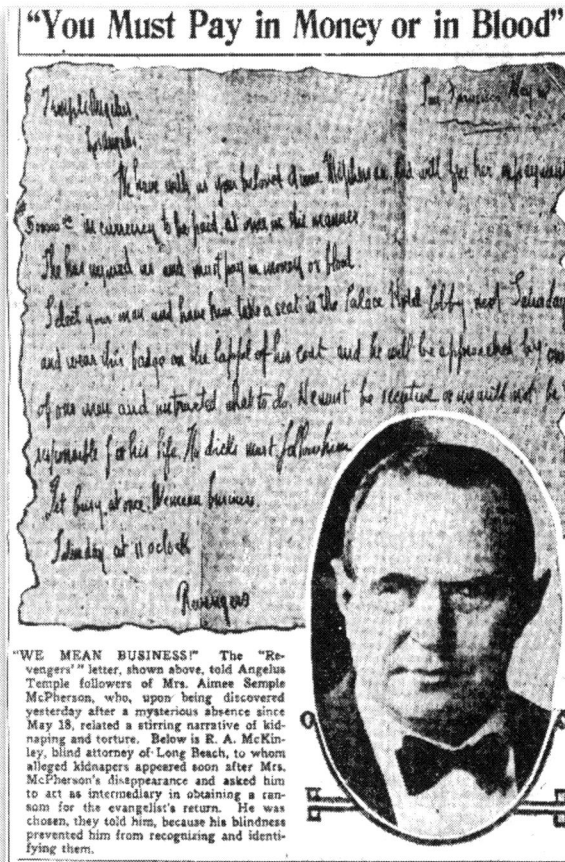

Photo insert of blind attorney R.A. McKinley

The ransom note No. 1 insert reads:

WE MEAN BUSINESS! The 'Revengers' letter, shown above, told Angelus Temple followers of Mrs. Aimee Semple McPherson, who, upon being discovered yesterday after a mysterious absence since May 18, related a stirring narrative of kidnaping and torture. Photo is R.A. McKinley, blind attorney of Long Beach, to whom alleged kidnappers appeared soon after Mrs. McPherson's disappearance and asked him to act as intermediary in obtaining a ransom for the evangelist's return. He was chosen, they told him because his blindness prevented him from recognizing and identifying them.

The ransom note No. 1 reads:

"Temple Angelus,
"Los Angeles

"We have with us your beloved Aimee McPherson, and will free Her on payment of $500,000 in currency to be paid at once in this manner.

"She has injured us and must Pay in money or blood.

"Select your man and have him Take a seat in the Palace Hotel Lobby next Saturday and wear this badge on the lapel of his coat and he will be approached by one of our men and instructed what to do. He must be secretive, or we will not be responsible for his life. No dicks must follow him.
"Get busy at once. We mean business.
"Saturday at 11 o'clock.

"REVENGERS."

San Francisco Examiner article also included a description of the purported kidnap suspects "Steve and Rose and third unnamed male," as provided by Aimee Semple McPherson from her hospital bed in Douglas, Arizona. Descriptions wired to Los Angeles County Sheriff William I. Traeger, by Douglas, Arizona, Sheriff McDonald, who stated in his wire, "Aimee McPherson *seems to have been kidnaped by the following persons:*"

Sheriff Wires Description of Kidnaper Trio

LOS ANGELES, June 23.—The following telegram was received late today by Sheriff Traeger from the sheriff at Douglas. It gives a description of the supposed kidnapers:

DOUGLAS, Ariz. June 23, 1926.

"William I. Traeger, Sheriff, Los Angeles County:

"Aimee McPherson seems to have been kidnaped by the following persons:

1—"Woman named 'Rose,' age 40, weight 145 pounds; large arms, black bobbed hair, brown eyes, even teeth, deep voice, business-like appearance.

2—"Man named Steve, weight 200, height 6 feet, complexion ruddy, clothes dark.

3—"Flat-chested man, bushy eyebrows, gray clothing, one upper tooth gold."

"McDonald, Sheriff."

San Francisco plainclothes detectives posing as Angelus Temple Church employees and wearing armbands that read, "Four Square Gospel," followed instructions and showed up in the lobby of the Palace Hotel with a wrapped bundle of "cash" on the following Saturday as instructed.

Additional detectives were posted throughout the lobby to assist in a possible arrest, but the kidnap suspects were a "no show" and made no contact.

Blind Long Beach Attorney R.A. McKinley

Blind Long Beach attorney R.A. McKinley
with his secretary Bernice Morris.

On June 2, 1926, a blind Long Beach attorney by the name of Russell A. McKinley entered the ever-increasingly bizarre McPherson fiasco by going to the District Attorney and reporting he had been approached by the purported Sister Aimee kidnappers.

Attorney McKinley related the following story to the DA:

> "Two men had accosted me on the street and told me they could procure Mrs. McPherson for the sum of $25,000 and would pay me $5,000 for opening the negotiations. They claimed they chose me because I was blind and, therefore, could not identify them."

McKinley went on to say that he then contacted Angelus Temple and Sister Aimee's mother, Mrs. Minnie Kennedy, who provided him with "four test questions" to determine if the suspects were legitimate or if they were attempting a hoax. McKinley was given a $1,000 retainer by Mrs. Kennedy and was awaiting further contact from the suspects.

On August 26, 1926, attorney McKinley was riding in a vehicle with two other individuals when the car they were in mysteriously ran off the roadway, flipped over, and all three passengers were pinned under the overturned vehicle and drowned in a mud and water-filled ditch.

Was it a freak accident?

HINT BLIND ATTORNEY IN AIMEE CASE "WAS PURPOSELY KILLED"

(*Stockton Independent*: Thursday Morning October 14, 1926)

Some suspicioned and speculated that it could well have been vehicular manslaughter where they were pursued by suspects in another car and "run off the roadway."

SKH Author's Note - No proof or any witnesses ever came forward to substantiate those suspicions, but for now, let us just put a mental pin in the possibility, to be reviewed at a future time and future crime.

Just three days after the "McKinley accident" the following article appeared in the *Los Angeles Sunday Times* on August 29, 1926:

M'PHERSON CASE LINK GIVEN

Secretary of Blind Lawyer Killed in Crash Admits Mystery Papers Bear on Inquiry

Mystery surrounding the contents of two documents taken from the clothing of Russell A. McKinley, blind Long Beach attorney, by his secretary, Miss Bernice Morris, following the former's death in an automobile accident late Wednesday night, partially was cleared yesterday afternoon when Miss Morris issued a statement in which she admitted the papers pertain to the Aimee Semple McPherson case.

Although she refused to reveal the details contained in the documents, a later statement issued by her indicates the papers bear on the contact McKinley said he had made with the asserted kidnappers of Mrs. McPherson.

CONFERENCE REVEALED

The first statement said:

"The papers received from the mortuary where Mr. McKinley's body was taken, indirectly deal with the McPherson case. They are correspondence with a third person who was interested in a solution of the kidnaping, and giving them publicity through the newspapers would only have made timid those with whom it was necessary to deal. Mr. McKinley's policy in relations with his clients was one of respectful silence, which I shall carry on until relieved of the responsibility."

Immediately after she issued the first statement, Miss Morris issued another in which she declared she had accompanied her employer on a secret trip to San Francisco on the 15th, where they conferred with Mrs. McPherson. The meeting, Miss Morris said, took place in the St. Francis Hotel. Although Mrs. McPherson was absent from her home for two days during the early part of the month, no mention that she had been in San Francisco was made. Effort to reach her last night for a statement brought the response that she was "in conference" and could not be disturbed. While admitting that the McPherson case had prompted the meeting, Miss Morris refused to go into detail as to its purpose or elaborate on her statement.

COMMENT REFUSED

The secretary's statements followed previous statements from both Mrs. McPherson and her mother, Mrs. Minnie Kennedy, that McKinley had formed a contact with one of the evangelist's asserted kidnappers and was nearing a solution to the case when he was killed.

In one statement issued by Mrs. Kennedy, she announced that "Steve," named as the ringleader of the kidnappers by the evangelist, had been located in a distant city and that many other important angles of the mystery were nearing solution.

The policy of silence as to the nature of several mysterious conferences held with the secretary by the temple pastor, her mother, and attorney, Roland Rich Woolley, was continued yesterday. None of the participants would answer questions in reference to the conferences.

It was rumored at the temple yesterday afternoon that "Rose," named by Mrs. McPherson as her guardian during the time she declares she was held captive, also had been located by McKinley, the fact being revealed in confidential memoranda supplied to the evangelist. However, nothing definite to support the rumor could be learned from any of the principals.

According to Mrs. McPherson, one of the men who kidnaped her is in Southern California and talked to her over the telephone a few nights before McKinley was killed. The temple leader was rumored to be conducting a search in an effort to locate the man and have him reveal the "inside" story of the asserted abduction.

"Although he only said a few words to me, I feel certain that I recognized his voice," she said.

SKH Author Note - While researching background on Long Beach attorney Russell A. McKinley, I came across a Facebook page entitled *The Clan of the MacQuillins of Antrim*, which provided some fascinating biographical information on their kinsman. Here are a few "highlights" from that source, dated December 18, 2018.

For additional information see link

https://www.facebook.com/rockinggg1950/posts/2070133126365863

Russell Alexander McKinley Jr.

- Nephew of 25th President of the United States William McKinley, who was assassinated in 1901.
- Totally blinded by an exploding fuse while working in a rock quarry.
- 1912-1926 - Successful lawyer practicing in Long Beach, California
- Prominent witness in the Aimee Semple McPherson scandal in 1926
- Quotation from a Long Beach AP (Associated Press) article:

"BLIND LAWYER DEAD WITH 2 STRANGERS; HELD IN MUD TRAP"
"Russell Alexander McKinley, Jr, and two companions drowned in an auto accident on Long Beach-Wilmington Road. They had taken a detour around the bridge construction. Their machine overturned in the soft mud, and the three were smothered in mud when the machine turned turtle."

Steve Hodel

The "Miss X" Mystery Unraveled

Lorraine Wiseman-Seilaff
Aimee Semple McPherson
Kenneth Ormiston and S.S. Hahn

Attorney
S.S. Hahn
circa 1923

Aimee and Kenneth Ormiston

In a complicated scenario that unfolded slowly in Los
Angeles over the six-month period between May and
December 1926, the public was titillated over the
suggestions of a scandalous love affair. That in truth,

Sister Aimee, rather than being the victim of kidnapping, was actually "involved in a 'Love Tryst' with her KFSG radio station manager, Kenneth G. Ormiston."

A half dozen reliable witnesses were located who were willing to testify to having seen the couple hiding out in a cottage in Carmel, California, a beautiful seaside community on the Pacific Ocean some 250 miles north of Los Angeles.

The DA's star witness was Mrs. Lorraine Wiseman-Seilaff, a member of Aimee's "flock" who was paid by Sister Aimee to claim she was the woman who visited Ken Ormiston in Carmel-By-the-Sea and was mistaken by witnesses as being McPherson due to their striking physical similarities. (See side-by-side comparison headshots of Lorraine and Aimee in newspaper article - page 306.)

However, late "in the game," Mrs. Wiseman flipped and admitted her perjury and became the star witness for the DA and the prosecution. Mrs. Wiseman made a deal with the DA to testify against Sister Aimee and "tell the truth."

She also decided to sue Sister Aimee and the Foursquare Church. She hired a prominent Los Angeles lawyer, **S.S. Hahn,** to represent and defend her in both the criminal and civil matters pending before the court.

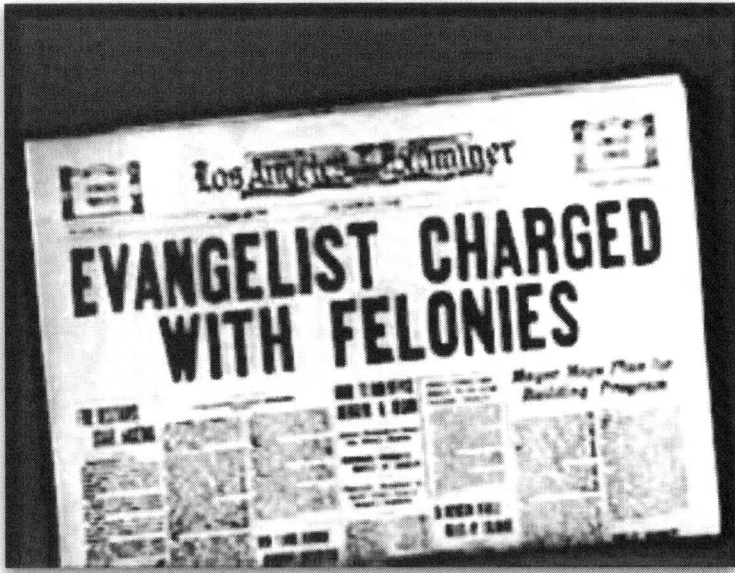

A few headlines from the summer/fall of 1926

SELL BROADWAY DEPARTMENT STORE

THREE CENTS CITY & COUNTY

EVENING HERALD

SPORTS THREE CENTS

SEIZE ORMISTON TRUNK AND NOTES IN N.Y. HOTEL

RADIO MAN NARROWLY ESCAPES CAPTURE

WRITING ON FOOD LIST CHANGED, CLAIM

Merritt Bares 'Love Ghosts' in Cour

ROWS, PEACE REVEALED ON STAND

RAISE MRS. MILLS' BODY FOR PROBE

$5,000,000 REPORTE PRICE O BIG DEA

REPORT KING FERDINAND NEAR DEATH IN RUMANIA

THREE CENTS CITY & COUNTY

EVENING HERALD

SPORTS COMPLETE N.Y. STOCKS

MRS. M'PHERSON FACING NEW CHARGES BY KEYES

FIND BODY LYING ON FLOOR OF OFFICE

POMONA-U.C.L.A. LINEUP

How Oxy Faced Whittier

Trojans, Bears in Annual Grid Clash

2 ARMENIAN QUAKES KILL HUNDREDS

BROWN TEAM SCORES ON YALE

COLIMA AND STRONG READY

TEAMS AWAIT WHISTLE IN SEASON'S BIG GAME

WOMAN IN X CASE TO SUE AIMEE FOR $500,000

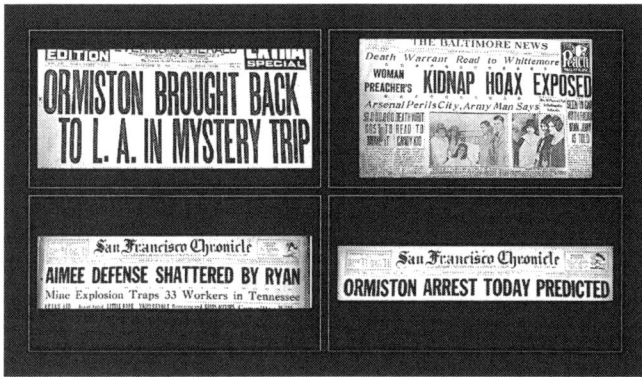

CLOSING FINANCIAL — Los Angeles Evening Express — SPORTS THREE CENTS

VOL. LVI, NO. 153.   56TH YEAR   TUESDAY, SEPTEMBER 21, 1926

STARTLING NEW M'PHERSON CASE EVIDENCE IS CLAIMED

EDITION — EXTRA SPECIAL

ORMISTON BROUGHT BACK TO L. A. IN MYSTERY TRIP

THE BALTIMORE NEWS

Death Warrant Read to Whittemore

WOMAN PREACHER'S **KIDNAP HOAX EXPOSED**

Arsenal Perils City, Army Man Says

San Francisco Chronicle

AIMEE DEFENSE SHATTERED BY RYAN

Mine Explosion Traps 33 Workers in Tennessee

San Francisco Chronicle

ORMISTON ARREST TODAY PREDICTED

THE SAN FRANCISCO EXAMINER: THURSDAY, SEPTEMBER 30, 1926

"Yes, I Saw Mrs. McPherson in the Ormiston Cottage at Carmel"

POSITIVE IDENTIFICATION by Mrs. Jeannette Parkes of Mrs. Aimee Semple McPherson as Kenneth G. Ormiston's companion at Carmel-by-the-Sea was not shaken in her cross-examination by Mrs. McPherson's attorney, W. I. Gilbert. Mrs. Parkes, whose Carmel home adjoins the celebrated cottage, is shown here testifying. Gilbert (1) is questioning her. Judge Blake is on the bench. Others are: (2) Mrs. Minnie Kennedy; (3) Mrs. McPherson; (4) Attorney S. S. Hahn, counsel for Mrs. Lorraine Wiseman-Seilaff; (5) Nick Harris, whose private detective agency has done some investigating for Mrs. McPherson; (6) District Attorney Asa Keyes.

Bottom of previous page (311), *San Francisco Examiner* photo of September 30, 1926, a witness testifies and positively identifies Sister Aimee as being at the Ormiston Cottage just days after her alleged "kidnaping."

"Yes, I Saw Mrs. McPherson in the Ormiston Cottage at Carmel"

Editor's Note - Though the image on page 311 is small and the people are difficult to recognize, the numbers in the photo identify the individuals listed below.

1) Attorney for McPherson, W.I. Gilbert (standing)
2) Mrs. Minnie Kennedy
3) Aimee McPherson
4) Attorney S.S. Hahn, attorney for Lorraine Wiseman-Seilaff
5) Nick Harris, whose private detective agency has done some investigating for Mrs. McPherson
6) District Attorney Asa Keyes.

Despite a strong case having been made, Los Angeles District Attorney Asa Keyes, believing that the evidence may not be enough to convict and with one star witnesses attorney Russell McKinley killed in an "accident" and his second, Mrs. Lorraine Wiseman-Seilaff raising new questions and allegations against Sister Aimee which he felt put her own "credibility in question"—Keyes dropped all charges against McPherson, Ormiston and related parties on January 10, 1927. Keyes decided he would leave it to the Court of Public Opinion. Case Closed.

Well, maybe not?

Ninety-four years after the fact, the "Kidnap of Aimee Semple McPherson" is unprovable.

The evidence strongly suggests that it was a HOAX. The motive? Possibly Sister Aimee saw it as a money-maker as large sums were raised for the church over the five missing weeks.

During her absence, the purported suspects "Steve, Rose" and a third unnamed man did make contact and arranged a date, time and place (Saturday, May 29, Lobby San Francisco's Palace Hotel) for the delivery of cash, but that plan was thwarted when the kidnappers claimed, "they spotted detectives in the lobby."

Personally, I doubt Aimee's mother, Mrs. Minnie Kennedy, was in on it and likely honestly believed her daughter had been kidnapped for ransom.

But the reason for this chapter is not to recite to you, my readers, a most curious and somewhat humorous historical "affair" from LA's "Roaring Twenties."

No. Instead, it has been to prepare and background you for something I believe is far more sinister.

"Steve" and "Rose" and the "Gold toothed Man".

A common error that I and many others fall prey to in our thinking when evaluating people, places, events, is to be—out of sync time-wise.

What do I mean?

In an earlier chapter on the Father Patrick Heslin murder, I noted that his lone kidnapper, who I believe was George Hodel would at that time have been weeks away from his fourteenth birthday. Immediately the mind says, "Oh, I can eliminate him—too young."

But not so.

Yes, "too young" *by today's standards.*

In 2021 we might doubt that a boy of almost fourteen would/could be driving a car. But, a hundred years ago, it was commonplace for a young man in his early teens to be driving. Not at all unusual.

This is what I mean by "out of sync with time and place." When it comes to the Sister Aimee investigation, we must think in 1926 time.

Our intellect must put itself in a Way-Back Machine and begin to think as if it is living in the Los Angeles of 1926.

In a city starting to burst its seams with new growth, consider the following: Prohibition. Gangsterism. City bosses like Kent Kane Parrot, LA's "de facto Mayor" who owned the city police and county sheriffs. Mayor George Cryer commonly known as "Parrot's Puppet." Massive graft, bootlegging, gambling, and prostitution.

Now let us put young George Hodel into that time and place and take a quick review and highlight what we know about him in the year 1926. I will refer to him by his initials-GHH.

(**SKH Author Note** - I will include my father's known biographical facts in regular type and what, based on my investigation, I believe *may have also been true, in italics.*)

- GHH is eighteen years old and living alone in his own separate private residence ("tea house") in Northeast Los Angeles, built by his parents for him for his fifteenth birthday.

- GHH has been kicked out of Caltech University in Pasadena after his first year because he was having an affair with a professor's wife, which broke up her marriage and the wife giving birth to the child, which she aptly named, "Folly."

- At age eighteen, GHH job descriptions have already included: Yellow Cab chauffeur driver, a crime reporter for the Los Angeles Record newspaper, a radio announcer for the Los Angeles Gas Company's classical music hour, Magazine Editor and publisher of his own private elitist magazine, "Fantasia."

- GHH and his teenage friend, John Huston, have been double dating with their two adolescent girlfriends, Dorothy Jean Harvey, and Emilia Lawson.

- GHH enjoys alcohol, cigars, fast women, and is a narcotic user, primarily frequenting "opium dens" in LA's Chinatown.

- GHH and Huston are close friends with artist Fred Sexton who is attending Art School. Sexton, at that time, was also known to be "involved in gambling and regularly running his own floating crap game."

- *GHH has probably committed the 1921 kidnap-murder of Father Patrick Heslin in the San Francisco Bay area and typed the ransom demand and sent it to the Catholic Church authorities, as summarized in an earlier chapter.*

- *GHH has probably committed the 1922 assassination murder of William Desmond Taylor (lying in wait, armed with a handgun outside the film director's residence) in Hollywood, California, as summarized in an earlier chapter.*

- *GHH and Fred Sexton are both likely known friendlies with Kent Kane Parrot, LA's top City Boss, and his gangster associates. (Based on photographs taken by GHH and included in his "one-man-show" as presented in an earlier chapter.)*

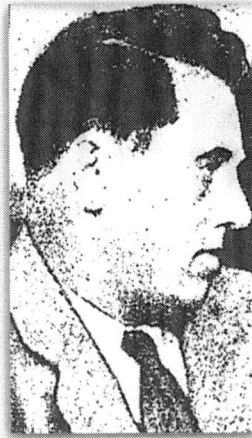

SKH Note - On left is a possible early photo of LA Politico and Crime Boss Kent Kane Parrot taken by GHH circa 1925, compared to the known photo of Parrot published in the Los Angeles Times ten years later. (1935)

Fred Sexton circa 1925

Photo taken by GHH of his close friend, artist Fred Sexton at
age seventeen. Sexton's daughter in viewing the photo in 2002
thought it "looked like her father, as a young man, but couldn't
be sure."

- We recall in a previous chapter that young
  George Hodel and William Desmond Taylor
  were both linked together by choosing Albert
  WITZEL, the same famous Hollywood star
  portrait photographer.

Well, here we are again in the Land of Deja Vu.
Albert **WITZEL** took both of the below photographs.

Aimee Semple McPherson c.1923

George Hill Hodel 1923

As described, this is the George Hodel of 1926 that we must understand and consider when we ask the question, Could the young man of eighteen be responsible for either "masterminding" or being a willing accomplice to the staging of the alleged May 18, 1926, kidnapping of Sister Aimee?

Based on his "track record," the answer is an unqualified—YES!

The Linkage

I believe that both 1926 McPherson Ransom Notes might well have been authored by George Hodel.

Why?

1. First, we have "the voice," an over-the-top dialogue that sounds identical to notes written both before and after the alleged Sister Aimee kidnapping as well as phone calls placed to press and victim family members.

2. These M.O./crime signatures match GHH's ransom demands and include deliberate misspellings, feigning illiteracy as well as threats to harm the victim and taunting telephone calls providing a location where victims can be found in the following GHH crimes:

1921 Father Heslin kidnap/murder
1924 Martin Sisters kidnap/murder
1930s (Numerous crimes yet to be described in "The
    Early Years" Part II)

1938 El Paso, Texas, Hazel and Nancy Frome,
    mother/daughter kidnap/murders.
1944 Georgette Bauerdorf kidnap/murder typed note.
1945-1946 Chicago "Lipstick Murders" notes and calls
    to family.
1967 Riverside Cheri Jo Bates murder and notes to
    press and family.
1968-9 "Zodiac" notes and calls in San Francisco Bay
    Area murders

3. "A Rose by any Other Name."

"Stardust and Rent Money," written **by Dorothy Harvey**, age 16 and published in her 1921 Benjamin Franklin High School Yearbook. Photo of Dorothy Harvey three years later, at age 19.

On the following page, 321, is my mother's short story **"Stardust and Rent Money,"** in full, as it appeared in her high school yearbook in 1921.

Star Dust and Rent Money

By Dorothy Harvey

(As printed in her 1921 Franklin High School Yearbook)

To him, who is blessed with an imagination, surroundings are immaterial, things to be considered only in the most extreme cases.

One of these cases presented itself to Rose, one morning, in the form of an irate landlady.

The landlady was a cautious soul, whom long acquaintance with park-bench, unsalaried humanity had made distrustful. "A week's salary in advance" was the slogan with which she greeted all boarders, particularly the hopeful paupers who expected tremendous sums of money next week, and whom she regarded with unbounded suspicion.

Rose was out of this hope-to-get-rich-quick type. In fact, she never thought of money except for its convenience, now and then, in disposing of certain troublesome, unenlightened people who persisted in thinking that money really counted and that sunsets, and singing birds, and all beautiful things did not matter.

But then, Rose had had her Dream, and the creditors and landlady had not. The Dream was the most wonderful thing in Rose's life. It had come to her one evening as she lay on the worn sofa in a little two by four attic room, looking up through the skylight at the myriads of stars above. She watched them as they whispered mysteriously among themselves, and as they arranged themselves, under the orders of the Brightest Star, in a glorious Idea; an Idea so beautiful and unearthly, that it had blinded her eyes with tears.

To say that she wrote it down would be an absurdity. She felt it down. And she guarded the paper containing the Idea, jealously; a secret too precious to be shared.

But stardust is not the stuff that rent is paid from, which brings us back to our starting point—the irate landlady.

The landlady, upon being admitted to the room, stated the reason for her visit without mincing matters in the least or troubling herself to be diplomatic.

She had, contrary to her usual policy of business, not only not insisted on Rose's paying in advance but had actually let her rent run for two whole weeks without putting her out. But matters had reached a climax. She could no longer bear the thought of having a boarder whose rent was not paid.

She delivered her ultimatum to Rose, who listened with a sinking heart. Two days' grace were given her. If at the end of two days, she failed to pay her rent, she would be without lodgings.

After the thunder and lightning left the sky, the rain came in torrents. Rose wept; not the tears of despair, but the tears of a mother who is compelled to sell her child as a slave. For Rose knew, even before the landlady left the room, that the idea would have to be sold.

You recall the poem, no doubt, for it caused a tremendous upheaval in American literature and became universally known. You doubtlessly envied the author of the poem her fame, as well as the fortune she made from it. But you didn't picture her in a little attic room weeping tears of sorrow and repentance as the stars gazed reproachfully at her through the skylight, now, did you? For, for her, they had been shattered, "the glory and the dream."

I would suggest that this short story, certainly would have been read by GHH who we know had dated Dorothy Harvey before his high school buddy John Huston eloped with Dorothy, marrying her in 1926. (This was the same year as the McPherson alleged kidnapping). I believe this tragic character could well have been George's inspiration for the McPherson kidnapping accomplice named—"Rose."

Forced by a greedy, money-hungry landlady to sell her child to pay the rent, young George Hodel would see to it that "Rose" would have her *revenge.*

4. A future "thoughtprint"?

"Steve," the author of the typed ransom note threatening to harm the bound and gagged Sister Aimee, writes in his note, "...if you insist a lighted cigar against a bare foot often gets results."

Then after her alleged escape, Sister Aimee from her hospital bed in Douglas, Arizona, tells the press, " They had burned me with a cigar on this finger, [exhibiting the burned scar] to make me tell the answers to questions they said my mother had asked to prove that I was alive. They threatened to cut off this finger (the second finger of the right hand, which has a long white scar thereon) so that my mother would know when she received it that they did have me captive." (Source of the quote, *El Paso Herald*, June 23, 1926)

SKH Note - Similarly, twelve years later in 1938, burned fingers figure prominently in the M.O. of a horrific crime near El Paso of a mother and daughter. Details of this double homicide are in my 2019 true-crime book *In The Mesquite* in which I attribute this

1938 kidnap/torture/murder of Hazel and Nancy Frome to GHH and Fred Sexton.

Below is a 1938 description of the injuries to Nancy Frome as reported by the El Paso coroner, Dr. Walter:

> "Eight separate burn scabs were observed to the back of the victim's right hand. One over each knuckle of the fingers. These wounds were inflicted by her killer pre-mortem by using either a cigarette or a cigar."

5. A Motive for his Madness?

McPherson's kidnapper, "Steve," *signs the first ransom note*, mailed from San Francisco to the church in Los Angeles as, "REVENGERS."

Then he *signs the second ransom note*, "AVENGERS."

GHH, in later handwritten and typed notes, will refer to the killing of his victims as "Divine Retribution" and, of course, in his 1947 "surreal masterpiece" crime, the kidnap/torture-murder of Elizabeth Short, he signs himself as, "BLACK DAHLIA AVENGER."

6. Sister Aimee in the telling of her abduction informs the press and public that she was chloroformed and rendered unconscious immediately after being thrown into the kidnapper's vehicle and was later bound and gagged with rope, but was able, "using a tin can" to cut through the bindings and escape.

George Hodel in at least five of his later kidnap/murders used a man's handkerchief soaked in chloroform to render his victims unconscious. In at least four of these killings he left the handkerchief next to or near the body. Many of his victims were also bound hand and foot and then strangled with a clothesline-type rope.

7. Murder Most Foul?

Fast forward now to the year 1944. Aimee's scandal of 1926 is nearly two decades old and in most people's minds—long forgotten.

America is at war. All that our country wants now is an end to the fighting and dying.

On the morning of September 27, 1944, the nation awoke to the following headline:

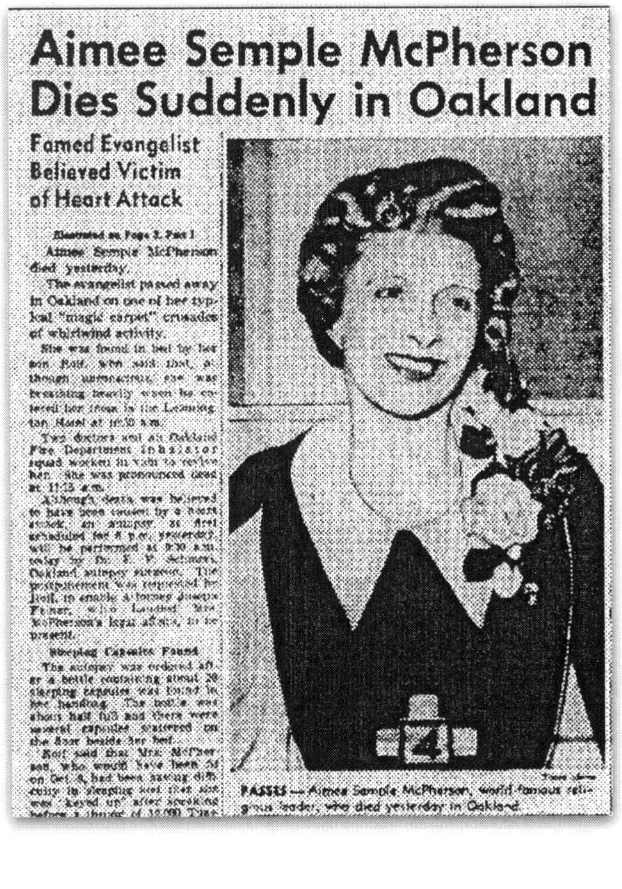

AIMEE SEMPLE MCPHERSON
DIES SUDDENLY IN OAKLAND

Los Angeles Times - Hotel Leamington, Oakland, Calif.

Aimee Semple McPherson Dies Suddenly in Oakland

Famed Evangelist Believed Victim of Heart Attack

Illustrated on Page 3, Part I

Aimee Semple McPherson died yesterday.

The evangelist passed away in Oakland on one of her typical "magic carpet" crusades of whirlwind activity.

She was found in bed by her son Rolf, who said that, although unconscious, she was breathing heavily when he entered her room in the Leamington Hotel at [illegible] a.m.

Two doctors and an Oakland Fire Department inhalator squad worked in vain to revive her. She was pronounced dead at 11:15 a.m.

Although death was believed to have been caused by a heart attack, an autopsy at first scheduled for 4 p.m. yesterday will be performed at [illegible] a.m. today by Dr. [illegible], Oakland autopsy surgeon. The postponement was requested by Rolf, to enable Attorney Joseph Fisher, who handled Mrs. McPherson's legal affairs, to be present.

Sleeping Capsules Found

The autopsy was ordered after a bottle containing about [illegible] sleeping capsules was found in her handbag. The bottle was about half full and there were several capsules scattered on the floor beside her bed.

Rolf said that Mrs. McPherson, who would have been [illegible] on Oct. [illegible], had been having difficulty in sleeping and that she was "keyed up" after speaking before a throng of [illegible]

Times photo

PASSES — Aimee Semple McPherson, world-famous religious leader, who died yesterday in Oakland.

Found in her bed by the maid at the luxurious Leamington
Hotel, in Oakland, California (Post Card below)

Sister Aimee's former home in Elsinore, California

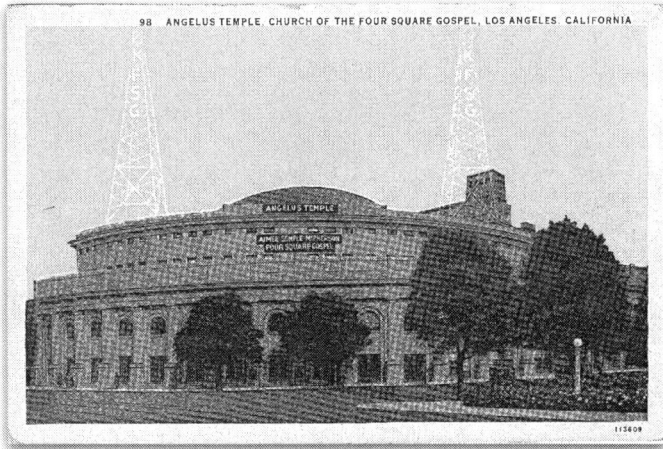

Sister Aimee's Angelus Temple near downtown Los Angeles with her own radio station KFSG (Two radio towers show faintly against sky.)

Sister Aimee's death was initially thought to be from a heart attack.

However, an empty prescription bottle was found on her bedspread along with a few red capsules.

An autopsy was conducted. The cause of death was found to be "due to an overdose of barbiturates," specifically, the drug that killed her was identified as "**Seconal**."

SKH Note re. the barbiturate-Seconal

"Secobarbital (Seconal) was patented in 1934 and marketed by Eli Lilly Company.
The drug comes as a white, odorless powder that is very soluble in water and alcohol.
Seconal is one of the most deadly drugs you can abuse because it has a low therapeutic to lethal ratio.
In other words, if you increase the amount you take by just a little (even an amount equivalent to a few grains of salt), your dose can become deadly. Seconal showed up in the autopsies of many celebrities who died of accidental drug overdoses such as Judy Garland, Jimi Hendrix, and Marilyn Monroe. Ingesting one gram of Seconal is usually serious, and two to ten grams can be fatal."

(Source: www.drugaddictiontreatment.com)

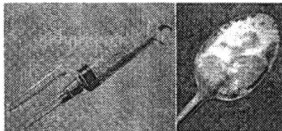

Pictured above is one teaspoon of powder = 5 grams

Her doctors were contacted and denied prescribing the drug for her. While authorities believed the Seconal prescription originated in Los Angeles, still the physician writing it was never identified.

Suicide? (No note and she was reportedly "in good spirits.") Accidental overdose? (Her doctor proffered the possibility she may have become confused and accidentally took too many capsules.) Or, forced overdose by person unknown?

We will never know.

What we DO KNOW is *that on that very same day, September 27, 1944,* the then-wife of Dr. George Hill Hodel, aka Dorothy Harvey Huston Hodel, quickly gathered her three young sons, Michael age 5, Steven age 3, and Kelvin age 2, and fled from the family home.

On that very day, Dorothy went directly to the downtown office of **S.S. Hahn,** attorney at law, where after a meeting and consultation, retained Mr. Hahn to represent her and had him file divorce papers from her then-husband, Dr. George Hill Hodel.

Sister Aimee's S.S. Hahn, you ask?

Yes, the very same S.S. Hahn that in 1926 represented and defended Mrs. Lorraine Wiseman, the prime witness for the prosecution who had testified against Aimee Semple McPherson and provided evidence that her "kidnap was a hoax."

Here is a scan from my mother's divorce papers from that time showing she initiated her divorce by separating from George Hodel on the very day of Sister Aimee's death.

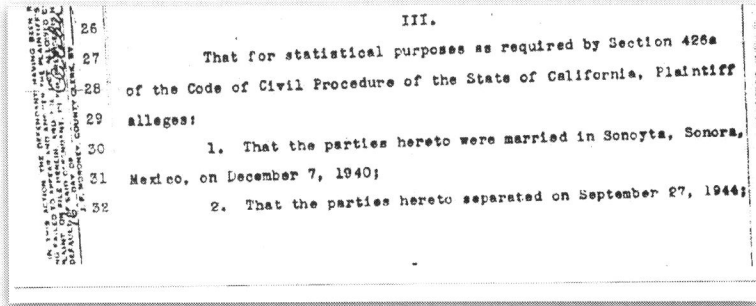

III.

That for statistical purposes as required by Section 426a
of the Code of Civil Procedure of the State of California, Plaintiff
alleges:

1. That the parties hereto were married in Sonoyta, Sonora, Mexico, on December 7, 1940;

2. That the parties hereto separated on September 27, 1944;

Section of S.S. Hahn-drawn divorce papers showing Dorothy Hodel separated from George on September 27, 1944.

SKH Note - It is interesting to take into account that the State of "Sonora, Mexico" was obviously a place of interest to GHH. He and my mother were married there in 1940. George and his later Filipina wife, Hortensia Laguda Lopez Starck, were also married in Sonora in 1952. It was also in the State of Sonora (Juarez) that GHH met and danced with Nancy and Hazel Frome in 1938 before their return to El Paso and their kidnap and murder the following day.

October 10, 1944, Ten thousand mourners attend
Sister Aimee funeral in Los Angeles

Let us assume that I am correct in my suspicions that George Hodel and Sister Aimee's acquaintance did go way back almost two decades to the mid-Twenties.

That George was, in fact, "Steve," the author of the Ransom Notes. That he and possibly his teen buddy Fred Sexton with or without Dorothy (aka "Rose") arranged and met with the blind Long Beach attorney Russell McKinley and asked him to be their financial intermediary—their facilitator.

Secret meetings occur both in Long Beach and in San Francisco. That McKinley's secretary, Bernice Morris, accompanies him to those meetings. Court testimony would later establish that Aimee McPherson paid attorney McKinley "one thousand dollars for his efforts to help locate the abductors."

Then, as we know, attorney McKinley as a passenger in the fated vehicle is crushed and killed when the car he is riding in with two others runs off the roadway and overturns in deep mud. (Either accidentally or on purpose, it matters not.)

However, I quote from an article in the *Honolulu Star-Bulletin* of October 14, 1926, that adds some meat to the bone:

ATTORNEYS IN AIMEE TRIAL WIELD FISTS

Physical Blows Mingled With Legal Attacks In Hearing of Evangelist

Clash Follows 'Liar' Statement: Important Documents Alleged Stolen

LOS ANGELES, Cal. October 14, 1926

Flying fists of two opposing attorneys found their targets today in the courtroom and threw into confusion the preliminary hearing of criminal conspiracy charges against Aimee Semple McPherson, woman evangelist and pastor of Angelus Temple.

The fight between the attorneys W.I. Gilbert, counsel for Mrs. McPherson, and S.S. Hahn, attorney for Mrs. Lorraine Wiseman Sielaff, occurred soon after the opening of today's session. The row began when Hahn objected that Gilbert had issued to newspapers statements that Mrs. Sielaff, the state's star witness and a co-defendant, with Mrs. McPherson, was a liar. After the two men had been separated, they were rebuked by Judge Blake, and the trial proceeded.

...

A hint that the blind attorney, R.A. McKinley, had been done to death, startled the court at Wednesday's hearing. Mrs. Lorraine Wiseman-Sielaff, testifying, said she had heard Bernice Morris, secretary to McKinley, voice the suspicion that "It might have been done on purpose."

McKinley was found dead several weeks ago with two other men, under an overturned automobile in a mudhole beside the road. Mrs. Sielaff testified that she had learned from conversations at Angelus Temple that $1000 had been paid McKinley for his alleged efforts to locate the abductors of Mrs. McPherson.

~ ~ ~

Sister Aimee escapes the clutches of "Steve and Rose and the man with the gold tooth," endures her waterless trek through the parched hundred degrees, snake-filled Sonora desert to an Arizona bordertown hospital. Several days of recovery, then her triumphant train ride home to the City of Angels, where she gathers her flock of true believers and a massive Hallelujah Celebration is held at her Angelus Temple.

All is good.

As I see it, from Day-One-At-The-Beach, May 18, 1926, there never was an abduction.

No man and woman couple approaching Sister Aimee with a "Come to the car and pray for our dying baby."

No, "cloth to the mouth with a sticky substance rendering me unconscious."

I think that there is an excellent chance that the "creative writing," the two ransom notes, and the approaching of the blind attorney Russell McKinley in Long Beach to be an "intermediary" with his secret follow-up meeting in San Francisco (to hoodwink McKinley into thinking this was a righteous kidnap) were all the work of one man—George Hodel.

Dorothy Harvey and Fred Sexton may have played minor supporting roles as ride-alongs to help convince a gullible McKinley and his secretary, Bernice Morris, but that was likely the full extent of their involvement.

From my perspective, it was all a paper caper.

Fool attorney McKinley, fool Aimee's mother, Mrs. Kennedy, fool the Four-Square flock, and fool the world.

To quote Sister Aimee's oft-repeated response to Doubting Thomases, "That's my story, and I'm sticking to it."

Forgive my divergence, let us return to October 1944 and the days and hours before Aimee's funeral.

October 9, 1944, had she survived, would have been Aimee Semple McPherson's fifty-fourth birthday.

The following day, October 10, 1944, the day of Aimee's funeral was Dr. George Hill Hodel's thirty-seventh birthday.

One might ask how did Dr. Hodel pass those hours immediately following her burial? Did he mourn her passing? Did he welcome in and celebrate his own birthday?

I know the answer.

He did neither.

On October 11, 1944, just hours after the cold body of Sister Aimee was laid to rest at Forest Lawn Cemetery, the suave, sophisticated doctor went dancing at the famous *Hollywood Canteen.* A USO-like, hugely popular club that offered free food, dancing, and entertainment to military service members. The only price of admission to the club was to wear their uniform. All else was "on the house."

George went to the Canteen and did what he did best —ever the predator; he followed a young woman (a volunteer Junior Hostess) from the club to her residence. He then forced entry into her apartment, assaulted and asphyxiated her and then placed the dead girl's body in her apartment bathtub, turned on the water and left the victim to be found by her neighbor tenant early the next morning.

On October 14, 1944, Dr. George Hill Hodel, Head of Los Angeles County Health Department, outdid himself. He made Page One of the *LA Times* with not one but TWO of his murders. A twofer!

In the below newspaper, the left-hand column reports the autopsy findings on *Hollywood Canteen* murder victim Georgette Bauerdorf's cause of death to be "asphyxiation at the hands of another." Her killer forced a nine-inch roll of elastic cloth from a medical ace bandage down her throat.

Below in the same newspaper, the middle column reports the autopsy findings on Sister Aimee Semple

McPherson, "Cause of death from an overdose of "Seconal" Barbiturate."

Los Angeles Times, October 14, 1944, front-page news reporting cause of death in what I believe are two of Dr. George Hill Hodel's murder victims: Georgette Bauerdorf and Aimee Semple McPherson

(See *Black Dahlia Avenger I and II* for full investigation and linkage to Bauerdorf investigation.)

Now let us move forward in time just seven months to May 9, 1945.

As previously summarized in *Black Dahlia Avenger I and II*, the evidence is presented that on this date, Dr. George Hill Hodel murdered his personal clinic secretary/girlfriend Ruth Spaulding, age twenty-seven.

How? By likely injecting her with a lethal dose of Seconal, which resulted in her death due to a "Barbiturate poisoning, overdose."

As previously described in my earlier publications, we know that GHH went to Ruth's apartment in downtown Los Angeles and called his wife (my mother) Dorothy, (the family was back living together while their divorce was still pending).

George telephoned Dorothy to "Come over to Ruth's apartment immediately—Ruth has attempted suicide."

Dorothy responded to find Ruth Spaulding in bed and unconscious but "still breathing."

George handed Dorothy several sets of manuscripts written by Ruth and told Dorothy "to burn them all." Dorothy took the writings which purportedly revealed and exposed some of GHH's past activities and did as ordered and left with the scripts and burned them in our kitchen home incinerator.

George remained at the apartment for several more hours. Once he was convinced that Ruth had become comatose, he called for a cab and took her to *Georgia Street Receiving Hospital,* just one mile distant from her apartment, where the doctors were unable to save her life, and she was pronounced dead in less than an hour.

The autopsy revealed the drug overdose on Seconal, and LAPD investigated the case.

In 2003 post-publication of *Black Dahlia Avenger,* an LAPD confidential source admitted to a *Los Angeles Times* columnist, Steve Lopez, that, "they suspected foul play and investigated Dr. George Hodel, Ruth's employer and her former lover. But, the cops were unable to establish any proof that he administered the barbiturates, and the case was ultimately labeled a 'Suicide'."

My later investigations revealed and produced actual letters between a female patient ("Mrs. X") of George Hodel's and his then secretary Ruth Spaulding. The correspondence revealed the laboratory owned by Dr. Hodel had provided false testing and an apparent intentional misdiagnosis. This resulted in the patient, Mrs. X, being informed she was "positive for a sexually transmitted disease" (Gonorrhea) when, in fact, she was not. (See the summary on this in *Black Dahlia Avenger II*.)

My initial thinking was that this might have been the reason for GHH intentionally overdosing his former girlfriend, Ruth, to "keep her quiet about Mrs. X." Add to that the fact that Ruth knew he was performing illegal abortions at the clinic, which we discovered through the later 1950 secret DA tape recordings. In those recordings, George admits to killing his secretary (Ruth Spaulding) and taking her at death's door to the Receiving Hospital.

Also, on that recording is a live conversation with a confederate, one Baron Ernst Harringa, in which he admits the crime. Addressing Harringa, GHH says, "Killed her. Maybe I did kill my secretary. Maybe they (LAPD) have figured it out."

However, now with this additional knowledge along with the timing of events, while the former may well have been contributory to his motive to kill her, I must consider the following possibilities.

We know from what my mother told my half-sister Tamar about the incident, that my mother suspected George intentionally overdosed Ruth.

We also know that George had "broken off the relationship with Ruth," who was madly in love with him and heartbroken. She was also truly angry with George— "Hell hath no fury like a woman scorned."

Ruth, as GHH's First Street Clinic secretary, would have known and had files on all his patients. We know for a fact that he doctored to the rich and famous as well as persons in high places in city hall and high-ranking officers with the police and sheriff's departments.

His confidential records had to include a Who's Who patient list of top Angelenos.

This list likely included the name of one Aimee Semple McPherson.

It is highly likely that the young boy genius of 1926, the faux kidnapper in the McPherson ransom note, the "Steve" of "Steve and Rose" two years after his Sister Aimee caper, in 1928 went on to pre-med at UC Berkeley, followed by four more years at UCSF to obtain his MD.

Then after doctoring in Arizona and New Mexico, he returns to Los Angeles, and joining LA County Health, he quickly rises to become the top VD czar in the county.

Now in a position of power and prestige, it would seem quite natural that Sister Aimee would be on his list of confidential private patients. Long-lost friends reunited with a unique shared secret from the long, long ago.

Ruth was privy to these files and may have known that Sister Aimee was receiving medical treatment and possibly a prescription for Seconal from Dr. George? She may have even been privy to the what and how of the 1926 scandal? (George, with his enormous ego and a few drinks in his belly, did like to talk. Especially when it came to wanting to impress pretty girlfriends.)

Sister Aimee was overdosed in September 1944. My best guesstimate is that George broke up with Ruth Spaulding shortly after that perhaps in December or early 1945?

Ruth, both saddened and furious with George for being "dumped," begins writing her manuscript, a tell-all?

My mother, Dorothy, in describing the Ruth Spaulding incident to my then fourteen-year-old half-sister Tamar, in 1949, at our Franklin Street home, after discovering that George had just had sexual relations with his daughter, informed Tamar:

> "Ruth had written two separate manuscripts. One used real names, and the other used fictional made-up names. When I was at Ruth's apartment with George, she was alive and breathing. He gave me her writings and told me to go home and burn them. I did."

George overdoses Ruth Spaulding on May 9, 1945, by likely injecting her with "Seconal" just seven short months after similarly injecting Aimee McPherson with "Seconal"—using the same barbiturate in both crimes.

As previously indicated, LAPD did suspect GHH and did actively investigate the Spaulding death as suspected foul play. However, GHH shortly after that quit his job at LA County Health Department, Chief of Hygiene, and joined UNRRA (United Nations Relief and Rehabilitation Agency). After being initially stationed in Washington, DC, at the end of 1945, in February 1946 was assigned and sent to Asia as Chief Regional Medical Officer to Hankow, China. (For those interested in his description of his year in China, see *The China Letter* [Thoughtprint Press 2020] by Dr. George Hill Hodel.

Dr. Hodel was assigned the honorary rank of "Lt. General" and remained abroad until unexpectedly returning to Los Angeles and resuming his doctoring in that city in September 1946.

Post Script to the Sister Aimee Story

Now, being sufficiently backgrounded in the Sister Aimee Scandal, we can see that it was a "Bad News" story for all the players. It don't get any *more noir* than that.

Sadly, there was one more coda to follow, which arrived in the summer of 1957.

Los Angeles Times, June 26, 1957

ATTY. HAHN DIES IN SWIMMING POOL
MYSTERY
Cement Weights on Neck

Cement Weights on Neck

FOUND DEAD—Atty. S. S. (Sammy) Hahn, found dead in pool at cabin.

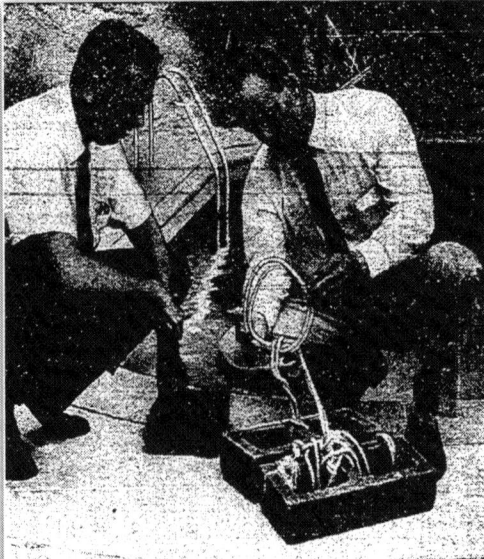

BLOCKS AROUND NECK—Building blocks tied with rope were around neck of Atty. S. S. Hahn when he was found drowned in swimming pool. Here Dep. F. L. Smongesky, left, and Sgt. Jim Wahlke, of Sheriff's homicide squad, examine them.

- photo bottom of previous page 340 -

**Sheriff's detectives posing with cement blocks
tied around attorney Hahn's neck when the body was
found at the bottom of the swimming pool**

I quote from that article:

"Atty. SS (Sammy) Hahn, 68, colorful legal counsel for top film celebrities and society figures, was found dead under mysterious circumstances in the swimming pool at his small isolated cabin in Tick Canyon yesterday.

The 5-foot lawyer, long a prominent figure in the Civic Center, was fully clothed, except for coat and necktie when he was found in the deep end of the pool.

ROPE AROUND NECK

A short length of rope was looped around his neck. Two 12-pound hollow cement blocks were tied to the ends. Det. Sgt. Jim Wahlke of the Sheriff's homicide squad, who investigated, said: "From all indications, it appears to be a suicide, but..."

There was some mystery, however, concerning a gash on the lawyer's forehead and the fact that no notes were found.

LACK OF NOTE QUESTIONED

"It wouldn't be like Sammy not to leave a note," mused Lt. Al Etzel, also of the homicide squad.

Hahn was found at 9:45 a.m. by Bob Nelson, 27, of 3903 Cloverdale Ave., a friend of the attorney's who had gone to the cabin to finish a painting job he had started there Monday.

Young Nelson said he pulled Hahn from the pool and tried artificial respiration. When it failed, he drove to a real estate office at Solemint Junction, five miles away, and called Newhall Sheriff's office.

...

In his autopsy report yesterday, Dr. Gerald K. Ridge, Coroner's office pathologist wrote:

"Uncomplicated case of drowning. Asphyxiation due to drowning. Nothing inconsistent with suicide. Nothing to show it was other than suicide."

REPORT OF BRUISES

Dr. Ridge went on to report that minor bruises on the right forehead apparently were sustained when he (Hahn) went into the pool; that there was no damage to the skull or brain.

And so, it went in 1950s Los Angeles. Head Injury, ropes around neck anchored with heavy cement blocks, found in the deep end of the pool, no note and the victim a   highly controversial criminal defense lawyer—"Obvious Suicide, case closed."

And closed it was. No further investigation needed.

I had intended to add one more 1920s crime that I believe my father committed, but on further reflection this past week, I have decided not to include it. At least not in the here and now.

As the case is very involved and will require a much lengthier explanation, I may, at a later time, present my investigation of that crime as a "standalone" book.

But, for now, let's let out our last roar for the *Roaring Twenties* and sip into the *Thirsty Thirties* "having one more for the road" as we get ready to begin examining my father's life and crimes in *Part II of The Early Years—The 1930s*.

Steve Hodel
Los Angeles, California
August 2020

Post Script
to the Attorney S.S. Hahn Mystery

In checking a reference in the 1926 newspaper archives, I chanced upon the below *Los Angeles Times* article from October 14, 1926.

In the Words of Hamlet, "It's Words, Words, Words"

H. S. HAHN
ATTORNEY AT LAW

LOS ANGELES CALIFORNIA

June 30, 1928

Mrs. Minnie Kennedy,
Angelus Temple,
Los Angeles, Cal.

Sister:--

            This is the name of our lawyer.   You will

hear from us thru him only.

            The Avengers

Introducing a Lot of Talk

Dep. Dist.-Attys. Dennison and Murray survey the growing transcript of the testimony taken so far in the McPherson case. Approximately 500,000 words now comprise the growing story. Below—The contents of the "avengers" letter, the high light of yesterday's session.

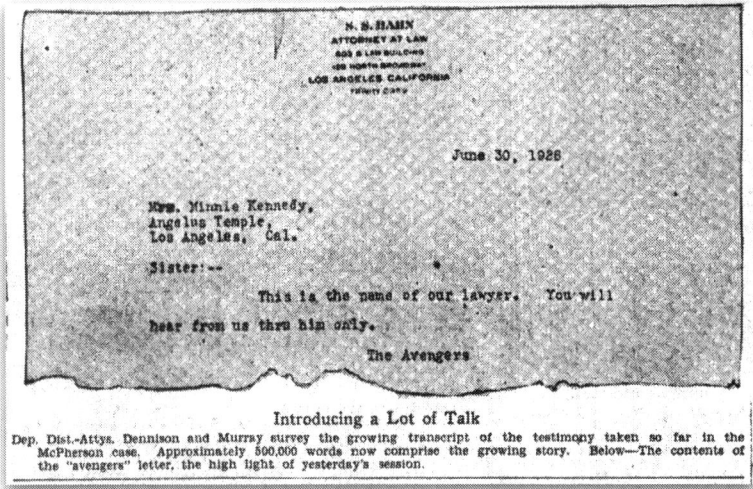

Introducing a Lot of Talk

Dep. Dist.-Attys. Dennison and Murray survey the growing transcript of the testimony taken so far in the McPherson case. Approximately 500,000 words now comprise the growing story. Below—The contents of the "avengers" letter, the high light of yesterday's session.

("The Avengers" letter appeared in the Los Angeles Times article October 14, 1926, seen on page 343 and as enlarged here on page 345.)

Los Angeles Times article references a letter (also shown on page 343 with enlargements on pages 344 & 345) introduced by the prosecution at Sister Aimee's Preliminary Hearing. The letter, purportedly from "The Avengers" to Mrs. Minnie Kennedy, dated on June 30, 1926, was written on the letterhead of attorney S.S. HAHN, his stationery, and read:

> **Sister: --**
> **This is the name of our lawyer. You will**
> **Hear from us thru him only.**
> **The Avengers**

Attorney S.S. Hahn, in court at the time of the letter's introduction, while admitting it was his stationery, vociferously denied any knowledge of the message. And, further disclaimed any connection to the "Avengers" as being his clients and informed the court he was "in Cuba at the time it was sent to Mrs. Kennedy at Angelus Temple." (See **LETTER OFFERED** on page 346.)

LETTER OFFERED

Camouflaged insinuations that Mrs. Wiseman was the author of an "Avenger" letter written to Mrs. McPherson were made in the questions asked by Attorney Gilbert when Mrs. Wiseman resumed the witness stand at the morning session.

Gilbert displayed a letter written on the stationery of S. S. Hahn, the "hoax woman's" counsel, dated June 30, and mailed July 1, reading as follows:

"Sister: This is the name of our lawyer. You will hear from us through him only.

(Signed) "THE AVENGERS."

The signature was typewritten. Hahn denied any knowledge of it, saying that he was in Cuba at the time it was written.

Although Mrs. Wiseman had testified that she never met Mr. Hahn until September, Gilbert asked:

"Did you write this letter?"

"I certainly did not," Mrs. Wiseman replied.

The letter was brought to court by Asst. U. S. Atty. Ohannesian. It had been known for some time that Federal authorities have been conducting independent investigation into letters directed to the leaders of the Angelus Temple congregation, including the ransom letters received at the Temple prior to Mrs. McPherson's reappearance.

Questions by Attorney Gilbert on cross-examination throughout the remainder of the session were directed for the purpose of impeaching Mrs. Wiseman's previous testimony.

Chapter 8

A Hundred-Year-Old Thoughtprint?

March 20, 2020
Los Angeles, California

On March 17, 2020, I received a short email from my friend, Robb Bindler.

Robb is an award-winning documentarian/filmmaker. He has been working closely with me researching for several years on a BDA/Zodiac Project in hopes of transforming the series of books into a television miniseries as an end result.

Robb had sent me some early speculations by Gareth Penn in which Penn had used his pseudonym "George Oakes" and had written to the FBI on May 26, 1981. At the bottom of this correspondence with the FBI Penn wrote the following:

SKH Note—In my book, *MOST EVIL I* (Dutton 2009) I credit Gareth Penn, *aka George Oakes,* with the discovery and linkage to Zodiac's crimes to a popular art movement known as *Land Art* or *Earthworks*, popularized in the Sixties at the Dwan Gallery in NYC.

> **Gareth,** a self-appointed Zodiacologist, using his **Penn** name (pun intended) of **Oakes**, wrote an article in *California Magazine* in November 1981 entitled, *"Portrait of the Artist as a Mass Murderer."* Penn is the son of an Army cryptographer who was a former employee of the California Attorney General's Office, and Gareth is a member of Mensa—the most famous high-IQ society in the world.

I sent a reply email to Robb on March 17:

> Will read the Gareth Penn material again you sent me, but this (above P.S.) just jumped out at me. A "market research questionnaire" sent to Capt. _____? Don't know what this is but sure would like to see the questionnaire and see if it was one of or could be traced back to GHH, whose full-time work then was analyzing his own Market Research Questionnaires.

Robb's immediate same-day response:

"That is suspicious. Needs some sleuthing for sure. Ever read this? 'Z' by Edwin Baird (publisher of Weird Tales Detective Mag and other magazines)."

SIGNED 'Z' BY EDWIN BAIRD

I had never seen any mention of the magazine or the "Z" short story, and as Robb had suggested, began my "immediate sleuthing."

Here is what I discovered:

A full reproduction of the original 1921 "Signed Z" twenty-six-page "novel"/short story as written by the publisher. I have reproduced Edwin Baird's "Z" novel in full at the end of this chapter. I recommend reading it in its entirety.

I believe that this 1921 "Z" serial killer story was, in fact, the original "inspiration" for my father's later "Z" signages as Zodiac.

As we know, young George loved pulp fiction and the sensationalized magazines of that day, and we need to look no further than his tabloid reportage in the *Los Angeles Record*, followed by promoting himself to Editor of his own bizarre, over the top publication, FANTASIA in 1925.

As of this writing, the first crime I have linked to my father occurred in **1921** when he was not yet fourteen. Mentally precocious, George Hodel would enter Pasadena's prestigious Caltech and begin his higher education in the fall of 1923 at the age of fifteen.

I believe George Hodel's "first crime" occurred approximately three weeks before the publication (August 27, 1921) of the fictional 'Z' serial crimes in Edwin Baird's *'Detective Story Magazine'*." (The kidnap/murder of Father Patrick Heslin on August 2, 1921, is summarized in Chapter 4 of this book.)

1967 and 1970 "Signed **Z**" Letters
in connected Zodiac Serial Murders

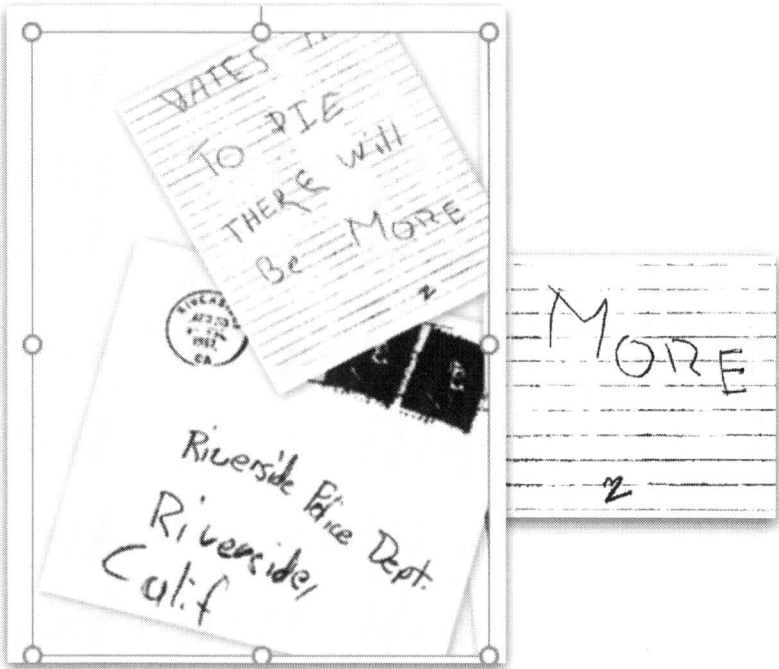

1966 Riverside Cheri Jo Bates murder
killer signs using just the letter "Z."

SKH Note - Uses the phrase: " THERE WILL BE MORE"

"Zodiac" in his 1970 San Francisco Halloween Card
sent to the *San Francisco Chronicle*, (George Hodel
worked for that newspaper in the 1930s, employed as
one of their columnist/reporters with his own weekly
column, *"Abroad In San Francisco"*) has used three
separate "clue" signatures all pointing to his real
identity.

Three clue signatory

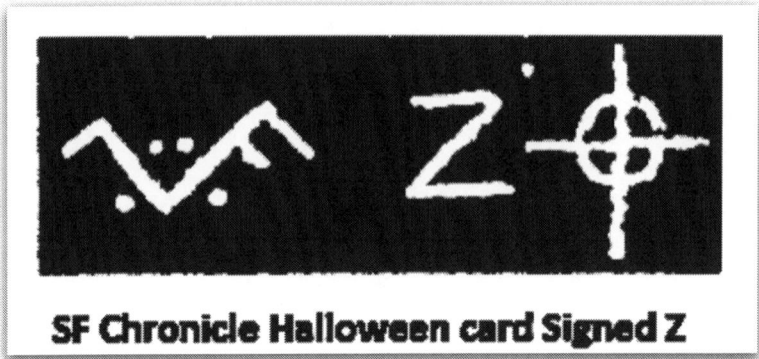

SF Chronicle Halloween card Signed Z

Ever the egomaniacal "master criminal," he boldly writes, "...**You Ache To Know My Name. And So I'll Clue You In.**"

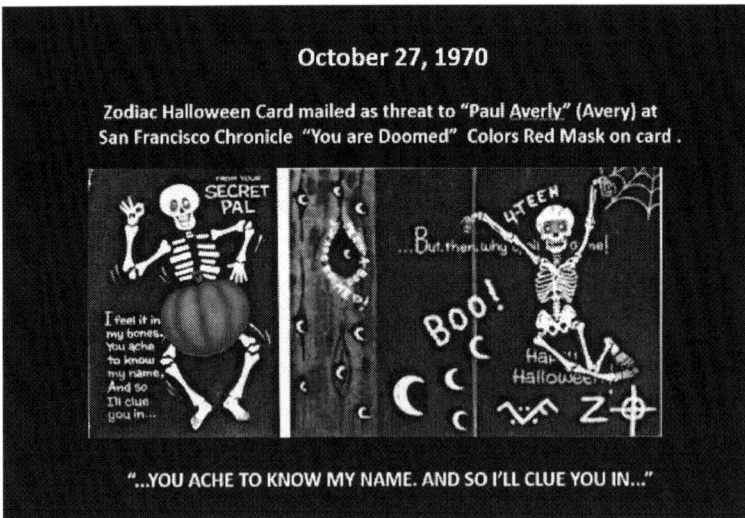

October 27, 1970

Zodiac Halloween Card mailed as threat to "Paul Averly" (Avery) at San Francisco Chronicle "You are Doomed" Colors Red Mask on card .

"...YOU ACHE TO KNOW MY NAME. AND SO I'LL CLUE YOU IN..."

And "clue us in" he does!

Clue No. 1 - Signing his name as "Z," (on Cheri Jo Bates murder note April 30, 1967 and the October 27, 1970 'Zodiac Halloween Card') I believe connects him to this hundred-year-old "thoughtprint," of the August 27, 1921 "Z" detective story, read by GHH just weeks after his first murder—the kidnap/execution of Father Heslin on August 2, 1921.

"Z" by Edwin Baird

Clue No. 2 - Signing his full name using the ancient Celtic alphabet known as Ogham, the cipher "cracked" by my friend and "French Connection," Mssr. Yves Person as presented in Most *Evil II* (Rare Bird Books 2015).

Most Evil II (Rare Bird Books 2015) – page 162

Below is shown a slightly more detailed rendering of the solution. (Courtesy of the artistry of my good friend, Robert "Dr. Watson" Sadler.):

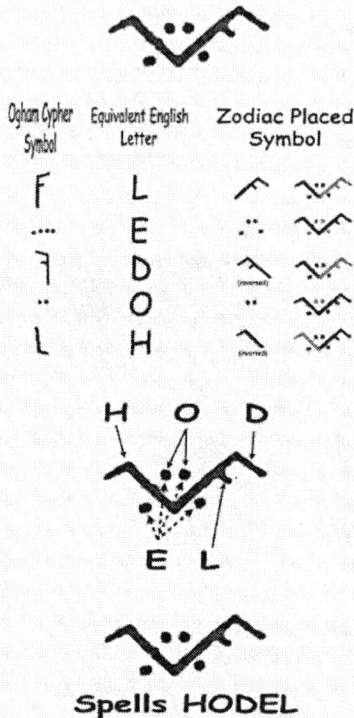

Ogham Cypher Symbol	Equivalent English Letter	Zodiac Placed Symbol	
F	L		
....	E		
˥	D		
..	O		
L	H		

Spells HODEL

Fig. 10.7

The decryption is perfect. Zodiac's signature reads **H O D E L.** Nothing is missing. No additional letters have been added or omitted.

Based on this decryption, it is my belief that Dr. George Hill Hodel, thoroughly convinced that he was a "master criminal" and that his high-genius insulated him from

Clue No. 3 - Signing his full name using the Zodiac cross and circle as his coded Sigil for his name.

(Full credit for identifying, creating, and presenting this "Sigil" signature to my attention goes to researcher/filmmaker Robb Bindler.)

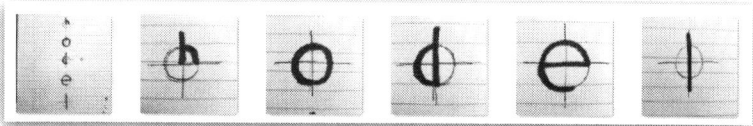

Above Circle & Cross Sigil "cracked" & illustrated to me
by Robb Bindler

rjs graphic

Summary of Serial Killer "Z"'s M.O. /Crime Signatures from Baird's short story

- Kills the victim by cutting his throat with a knife slashing the jugular.
- Calls all the local newspapers "This is Z speaking..." informs them of his crime.
- Robbery not the motive—money, watch, etc. left on the victim's person.
- Shumway (reporter at The Standard) answers phone, caller says, "This is Z calling, and We just killed Ashfield of the Western Trust. Look for apple seeds." Caller hung up.
- Second slaying, same suspect, throat cut in his office. Z again called all city editors of newspapers.

- Suspect Z a tall skinny man wearing an overcoat.
- Both crimes letter left with a crudely written letter Z.
- One thing I'm sure of said Shumway, "This man has just begun to kill."
- "The police department, angered by the boldness of the unknown murderer and stimulated by the big reward, had taken extraordinary measures to capture him."
- Z shoots third victim banker, Frank Eggleston, through office window from across the street, left rifle and note—"I told you so." Signed Z.
- Envelope sent to the newspaper office; angular H.W. addressed, "City Editor, Herald." Letter with a large black "Z" with the message: "Walter E. Bubbell, president of the Midland Trust & Savings Bank, will die before four p.m. Today, Friday, and J.D. Hoyt, president of the State Bank of Oakdale, will die at nine-fifteen a.m. tomorrow, Saturday. Z."
- The fourth victim was slain by Z, who mailed him a sampling of a new kind of sanitary drinking cup which he drank from and was poisoned.
- Z tricked and caught by Shumway confesses, "I am the man that America is talking about tonight. You are nothing! ...I am the celebrated Z!"
- Z's motive for the murders was that of an Avenger. He blamed all bankers as being

the cause of him going bankrupt and sought revenge.

The graphics on the following pages (359-361) come from the graphic that demonstrates the "Coincidence or Potential Source" of three significant comparative "thoughtprints."

1920s - Baird's fictional murderer, "Z," uses the phrase: "This is Z calling..."

1940s - In the Hodel household, George would often, over the intercom, say to his children: "This is God speaking..."

1970s - In communications to police and media the serial killer calling himself 'Zodiac' or 'the Zodiac' would often use the phrase: "This is the Zodiac speaking..."

Coincidence or Potential Source

"This is God speaking..."

1921
"This is Z calling..."

"Z" - Alias used by
Fictional Murderer in Short Story
by Edwin Baird published 8.21.1921
Detective Story Magazine

1970s
"This is the Zodiac speaking..."

"Zodiac" - Alias used by
Real-Life Murderer in Letters
sent to Police or Media
(6 of 9 Letters using the phrase)

graphic by rjs

1921
"This is Z calling..."

"Z" - Alias used by
Fictional Murderer in Short Story
by Edwin Baird published 8.21.1921
Detective Story Magazine

36   Detective Story Magazine

ficed to show that he was dead, and the crimson-stained rug, the deep gash in his neck, showed that death had come in a violent manner.

CHAPTER II.
APPLE SEEDS.

IT was characteristic of Shumway that his first thought was for his paper. There was a telephone a few feet away. He crossed to it swiftly and called his office.

"The first thing to do," he said to Pierce, after describing the scene at the bank, "is to learn who phoned you about this murder. Maybe you already know who it was. Eh?"

"No, I don't," said Pierce over the wire. "It was a man's voice, and he merely said, 'This is Z calling. I've just killed Reeves of the Second National.' Then he hung up. I tried to establish the connection but couldn't make it. We're tracing the call now, or trying to."

"Good! We've got to find him," insisted Shumway. "There's a real mystery here, and this unknown Z is probably the only person who can clear it up. He phoned you about three fifty-seven, or between three fifty-five and three fifty-nine. I remember looking at the clock."

"Other papers there?" asked Pierce.

"All of them. He phoned them, too. They're in the directors' room now," said Shumway, rising from the desk with the receiver to his ear, "so I'd better choke off. Call you back in a few minutes." He snapped the receiver on its hook and hurried back to the long, paneled room, where lay the body of the murdered banker.

The room was rapidly filling with excited persons. Two of the evening newspaper reporters were quarreling over a telephone. At another telephone stood Simpson, calling the police in an excited tone of voice.

Several of the other bank officials, attracted by the unwonted commotion, stood gaping in speechless horror at Reeves' dead body, as if unable to believe their eyes. A number of minor employees, similarly drawn to the chamber of death, clogged the doorway, whispering excitedly to one another, craning their necks to see what had happened. The bank, peacefully dozing a few minutes ago, was now buzzing with alarm.

It was also characteristic of Shumway that, when people around him became excited, he grew calm. Now, in the midst of all this frantic agitation, he was cool master of his thoughts, and his mind was working with the precision of a piece of perfect mechanism. Heedless of the feverish babble in the room, he concentrated all his faculties on one thing alone: Who killed Reeves? Rapidly he marshaled all the known facts, adding to them, as he inspected the room and questioned the bank officials. These facts, when brought together, were arrayed in his mind as follows: First, Reeves had entered the directors' room, unknown to his associates, between three and four o'clock this afternoon; second, also unknown to his associates, or to any other person in the bank, he had met a violent death there; third, so far as was known he had no enemies and no cause to take his own life; fourth, his assailant, assuming it was murder and not suicide, had gained access to the directors' room by a private passageway which led to a corridor on the second floor of the bank building; fifth, since the body was still warm when found, Reeves had died only a few minutes before.

As Shumway mentally noted his fifth fact it came to him that the banker undoubtedly was still alive when the mysterious Z had telephoned to *The Standard*. This, of course, brought him back to the important question of who this anonymous person was, and

1970s
"This is the **Zodiac** speaking..."

"**Zodiac**" - Alias used by
Real-Life Murderer in Letters
sent to Police or Media
(*6 of 9 Letters using the phrase*)

Dear Editor
This is the Zodiac speaking I
am back with you. Tell herb caen
I am here, I have always been here.

Dear Channel Nwe 5
This is the Zodiac speaking. You people
in LA are in for a treat. In the next three
weeks you are finally gona have something

This is the Zodiac speaking
By the way have you cracked
the last cipher I sent you?
My name is —

This is the Zodiac speaking

I have become very upset with
the people of San Fran Bay
Area. They have **not** complied

This is the Zodiac speaking.
I am the murderer of the
taxi driver over by
Washington St & Maple St last

This is the Zodiac speaking I
am still out here an creck proof. I want you
to know about my latest slaves that I

MO and Crime Signatures in Fictional
1921 "Z" Serial Murders
(In bold from the written short story pages 363 - 388)

Compared to

GHH Crime Signatures used by him as Black Dahlia Avenger, Lipstick Killer, Manila Jigsaw Murderer, In The Mesquite Murders and Zodiac
(in italics)

BDA   = Black Dahlia Avenger
CLK   = Chicago Lipstick Killer
ITM   = In The Mesquite Murders
MJM   = Manila Jigsaw Murder
Z   = Zodiac
LWM   =Los Angeles

- Kills several of the victims by cutting their throat with a knife and or slashing body. (*BDA, LWM, CLK, MJM, Z*)

- Uses a rifle or handgun to shoot the victim. (*ITM, CLK, Z*)

- Calls the City Editor of the local newspaper, "This is Z speaking," informs them of his crime. (*BDA, CLK, Z*)

- Robbery not the motive, money, watch, jewelry, etc., left on the victim's person. (*ITM, BDA, LWM, CLK, MJM, Z*)

- Crudely written Note or Crime letter. (*CLK, LWM BDA, Z*)

- One thing I'm sure of said Shumway, "This man has just begun to kill." Killer promises, "There will be more." (*BDA, LWM, Z, CLK*)

- "The police department, angered by the boldness of the unknown killer and stimulated by the big reward, and the killer's public taunts took extraordinary measures to capture him." (*CLK, LWM, BDA, Z*)

- Envelope sent to the newspaper office; printed handwriting addressed, "City Editor, Herald." (*CLK, BDA, Z*)

- Mails letter to relative of intended victim (daughter) threatening to kill family member. (*CLK, Z*)

AUG. 27, 1921   15 CENTS

DETECTIVE

STORY MAGAZINE

EVERY WEEK

"Z"

By Edwin Baird

DETECTIVE STORY MAGAZINE
E V E R Y   W E E K

Vol. XLII   Contents for August 27, 1921   No. 6

Publication issued every week by Street & Smith Corporation, 79-89 Seventh Avenue, New York City. ORMOND G. SMITH, President; GEORGE C. SMITH, Treasurer; GEORGE C. SMITH, JR., Secretary. Copyright, 1921, by Street & Smith Corporation, New York. Copyright, 1921, by Street & Smith Corporation, Great Britain. All Rights Reserved. Publishers everywhere are cautioned against using any of the contents of this Magazine either wholly or in part. Entered as Second-class Matter, September 4, 1917 at the Post Office at New York, N. Y., under Act of Congress of March 3, 1879. Canadian subscription, $7.54. Foreign, $8.54.

WARNING—Do not subscribe through agents unknown to you. Complaints are daily made by persons thus victimized. IMPORTANT—Authors, agents and publishers are requested to note that this firm does not hold itself responsible for loss of unsolicited manuscripts while at this office or in transit; and that it cannot undertake to hold uncalled for manuscripts for a longer period than six months. If the return of manuscript is expected, postage should be inclosed.

YEARLY SUBSCRIPTION, $6.00   **SINGLE COPIES, 15 CENTS**

" Z "

by Edwin Baird

CHAPTER I.

IN THE DIRECTORS' ROOM.

THE star reporter of *The Evening Standard*, Waldron Shumway, covered up his typewriter and glanced at the clock above the city desk. The hands pointed to three fifty-five.

Pierce, the city editor, was sitting easily back in his swivel chair, smoking a cigar and glancing through the early editions of the other afternoon papers. His assistant was reading a magazine. Fanny Fletcher, feature writer, was chatting lazily with Menns, the music critic, about last night's opera.

The financial edition had gone to press, and the dynamic tension was over for the moment. The local room was languorously peaceful, resting from the day's hard grind. Shumway, pushing his typewriter aside, rose from his desk, thinking of the date he had for to-night with Katharine Hoyt. He and Katharine were going to a new musical show and afterward to supper.

Whistling blithely he started toward his locker for his hat and overcoat, and then, all at once, he became aware of a sudden commotion at the city desk. Turning he saw Pierce talking excitedly at the telephone, while Barker, his assistant, had tossed aside his magazine and was hurrying to the private office of Carmody, the managing editor. The air tingled with electric tension.

These things at once told Shumway that a big story was "breaking." He was hastening to the city desk even before Pierce called sharply: "Shumway!"

"What's happened, Pierce?"

"Plenty! Henry W. Reeves, president of the Second National Bank, has just been murdered!"

"Where?"

"At the bank. Hurry!"

Shumway sped back to the locker, seized his hat and overcoat, and rushed for the street. As he dashed from the local room, struggling into his overcoat while he ran, his eye chanced to encounter the clock on the wall. The hands pointed to three fifty-nine.

Walking rapidly toward the Second National Bank building, which was only four blocks away, Shumway visualized the scene that he supposed awaited him there: the startled officials, the frightened clerks, the confusion and excitement, the curious crowd outside the bank, the ambulance, and policemen. But for what he really found he was totally unprepared.

Since it was after banking hours, the massive front doors were closed and bolted. But, when he entered the bank, through the employees' private entrance, where he was admitted on the presentation of his reporter's card, he was surprised to see that there were no visible signs of anything unusual.

The clerks and tellers were in their cages, clearly intent upon their routine duties. Several of the executives were at their desks, similarly oblivious to all except the work before them. A sleepy-looking janitor was methodically mopping the marble-tiled floor. Except for the rhythmic swish of his mop, scarcely a sound disturbed the stillness.

There was nothing here to indicate that a murder had been committed, or that anything out of the ordinary had happened. Shumway, irresolute and puzzled, was wondering if somebody had hoaxed his city editor when he heard his name called. Turning to look, he saw Nat Sloan of *The Evening Times*.

"Who killed him?" asked Sloan, breathing like a spent runner.

"Who killed who?"

"Reeves. He's dead, isn't he? Murdered?"

"Don't know yet. I haven't seen him."

"Somebody phoned my office," Sloan declared, still breathing hard. "Said old Reeves had been croaked. Wasn't more than ten minutes ago. What d'you know about that?"

"I know this much," said Shumway, nodding toward the marble steps that led to the bank floor, "the same message has been telephoned to every newspaper office in town."

Up the steps swarmed a phalanx of eager newspapermen, representing *The Evening Star*, *The Evening Dispatch*, *The Morning Post*, and *The Morning Sun*.

It speedily developed that all had received the same communication which had brought Sloan and Shumway to the bank. After a hasty consultation all agreed that they were victims of a practical joker.

"Still," said Shumway, bending his gaze on a desk in the far corner, "we've got to make sure of that. That's Reeves' desk, over there near the window, and Reeves is not there. We've got to find Reeves."

"You'll find him at his club," said *The Sun* reporter, "drinking his favorite hooch. I know Reeves."

"Go find him, then," said Sloan, "and bring him here so I can see him."

"I pass the buck to Shumway. He knows him even better than I."

"Accepted with pleasure," Shumway said, and, leaving his colleagues, he strode the length of the big rotunda and stopped before a mahogany desk behind a mahogany railing, where sat a slender, elderly gentleman, wearing gold-rimmed spectacles. Shumway recognized this official as G. N. Simpson, from whom he had often received financial news for his paper.

"Excuse me, Mr. Simpson," he said pleasantly. "I wonder if I may see Mr. Reeves for a moment?"

Mr. Simpson glanced briefly up from the work before him. "You'll find him at that desk in the corner," he said, carefully signing a letter.

Shumway made an elaborate pretense of inspecting the corner desk. "But there's nobody at that desk, Mr. Simpson."

Mr. Simpson put down his pen with grave deliberation and turned and looked over his shoulder.

"Strange!" he murmured, patently surprised. "He was there a few minutes ago. He's probably in the directors' room. Who wants to see him?"

"Shumway, of *The Evening Standard*."

"I'll tell him you're here," said the elderly Simpson, and he rose from his desk and moved toward a mahogany door, some thirty feet away.

Shumway, following him narrowly with his eyes, saw him casually open the door, as if to cross the threshold, then violently start and stagger backward, as though struck in the face by an invisible hand. Then he swiftly entered the room and closed the door behind him.

In another moment Shumway had vaulted the mahogany railing and was running toward the closed door. He flung the door open, every sense quiveringly alert, and what he beheld in the directors' room confirmed his wild suspicion. Sprawling unnaturally across the thick rug, beside an overturned chair, lay the body of Henry Reeves, president of the bank. A glance sufficed to show that he was dead, and the crimson-stained rug, the deep gash in his neck, showed that death had come in a violent manner.

CHAPTER II.
APPLE SEEDS.

IT was characteristic of Shumway that his first thought was for his paper. There was a telephone a few feet away. He crossed to it swiftly and called his office.

"The first thing to do," he said to Pierce, after describing the scene at the bank, "is to learn who phoned you about this murder. Maybe you already know who it was. Eh?"

"No, I don't," said Pierce over the wire. "It was a man's voice, and he merely said, 'This is Z calling. I've just killed Reeves of the Second National.' Then he hung up. I tried to reëstablish the connection, but couldn't make it. We're tracing the call now, or trying to."

"Good! We've got to find him," insisted Shumway. "There's a real mystery here, and this unknown Z is probably the only person who can clear it up. He phoned you about three fifty-seven, or between three fifty-five and three fifty-nine. I remember looking at the clock."

"Other papers there?" asked Pierce.

"All of them. He phoned them, too. They're in the directors' room now," said Shumway, rising from the desk with the receiver to his ear, "so I'd better choke off. Call you back in a few minutes." He snapped the receiver on its hook and hurried back to the long, paneled room, where lay the body of the murdered banker.

The room was rapidly filling with excited persons. Two of the evening newspaper reporters were quarreling over a telephone. At another telephone stood Simpson, calling the police in an excited tone of voice.

Several of the other bank officials, attracted by the unwonted commotion, stood gaping in speechless horror at Reeves' dead body, as if unable to believe their eyes. A number of minor employees, similarly drawn to the chamber of death, clogged the doorway, whispering excitedly to one another, craning their necks to see what had happened. The bank, peacefully dozing a few minutes ago, was now buzzing with alarm.

It was also characteristic of Shumway that, when people around him became excited, he grew calm. Now, in the midst of all this frantic agitation, he was cool master of his thoughts, and his mind was working with the precision of a piece of perfect mechanism.

Heedless of the feverish babble in the room, he concentrated all his faculties on one thing alone: Who killed Reeves? Rapidly he marshaled all the known facts, adding to them, as he inspected the room and questioned the bank officials. These facts, when brought together, were arrayed in his mind as follows: First, Reeves had entered the directors' room, unknown to his associates, between three and four o'clock this afternoon; second, also unknown to his associates, or to any other person in the bank, he had met a violent death there; third, so far as was known he had no enemies and no cause to take his own life; fourth, his assailant, assuming it was murder and not suicide, had gained access to the directors' room by a private passageway which led to a corridor on the second floor of the bank building; fifth, since the body was still warm when found, Reeves had died only a few minutes before.

As Shumway mentally noted his fifth fact it came to him that the banker undoubtedly was still alive when the mysterious Z had telephoned to *The Standard*. This, of course, brought him back to the important question of who this anonymous person was, and that bred other baffling questions which Shumway quickly classified thus: First, assuming the unknown Z had murdered Reeves, what was his motive? Second, if he had committed the murder, why had he telephoned the newspapers about it? Third, if he hadn't committed the murder how had he known of it before the banker was dead?

These and other puzzling questions hinged clearly enough on the apprehension of Z, and Shumway, having made a hasty inspection of the room and questioned those who might shed light on the mystery, started briskly back to the telephone, intending to call Pierce again. As he shoved his way through the frightened crowd, which now filled the big room, he chanced to pass near the body of the dead bank president. He paused for a moment to gaze down at it, his brows knitted in perplexity.

Reeves in falling had evidently struck one of the heavy chairs and upset it. His left hand rested on a rung of the chair, and his right arm was flung out horizontally from his body. He lay with his head thrown back, and it was apparent that a severed jugular vein had sealed his fate.

Suddenly Shumway stooped and picked from the rug, beside the body, three tiny brown objects which he perceived to be apple seeds. He quietly inclosed these in his palm; and then he saw something that seemed to have a deeper significance, something that piqued his interest sharply. The outstretched right hand of the dead man clutched a ragged sheet of red paper.

Shumway would have given much to have possessed that bit of red paper, and for a moment he rashly thought of taking it. But he knew the danger of doing that before the coroner's arrival, knew he was courting trouble in concealing even the apple seeds. Besides, Simpson and his fellow officials had recovered from their shock and were now clearing the room.

Ejected with the rest of the crowd, Shumway put the apple seeds in a vest pocket, then stepped to a telephone and called his office.

"We've traced the call!" Pierce jubilantly told him. "It came from the drug store two doors north of the bank. I've got two men on the way there."

"I'll be there first," said Shumway and bolted for the street.

Entering the crowded drug store, he wedged his way to the cashier's cage and said to the proud young woman there: "About five minutes to four this afternoon you sold a telephone slug, or maybe five or six, to a man who was eating an apple. Do you remember what that man looked like?"

The young woman surveyed him haughtily. "What's eatin' you?" she inquired with superb disdain. "We got ten public booths in this store, and I sell a thousand slugs a day. Beat it!"

Shumway didn't beat it. Instead he handed her a ten-dollar bill.

"Think it over," he told her earnestly, "and try to remember. I'll return in a minute."

He crossed to the first telephone booth, saw it was occupied by a woman in furs, and tried the next one. Searching the floor he found nothing more important that a cigar stump and a burnt match; he scanned the floor of the third booth, likewise unsuccessfully. The fourth was occupied, and he moved on.

When he opened the door of the seventh booth and looked closely at the floor he uttered a low cry of triumph and plucked from a corner a fresh apple core, recently thrown there. He entered the booth, closed the door, which automatically lighted the lamp overhead, and with his thumb nail pried a seed from the apple core and compared it with those in his vest pocket.

They matched as perfectly as the buttons on his coat. Pocketing his possessions he sought the proprietor of the store and quietly told him what had

38   Detective Story Magazine

happened. His fellow workers from *The Standard* came in at this juncture, and Shumway, knowing the coroner had probably arrived by now, left them in charge of the drug-store "angle" and hurried back to the bank.

When he entered the directors' room he found the coroner, whom he knew intimately, examining the body of the slain bank president. Two detective sergeants, whom he also knew, were inspecting the room, and the doors were guarded by two patrolmen.

But Shumway's eyes went first of all to the right hand of the dead man. It was empty. "There was a bit of red paper in his right hand, Tom," he said casually to the coroner. "You got it, I suppose?"

The coroner, kneeling beside the body, looked up over his shoulder. "Oh, hello, Shumway! Yes, I found the paper. It's on the table there. I can't make anything of it."

Shumway's eyes, darting instantly to the table, beheld the ragged piece of paper, and involuntarily he gasped with amazement. Surely this was carrying the thing too far! Zigzagging crazily across the red surface, in heavy black lines, was the crude, gigantic letter Z.

CHAPTER III.
UNDER THE MICROSCOPE.

DURING his several years experience in metropolitan newspaper work, Shumway had encountered many peculiar criminals, but here was one quite new to him.

Here was one who walked boldly into a bank, stabbed the president to death, left his calling card in his victim's hand, scattered other evidence about, then calmly walked out and told the newspapers all about it and got away. The brazenness of the thing, to say the least, was disconcerting.

Examining the sheet of scarlet paper under a reading glass, which he found in the room, Shumway discerned it was of strong linen texture, that it contained two faint finger prints, and that the letter Z was roughly drawn with a soft, black crayon.

And now the coroner, emptying Reeves' pockets, drew forth a second sheet of like description. This, too, was scrutinized by Shumway who, unperceived, pinched off a corner that bore a thumb print and quietly concealed it in his hand.

Tantalized by the multiplicity of clews, he waited till the coroner's investigation was finished, and, discovering nothing further of note, he then returned to the drug store.

The cashier had been searching her memory, and she now vaguely described to him a number of men to whom she had sold telephone slugs today. The proprietor supplied a description of others whom he had seen in the store that afternoon, and who, so he thought, had "acted suspiciously."

Shumway wrote down the salient points, though he felt it was futile, like describing small objects lost in the sea.

The musical show, which he had eagerly anticipated seeing that night, was to him and Katharine a failure. In the circumstances it could not have been otherwise.

Katharine's father, J. D. Hoyt, president of the State Bank of Oakdale, and a warm friend of the murdered Reeves. The dinner-table talk in her home that evening, centering almost exclusively on the tragedy at the Second National, had not been conducive to joyousness.

Her mood, therefore, was dismal, and Shumway unconsciously contributed thereto. For the first time since she had known him he was preoccupied in her presence and inattentive to her. He was similarly heedless of the bright performance. Although he stared steadily at the stage, his mind took no cognizance of what happened there. He was, in fact, completely buried in his thoughts and oblivious to everything around him.

Shumway's brain was working hard on a plan to trap the mysterious Z. It was only a nebulous plan as yet, but—— Suddenly he rose and, with a hasty apology, went to the nearest telephone booth and called the city editor of *The Morning Sun*.

"Hello, McLaughlin? . . . Shumway talking. Want to ask a small favor. Just for my own information, would you mind telling me exactly what this anonymous bird, known as Z, said to you over the phone this afternoon?"

"As nearly as I can remember," McLaughlin answered, "he said: 'This is Z speaking. I've just killed Reeves of the Second National.'"

"You sure he said nothing else?"

"Nothing else that I recall. Oh, wait a second. He did say something else at that. Something nutty, as I remember. Something about apple seeds, I think."

Shumway suppressed his swift throb of elation and asked in a puzzled tone: "Did you say 'apple seeds,' old man?"

"'Apple seeds' is what I said."

"What'd he say about apple seeds?"

"Can't remember his words exactly, but it was something about looking for apple seeds. He was clearly off his nut."

Further interrogation failing to elicit anything more definite, Shumway called *The Morning Post*. Randall, night city editor, possessed a better memory.

"I recall his words perfectly," said Randall. "'This is Z calling,' he said to me. 'I've just killed Reeves of the Second National. Look for the apple seeds.' What he meant by that last crack, Heaven only knows! Have you any idea what he was driving at?"

Shumway answered evasively and then phoned Pierce at his home.

"Why, yes," said Pierce. "Now that you remind me of it, he did say something about apple seeds, but I attached no particular importance to it. The fact is that, when he mentioned killing Reeves, I cut in with a question, and his chatter about apple seeds was lost. What do you see in it, Shumway? What's on your mind?"

"I can't tell you now," said Shumway and returned to his seat in the theater, treading on air.

His plan was not so nebulous now. In fact it was shaping itself beautifully in his mind, and he was jubilant.

When he sat down beside Katharine, however, he saw that no such joy was hers. The curtain was down, and the lights were up, and she looked at him with disapproval. "Where on earth have you been?" she asked, a touch of coolness in her voice. "You missed the best part of the first act."

"I don't care!" he answered lightly. "I'd far rather sit and talk with you."

"If you'll pardon my saying so, I think it's high time. You've pointedly ignored me the entire evening."

"I'll make up for it now," he promised and reassuringly patted her hand. "From now on I shall devote myself to you exclusively."

Straightway he excluded all thought of the mystery, which hitherto had occupied his mind, and paid homage to her. And later, when they sat vis-à-vis at a charming after-theater supper in a sparkling restaurant, he smiled into her starry eyes across the pink-shaded, lamplit table, and wove a dream about her loveliness. Some day, he fondly whispered to himself, she would face him thus across the breakfast table!

When at last he reached home, however, he put all such thoughts aside. It was nearly two o'clock when he let himself into his room, for the suburban town of Oakdale was a good twelve miles from his lodgings, but he did not immediately prepare for bed.

Instead he closed and locked the

door, lowered the window shades and attached a high-powered electric bulb to the reading lamp on his table. He then brought forth the bit of red paper and the apple core and seeds, and for upward of an hour he studied them with a powerful microscope. Of particular interest to him were the marks of the teeth in the apple core and the thumb print on the paper.

When he turned out the light and got into bed he was well satisfied with his progress. His plan to capture Z seemed perfect.

CHAPTER IV.

A MESSAGE FROM Z.

HE was up before seven o'clock, and thirty minutes later he occupied a stool in a lunch room round the corner, simultaneously breakfasting and reading the morning newspapers.

The Reeves story, of course, had been "played up" heavily in both morning papers, and was liberally embellished with pictures of the slain banker and members of his family, photographs of the bank, more photographs of the coroner and detectives "searching for clews," and a diagram of the directors' room, with a maltese cross indicating the spot where the body was found. A perusal of the text, however, failed to disclose anything beyond what Shumway already knew.

At least one important thing, and this only contributed to the mystery, had been definitely established: Robbery was not the motive. Several hundred dollars in currency had been found on the dead man's body, and his costly gold watch, a pearl scarfpin, and other objects of considerable value were found intact.

But Shumway had already ascertained that the unknown murderer had stolen nothing; and last night, while studying the several peculiar phases of the crime, he had, he believed, discovered the thing that actuated it. Upon

this thing he had decided to base his procedure to-day.

After breakfast he telephoned his office and said to Pierce:

"I'm working on the Reeves story. I've an idea of my own I'd like to follow up if I can have two or three hours to do as I please. It may mean a big scoop for us, or it may mean nothing. I can't tell yet. Shall I go ahead?"

"Sure!" said the city editor. "But what is this idea, Shumway?"

"I'll tell you as soon as I get to the office, and I ought to be there before eleven."

"All right, hop to it," said Pierce and hung up the receiver.

Shumway then went to a large dental supply house and asked to see the proprietor.

"I'm from The Standard," he said to this gentleman, "and I want a good feature story on the newest discoveries in dentistry. I should particularly like to get the latest dope on bridgework, false teeth, and dental surgery. Can you fix me up?"

"I can and will," said the beaming proprietor, clearly pleased by the prospect of free publicity. "We have a wonderful plant here, and I'll be glad to show you through it."

"I'd rather not put you to so much trouble," protested Shumway, "but I should like to see the place where you make false teeth, and I wish you would explain how they are fitted to people's mouths."

"Delighted! We have a wonderful laboratory, biggest in the city. Step this way, please."

An hour had passed before Shumway emerged to the street again, but he felt that the hour had been well spent. He next called upon a noted finger-print expert and interviewed him for thirty minutes, ostensibly for the purpose of writing a story concerning the various characteristics of thumb prints.

From there he went to a department store and bought a soft black crayon. Then he visited in turn three stationers, and, though he was unable to find exactly what he wanted, a bright red paper of stout linen texture, he found something that he thought might answer his purpose, a cherry-colored wrapping paper. He bought two pounds, then started for his office.

On his way there he stopped at a fruit store and carefully selected and bought four apples of different varieties. At a second store he found two more varieties, unobtainable at the first place, and he bought one of each kind.

It was five minutes of eleven when he entered the local room of *The Standard*, and the incessant clatter of many typewriters, the scurrying copy boys, the industrious reporters, the nervous tension in the air, all were familiar signs to him of the home-edition deadline. Placing his purchases in his locker, he walked toward the city desk, always the center of feverish activity when an edition was going to press.

Pierce was conferring with the make-up editor, and for the moment his desk was left in charge of Barker, his assistant. Barker was handling a steady stream of copy, which flowed from the machines of three rewrite men and five reporters, and trying to answer two telephones at once. He nodded toward the third phone, as Shumway stopped beside the desk.

"Answer that, will you, Shumway?"

Shumway picked up the telephone and placed the receiver to his ear. "Hello?" said he.

"This is Z calling," said a deep masculine voice. "I've just killed Ashfield of the Western Trust. Look for the apple seeds."

Shumway's strong fingers spasmodically gripped the telephone instrument, and, for a breathless instant, he listened tensely, the receiver glued to his ear, every sense quiveringly alive. Then, as

no further sound came, he said clearly and distinctly in a tone of stern authority: "I don't believe a word you say. I think you're lying to us."

But it was no use. The telephone connection had been broken.

Instantly, for he realized the value of every second, he got *The Standard* switchboard operator on the wire. "Trace that call!" he said sharply. "The last one you got for the city desk. Drop everything else and trace it! It's of the utmost importance." Then he whirled round to Pierce, who was still talking with the make-up man, quite unaware of what had happened. "L. D. Ashfield, president of the Western Trust, has just been murdered!" he said. Heedless of the quick excitement that seized all within sound of his voice, and the babble of questions that were shot at him, he went on: "Better call up every public telephone booth within two blocks of the bank. I'd put at least five men on it, Pierce. Then call up the bank and ask for Harris, first vice president. We've got to work fast! Every second is precious. I've——"

"Is this another Z killing?" Pierce demanded.

"Yes! Just got his message over the phone. Miss Mandel is tracing the call. Mustn't lose a moment. I'm off for the bank. Be there in five minutes."

He was already hurrying toward the door. Not waiting to get his overcoat, he sped down the stairs and out into the street. A taxicab stood at the curb. "Western Trust, and make it snappy!" he said to the chauffeur, as he sprang into the vehicle.

CHAPTER V.

CARMODY CONSENTS.

THE circumstances surrounding the mysterious slaying of President Ashfield of the Western Trust Company were, as Shumway quickly discerned, almost identical with those that attended the murder of President Reeves of the Second National Bank.

That the same person had committed both crimes there could be no doubt. Ashfield had been stabbed to death in his private office, not more than twenty minutes ago, or shortly before eleven o'clock, by an unknown man who had entered and left the room without attracting attention. The slayer had then telephoned the city editors of all the newspapers the same weird message that had startled them yesterday.

Ashfield's body had been found by an office boy, John Simmons, only a few minutes before the newspaper men arrived. When Shumway hastened into the bank he found this frightened lad surrounded by a group of men who were excitedly plying him with questions.

Listening unobtrusively, Shumway learned that the boy had admitted the murderer to the banker's private office and a little later had seen him depart, but could give no adequate description of him.

"He was tall and skinny," said the trembling youth in answer to a question, "and I guess that's all I can remember about him, 'cept that he wore a long overcoat."

"Was he dark or light-haired?" somebody asked.

"I guess he was dark. No, he was light. I'm not sure which. He wasn't in Mr. Ashfield's office more'n two or three minutes," declared the boy defensively, "and I don't see how he could 'a' done much in just that little time."

"You saw him come out?"

"Yes, sir. He come out and closed the door and walked away, just like nothin' had happened."

"Which way did he go?"

"I didn't notice where he went. I wasn't payin' much attention. I guess he went out in the street. I don't know."

"What happened next?"

"Well, pretty soon Miss Nichols give me some letters for Mr. Ashfield to sign, and I went to his office and opened the door, and I saw him sittin' there at the desk, all slumped over, and his face was smeared with crimson stains." The boy, overcome by the memory of the horror he had seen, was unable to continue.

"How did you happen to let this man in?" one of his questioners asked. "What did he say to you?"

"Well, he said he wanted to see Mr. Ashfield, and when I asked him for his card he said, 'Never mind the card; just tell 'im Mr. Zander wants to see 'im on some very important business.' Well, I told Mr. Ashfield that, and he said to tell the gentleman to come in. Well, the man went in, and he wasn't in there more'n two or three minutes before he come out again."

Shumway hurried on to Ashfield's office, shoved his way through the crowd of people standing about the doorway and in one swift glance took in the scene within the room. The dead banker sat in a deep swivel chair before his desk, his face buried in his arms, resting upon the plate-glass top.

His back was toward the door, and Shumway divined that the murderer had slipped noiselessly up behind him, cut his throat, then stepped from the room as casually as he had entered. Ashfield had pitched forward on his face and now lay as he had fallen.

Entering the room Shumway's eyes darted to the dead man's right hand, clenched beside his head; and, yes, there it was! A bit of paper, as red as the stains on the desk, protruded from his fingers, Z's calling card.

Kneeling, he searched the rug around the chair, and when he rose he held in his palm three apple seeds. An irate bank official confronted him, seized him, and pointed angrily to the door.

"Get out! You've no business in here. Clear out!"

"Z"   43

"Of course I will," said Shumway, "if it'll ease your mind. I don't blame you a bit for losing your head."

Outside the door he was besieged by a half dozen of his colleagues who had been denied admittance to the room. All talking at once, they plied him with eager questions: "What'd you find, Shumway? Is he dead? Who killed him? How was he killed? What'd you see in there? See anything of any apple seeds? The boss said——"

Shumway, genial though noncommittal, good-naturedly shook them off and hurried to the public telephone booth, near the main entrance to the bank, and called his office.

"We've traced the call," Pierce told him. "It came from the public booth in the Western Trust building."

"I'm telephoning in that booth now," said Shumway.

"Good gosh! Search it, man! Maybe he's left a clew. Look around! He may still be in the bank or in the neighborhood."

Shumway slowly replaced the receiver on the hook, his brows knitted in deep thought, inspected the narrow shelf in the booth and the telephone directory lying there, then searched the floor. Finding nothing, he stepped from the booth and swept his gaze keenly around the bank. It was buzzing with noon-day customers, none of whom suspected anything amiss.

"A tall, skinny man in a long overcoat," so the boy had said.

He glanced toward the boy, saw his questioners had been augmented by the newspaper men and two plain-clothes detectives, and sauntered to the rear of the bank and back, scrutinizing all around him. He then walked outside and as far as the corner, eying every person who appeared to be loitering in the neighborhood.

The quest was hopeless, as he feared it would be, yet at least he had obeyed Pierce's instructions.

The coroner had arrived when he returned to the bank, and he learned that Ashfield's death was caused by a severed jugular vein, that nothing had been stolen from him or from his office, and that the sheet of red paper, found in his hand, bore a crude black letter Z.

He now sought the boy Simmons, took him aside and contrived to have a few minutes' private talk with him. "This man who entered Mr. Ashfield's office," he said to the lad, "was eating an apple when you saw him, wasn't he?"

"Well, if I didn't forget all about that!" exclaimed the boy. "How'd you know he was eatin' an apple?"

"While he was eating the apple," pursued Shumway, "or while he was talking, did you notice his mouth?"

"Well, yes, I guess so."

"Then you saw his teeth. Think hard now! What sort of teeth did he have?"

With a visible effort, the boy prodded his memory. Suddenly his face brightened. "I remember now! He had one of his front teeth gone. I think it was this one here." He indicated with his finger the position of the missing tooth.

"Did he look you in the eye while he was talking to you? Or how did he act?"

"I guess I don't remember about that. I looked up and saw him standin' there, eatin' an apple, and, when he said he wanted to see Mr. Ashfield and I asked him for his card, he sorta grinned, and I saw one of his teeth was gone. That's about all I remember about 'im."

"All right, Johnny. Here's a half dollar for you."

Further inquiry disclosed that no other person had observed the man except Mr. Ashfield's secretary, Miss Nichols; and she, busily typing at her desk, had given him only a fleeting glance as he entered her employer's office. She corroborated Johnny's statement that he was tall and thin and wore a long overcoat, but could recall nothing else that might help to identify him.

After "cleaning up" on the story and ascertaining that it corresponded in all its salient details with the murder committed yesterday, Shumway started back to his office.

This second peculiar murder, treading hard on the heels of the first, did not puzzle him or complicate the mystery, but rather substantiated the theory that he had already formed. Nor was he persuaded to alter the plan carefully conceived last evening. Indeed he was now more than ever firmly convinced that this plan offered the only quick way of trapping the murderer.

Late that afternoon, when the final edition had gone to press, he outlined the plan to Pierce and to Michael Carmody, the managing editor, in the latter's office. When he had finished, Carmody shook his head dubiously. "It sounds too fantastic to me, Shumway. What do you think of it, Pierce?"

"I'll say this for Shumway," replied the city editor, "he's solved more crime mysteries and caught more crooks than any other man on my staff, if not more than all the rest combined. This present scheme of his, I admit, seems pretty extravagant, but I know Shumway. I'm willing to take a chance on it."

"Very well, then," said Carmody, turning back to Shumway. "Go ahead with your plan and draw on the paper for whatever money you need. You'll be needing some cash right away, I take it, so I'll give you an order on the cashier now."

"Thanks," said Shumway briefly. "I can't guarantee, of course, that I'll catch this bird within a certain length of time, or even that I'll catch him at all, but, unless I'm sadly mistaken, I'll be able to hand him over to the police inside of forty-eight hours.

"There's one thing sure," he earnestly added. "If he's not caught pretty soon he'll commit more murders. The two

we've already had are, I am sure, only the forerunner of others. This man has just begun to kill."

CHAPTER VI.
A SHACK ON STEEL STREET.

NOW that he had authority to go ahead, Shumway immediately set and baited the trap which Carmody, justifiably perhaps, had characterized as "too bizarre."

His first act upon leaving the managing editor's office was to write a postscript story, to be run on the first page of all editions of the next day's *Standard*, concerning a mythical Professor Zipf, self-styled banking expert.

Written in straight "newspaper style," with no undue embellishment, the story stated that Professor Zipf, reduced to poverty by the collapse of a bank in which he had deposited his life's savings, now lived in a wretched hovel. Here he was engaged in writing a book that would "expose the evils of the banking system." Shumway wrote:

Professor Zipf was found by a *Standard* reporter in a poor neighborhood, living alone in a dilapidated shanty, meagerly furnished and heated only by a rusty oil stove. He sat at a crude pine table, busily writing, when the reporter found him.

At first he was unwilling to talk, but eventually he consented to an interview, when it was pointed out to him that this might aid him in finding a publisher for his book. Among other things he said that his diet consisted chiefly of apples which he declared to be the most healthful of foods. A large bowl of the fruit was on the table beside his writing pad, and he ate one of these while speaking with the reporter from *The Standard*.

Then followed a lengthy interview in which Professor Zipf described how his life had been ruined by an "inexcusable bank failure," how his home had been destroyed, and how his book, when published, would "shake our nefarious banking system to its rotten foundation."

Shumway, uncommonly painstaking

in writing the story, carefully omitted one salient point: The exact whereabouts of Professor Zipf. Beyond the vague information that he lived in a "poor neighborhood," there was no clew to his street address.

He gave the copy to Carmody for approval, then wrapped up the things he had bought that morning and called at the office of an old and trusted friend, one Robert Cooper, a salesman for the real estate firm of D. L. Rothschild & Co.

"Bobby, old man, I'm in the market for a house."

"You're out of luck," said Bobby.

"I'm in the market," said Shumway unperturbed, "for the meanest, ugliest, dirtiest tumble-down shack in town; and it's got to be in a street of the same description. The more slovenly the street the better."

"In these days," said Bobby Cooper, "with houses scarce as snowballs in June, that's the only sort of place you can find. But what's the joke?"

Shumway convinced him he wasn't joking, and young Cooper inspected his card index and plucked forth a card and studied it.

"How's this sound?" he asked. "Here's a three-room cottage on Steel Street, that's a tenement district, you know, and there's no plumbing, no electricity, no gas, no heat. The house, which has been unoccupied for several years, is in a state of general disrepair."

"Have you got a sign on it?" Shumway interrupted.

"No; and we'd hardly care to put one on. We don't want the name of our firm associated with such a hut. As a matter of fact we're not offering it either for sale or rent. The old man owns the property, as well as several adjoining lots, and he's planning to erect a modern structure, flats and stores, as soon as building gets back to normal."

"I'll rent the house," said Shumway, "at your own figure, if you'll nail a 'For Rent' sign on it."

"I suppose I could manage that. How long will you want the house, old man?"

"Not more than a week, probably less, but I'll pay you a month's rent in advance on one other condition. Within twenty-four hours, perhaps tomorrow morning, a number of men will be asking you for the name of the person who rented this house. To all of them you are to say that the house has not been rented, will not be rented, and is soon to be torn down. Tell 'em nobody is living there, that your sign was placed on the house by mistake."

"I suppose I could manage that, too. If you want to see the shack, old man, I can——"

"Not now, Bobby. I'll take your word that it's what I want, and I'll move in sometime to-morrow. Meanwhile get that sign up. Better do the job yourself. I wish you'd do it tonight with as little fuss as possible, for I don't want the neighbors to see you. If you drive out in your car, park it several blocks from the house and go the rest of the way afoot."

"It shall be done," Bobby promised. "And now, not that I care a cent, of course, would you mind explaining all this dark, deep mystery?"

"I can't tell you just yet, Bobby. You'll pardon me, won't you? At the present moment only two persons, besides myself, know why I'm doing this. In less than forty-eight hours, if all goes well, it will be known by many times two millions."

CHAPTER VII.
SETTING THE STAGE.

LEAVING the real estate office, with a key to the cottage in his pocket, Shumway went to a secondhand furniture store in a crowded neighborhood and bought three broken chairs, a cheap kitchen table, an old glass jar, grievously cracked and chipped, a portable bookcase of like description, three blankets and a mattress, sundry cooking utensils, a kerosene lamp, and a stove.

He paid the proprietor, saying he would return for the goods in an hour, then boarded a street car. rode to another part of the city and alighted near a garage that made a specialty of renting automobiles.

"I'm showing some out-of-town friends around to-night," he said to the owner, with whom he was slightly acquainted, "and I want a closed car for about four hours. I'll drive it myself."

Ten minutes later, in an ancient limousine, he was traveling back in the direction from which he had come. He stopped en route at an old book store and from the dusty shelves selected two dozen odd books on banks and banking. These he bought and placed in the car.

Further on he passed a lighted pawnshop, and, two blocks away, he stopped the car, removed his hat and overcoat and walked back to the shop and addressed himself to a phlegmatic young man behind a show case filled with revolvers. "Coupla guys stuck me up down the street. Got my hat and coat. All I managed to save was a five-dollar bill. I'd like to get home without freezing. Can you fix me up?"

He left the pawnshop wearing a shabby overcoat, that reached well below his knees, and a discarded felt hat, both of which gave him a quite disreputable appearance. He made two more purchases before reaching the secondhand furniture store. At a corner grocery he bought a half dozen old gunny bags, and at a hardware store a package of carpet tacks.

It was nearly ten o'clock that night, with a north wind blowing freezingly, when he steered the aged limousine, heavily freighted with secondhand chat-

tels, into the alley back of No. 2715 Steel Street. Having darkened his lamps, he proceeded slowly, cautiously, with the least possible amount of noise, eyes and ears keenly alert.

Luckily the cold had frigidly sealed the denizens of this teeming district within their miserable homes, and his arrival in their squalid midst was unobserved.

Wearing the tattered hat and overcoat he entered the tumble-down cottage and, so far as he could determine in the darkness, for he dared not strike a match, it was all that Cooper had claimed. The rotting floor gave soggily beneath his feet, the wind whistled through the broken windows, and the rooms seemed moldy with decay.

Without delay he lugged the goods from the automobile across the small back yard, littered with all manner of refuse, and placed them in the shanty. Then he rubbed the gunny sacks in the dust on the floor and tacked them over the windows.

He now locked the door, returned to his car and drove silently away. As he emerged from the dark alley, his lamps still unlit, he paused to look back upon his surrounding, palely illumined by the moon. He was reasonably sure that no eye had seen him arrive or depart.

Hard upon midnight Shumway entered his own rooms, carrying the disreputable hat and overcoat in a roll beneath his arm. Bolting the hall door behind him, he lowered the shades, switched on the lights and settled down to the remainder of his nights' work. He was glad for the warmth and the cheer, which were doubly welcome after the squalor of the cottage that he had just left.

With a pot of coffee, fragrantly steaming on an alcohol stove beside him, he bisected the apples, which he had bought that morning, and removed the seeds and compared them, beneath his microscope, with those found beside the murdered bankers. When at length he had perfectly matched the seeds, he made a notation in his memorandum book and turned his attention to the cherry-colored wrapping paper.

Spreading this paper upon the table, he cut it into sheets, eight by eleven inches in size, and then, with the soft, black crayon, which he had bought at the department store, he printed upon each ruddy sheet a tremendous letter Z.

CHAPTER VIII.

ANOTHER CALLING CARD.

ARISING at six next morning, he examined his face in the bathroom mirror, and decided not to shave. Ordinarily a punctilious young man about his personal appearance, he now proceeded to make himself as disreputable-looking as possible.

He donned a pair of moth-eaten trousers, a soiled shirt and collar, a faded necktie, an old coat and vest, and shoes worn beyond repair. He then partially concealed his unkempt appearance with his stylish hat and smart overcoat which he buttoned around his neck. With the coat and hat from the pawnshop, wrapped in newspaper, he started forth.

In the next block he entered a saloon which ostensibly had become a "soft-drink parlor." To strangers this place was "dry," but the proprietor's friends could obtain something more stimulating than malted milk.

The proprietor knew Shumway, and Shumway departed a little later with a quart of whisky in the newspaper parcel under his arm. Thus far, at least, his plans for this day were proceeding nicely.

Upon entering the office of *The Standard*, however, these plans received an unexpected jolt. Pierce, visibly excited, hurried him into Carmody's office and gave him a long envelope of bright-

red hue, addressed in angular handwriting to "City Editor, Herald."

"It came in this morning's mail," said Pierce. "Read it."

Shumway drew from the envelope a sheet of red paper which he instantly recognized as Z's calling card. On one side was printed a huge black Z, on the other this message was written:

Frank W. Eggleston, President of the Merchants' Bank, will be killed at one forty-five p. m. on the day you receive this message.

"Every paper in town," Pierce went on, "got one of those things in the mail this morning. I tried to get you on the phone at home, but they said you'd left. What d'you think of it, Shumway?"

Shumway, examining the missive by the light at the window, saw that the Z was the same as those he had seen before; that the superscription was jerkily written with black ink and the message with a soft black lead pencil, the handwriting of both being the same, and that the communication was correctly spelled and punctuated. The postmark revealed that the letter had been mailed at the main post office at five o'clock yesterday afternoon.

"It seems genuine enough," he said, handing it back to Pierce. "Of course, it may only be the work of a harmless crank, but I think not."

"You think, then, it was written by the person who killed Reeves and Ashfield?"

Shumway nodded affirmatively. "It's the same as his other calling cards, same sort of paper and same black crayon. I've no doubt he'll try to kill Eggleston to-day, just as he says he will. Where's Carmody?"

"Attending a publishers' meeting."

"Gosh! At this hour?"

"It's an emergency session, called twenty minutes ago by all the papers, when it became known that all had received that message. They're considering the question of suppressing it. This thing's getting mighty serious, Shumway."

"Right! The police——"

"The chief of police," Pierce interrupted, "got one, too! So did Captain Grimm of the detective bureau. And so did Eggleston. He apparently overlooked nobody."

Shumway glanced at his watch. "I can see this is going to be my busy day. First I've got to hustle out to that shack I rented. The address, by the way, in case you happen to need it, is 2715 Steel Street."

"That reminds me of something," said Pierce, writing down the address, "that will probably interest you: *The Standard* is offering five thousand dollars for the arrest of Z."

"I can use it quite neatly," Shumway said, and called back over his shoulder, as he started for the door: "I'll need it pretty soon to set up housekeeping."

Within an hour he entered the tumble-down cottage from the rear, carrying the newspaper parcel and a loaded market basket, and locked the door behind him. Upon the kitchen table in the front room he placed the contents of this basket, a can of kerosene, some writing materials, an earthen pot, a long-pronged fork, a paper lamp shade, two jelly glasses, a hammer and chisel, and a dozen Baldwin apples.

He perforated two of the apples with his fork, placed them in the earthen pot and upon them poured a pint of whisky. Then, working carefully with hammer and chisel, he pried loose two of the rotting boards in the floor, concealed the apples and whisky in the aperture, nailed the boards down and placed the table and chairs over the spot.

The next forty minutes were devoted to giving the cottage an appearance of long habitation. The books were arranged in the secondhand bookcase, the mattress and blankets were spread on the floor, the lamp and stove were cleaned and filled, the writing materials were spread on the table. He also put the glass jar on the table and filled it with six of the bright-red apples.

For two hours thereafter, with the kerosene stove lighted, he sat at the table and made copious notes from one of the books on banking. He wore the hat and coat from the pawnshop, his own coat and hat hanging in the rear room.

A few minutes before twelve o'clock he heard footsteps outside the house, then a knock on the door. He rose, took an apple from the jar, and walked to the window, eating it. Two newspaper reporters stood outside.

Shumway hastily removed the overcoat and hat, hid them beneath the mattress on the floor, and, wearing his more presentable apparel, greeted them cordially. "It's no use, boys. I've been waiting three hours for Professor Zipf, and there's nothing doing."

One of the reporters exhibited an early edition of *The Standard* and indicated the Zipf story on the first page. "What about this interview? Who wrote that?"

"A cub named Schiller. I came here this morning for a follow-up story, bought some apples for the professor on the way out, and I found nothing. Nobody around here ever heard of Professor Zipf. I called up D. L. Rothschild & Co., agents for the house, and they told me it hadn't been rented. You might try your luck with them. Ask for Robert Cooper."

"We'd better take a look inside first."

"Step right in," said Shumway, "and make yourselves at home. I bought some oil for the professor's stove and helped myself to one of his books; but it's been disagreeable waiting for him, and I'm ready to give it up."

The reporters poked through the rooms, kicked at the mattress, read the titles of the books, examined the papers on the table, and decided it was useless to wait any longer for the "nutty professor."

"It's a rotten assignment, anyway," said one.

Shumway heartily agreed and conducted them to a corner drug store and ordered hot coffee and sandwiches. While his confrères were consuming this repast, he went to the telephone booth and called his office.

"Two unknown men," Pierce told him, "telephoned for Zipf's address. One said he was a publisher."

"I'm lunching with them now," said Shumway. "One is Tom Knox of *The Star*, and the other is William Mandel of *The Dispatch*, both charming fellows. Any further developments?"

"Plenty! We've learned that every banker in town got one of those anonymous messages this morning, and the Bankers' Association has held a special meeting and offered a reward of twenty-five thousand dollars for the arrest of the person who murdered Reeves and Ashfield. That means thirty thousand for you, my boy, if your plan succeeds."

CHAPTER IX.
AT ONE-FORTY SIX.

WHEN Shumway reached the Merchants' Bank, about one o'clock that afternoon, he perceived a dozen uniformed policemen in the neighborhood and as many more plain-clothes men, mingling with the crowds in the street in a casual, unobtrusive manner. Since the Newspaper Publishers' Association, at the special conference this morning, had agreed to print nothing concerning the threat against Eggleston's life, the people streaming to and from the bank building never suspected the cause of the policemen's presence.

The police department, angered by the boldness of the unknown murderer and stimulated by the big reward, had taken extraordinary measures to capture him. Every door to the bank was heavily guarded, and every policeman in the downtown district had been put on his mettle.

4F—DS

Ascending to the bank floor, Shumway discerned a dozen more plainclothes guards stationed quietly at strategic points. The Bankers' Association had retained a private detective agency, and the representatives of this agency were also present.

He found President Eggleston in his private office, exchanging witticisms with the newspaper men. The private detectives, with characteristic self-importance, had attempted to eject the reporters from the bank, but Eggleston, also characteristically, had forbidden this.

"Let 'em stay," he said in his bluff fashion. "If there's going to be a killing in my bank I want the press to know about it. But there won't be any killing," he added emphatically, and, rising from his great desk, he illustrated to the reporters, with elaborate detail, the "utter impossibility" of such a thing.

His office could be entered, he pointed out, only through the door leading to the bank, and that door was now guarded by three armed men, and it would be so guarded all afternoon. The massive plate-glass window, facing the street, was securely locked on the inside and could not be opened from without.

Besides, he went on, the window was a sheer forty feet above the sidewalk and more than ten feet from the window above. There was no fire escape near the window, and a half dozen men were guarding it, both in the street below and the window above.

"So you see," he finished laughingly, "there's no hope for you boys getting any news here to-day. Sorry to disappoint you, but there'll be no killing. Not to-day, at any rate. There's not one chance in twenty million."

They went out, leaving him alone with his secretary, a dark-haired young woman, who, throughout the "demonstration," had sat quietly beside his desk, staring absently at the stenographic notebook in her lap.

It was quite apparent to Shumway that Eggleston's jovial bravado was mostly sham. Beneath the banker's blustering manner he detected an undercurrent of fear which seemed substantiated by the remarkable precautions he had taken.

And, after all, who could blame him? With the atrocious murder of his fellow bankers, Reeves and Ashfield, still fresh in his mind, no wonder he was alarmed!

Shumway, last to leave the office, glanced back at the door and saw the bank president sitting at his desk, dictating a letter to his secretary.

A huge clock on the wall informed him it was fifteen minutes past one. Shumway strolled through the bank, remarking that the detectives outnumbered the customers. He walked back toward Eggleston's private office. Three men stood guard outside the door, and a short distance away stood two more, narrowly eying every person who approached.

The street outside, as Shumway knew, was carefully watched, and so were all the adjacent streets. The window of the banker's office was guarded by at least a dozen men. "Not one chance in twenty million," Eggleston had said, and it seemed he was right.

Shumway joined the group of newspaper men who were sitting outside the door, enjoying the expensive cigars which Eggleston had given to them. It was now twenty-five minutes past one.

The minutes sped past, or dragged slowly along, according to your mood, while the reporters bantered one another, "kidded" the detectives, smoked the cigars, spent the reward money, and watched the big clock on the wall.

At thirty-eight minutes after one, Eggleston's secretary came from his office, closed the door behind her and walked to her desk. Shumway, observing her closely, saw her seat herself at the desk, insert a letterhead in her typewriter and open her notebook. He noticed her fingers were trembling.

For perhaps a minute she studied her notes, a perplexed frown on her brow, then she rose abruptly with a quick, nervous movement and returned to the office, taking the notebook with her.

At one forty-three she again emerged, again closed the door behind her and crossed to her desk, studiously ignoring the eyes watching her. Her face was pale. She was palpably frightened, ill at ease.

It was one forty-four, one minute from the fatal hour. The reporters had ceased their chatter and were silently watching the clock. The guards at the door were exhibiting signs of nervousness. One of them placed his hand on the knob, as if minded to open it and look within, but refrained, evidently fearing the act would betray his excitation.

The giant minute hand of the clock crept slowly, inevitably toward the figure nine. The dozen men who were watching it almost held their breath, as it touched the three-quarter mark, and when it gradually moved on, the merest fraction, there was an almost audible sigh of relief. The suspense was over! The fateful moment had come and gone.

The hand was hovering at one forty-six when Eggleston's secretary, who had made several ineffectual attempts to type a letter, sprang from her chair, her face pale as death, and hurried to his office. Ignoring the detectives, she flung the door open, and then, just as she was crossing the threshold, she uttered a piercing scream and fell unconscious to the floor.

Shumway, who had been watching

her instead of the clock, leaped to his feet and rushed to the room. His eyes darted instantly to Eggleston, and he saw why she had fainted. Eggleston was dead!

CHAPTER X.
"I TOLD YOU SO."

IN the midst of the ensuing panic, Shumway kept a level head. Detectives, reporters, bank employees, all crowded pell-mell into Eggleston's office, all talking excitedly, all asking questions which nobody answered.

The unconscious young woman was carried to a divan. Somebody telephoned for a doctor. Somebody else dashed madly downstairs to spread the alarm. A group gathered quickly at the desk where the dead man sat. There was much confusion.

Shumway, standing near the door, heard a voice say: "He's shot through the head; it killed him instantly."

Two answers immediately presented themselves: Suicide and the dark-haired secretary. The first he promptly put aside. As for the second—but that, too, he saw, was highly improbable. True, the girl might have killed him, but no shot had been heard.

And then suddenly he perceived the correct solution, and, such was its obviousness, he wondered he hadn't seen it at once.

Without a word he turned and sped quietly from the bank and hastened across the street to an old office building, directly opposite. On the third floor of this aged building he found what he sought, a small room, recently vacated, facing the street and commanding an unobstructed view of Eggleston's private office.

Beside the open window stood a .45 caliber rifle, mute evidence of the tragedy that had just been enacted here. From the litter on the floor he plucked a half-eaten Baldwin apple, and nearby he found a rifle case; but of more immediate interest to him was the sheet of red paper attached to the barrel of the rifle.

Scrawled across this ruby-colored sheet, which bore the fatal letter Z in the angular handwriting he had seen that morning, were four brief words, forming a grim, ironical sentence:

"I told you so!"

Hurried inquiry in the adjacent offices and questioning of the elevator starter and operators revealed nothing of value. The people in the next office said they had heard "some sort of report" a few minutes ago, but hadn't paid it much attention, supposing it to be only the slamming of a door. Nobody had seen a man of Z's description, nor had anybody noticed "anything unusual."

Shumway telephoned the story to his paper and ran back to the vacant room. Looking across the street into Eggleston's office, he saw that the frantic men therein had discovered the bullet hole in the plate-glass window and were excitedly gesticulating his way.

In ten minutes they were swarming through the building, carefully searching every office, minutely examining the "death chamber," combing the litter there for clews, interrogating all.

The alarm went forth. A hue and cry went up. The police dragnet was spread throughout the downtown streets and drawn in and thrown farther out. A dozen or more "suspects" were arrested. When all was done, the entire result came merely to this: Z had again committed murder, and again he had eluded the law.

CHAPTER XI.
ANOTHER RED ENVELOPE.

THAT night Shumway sat in his shanty copying long passages from the book on banking, until well past twelve o'clock.

His lonely vigil was interrupted by

an amateur sleuth, eagerly seeking fame and fortune, and by two newspaper men, one from *The Morning Post*, the other from *The Morning Sun*, whom he disposed of in somewhat the same manner that had proved effective in the case of the afternoon reporters.

About one o'clock he wrapped himself in the blankets on the floor and fell asleep. He left the oil stove burning, the kerosene lamp lit on the table, and the door to the cabin unlatched. He awoke with a start to find himself in darkness and the room freezingly cold. The lamp and stove had burned out. He struck a match and looked at his watch. It lacked twenty minutes of five.

Further sleep being impossible, he sprang from his comfortless couch, violently waving his arms to excite warmth, and went to an owl lunch room for some hot coffee. Then he boarded a downtown street car and, before six o'clock, entered the local room of *The Standard*. Barker, who was on the early shift, sat at the city desk, clipping the morning newspapers. He looked up in surprise. "Hello! What brings you down so early?"

"Couldn't sleep," said Shumway. "Has the mail come yet?"

"Not due for an hour. But here's something that will interest you." Barker with his shears indicated a "box" on the first page of *The Morning Sun*, announcing a reward of five thousand dollars offered by that paper for the arrest of the person or persons who had slain Henry W. Reeves, L. D. Ashfield, and Frank W. Eggleston.

Beyond this announcement the morning papers contained little that was new or really important, notwithstanding each of them devoted several columns to the murder mystery which was declared to be the most baffling in the annals of the city.

The police and detective departments were engaged in the greatest man hunt in their history. Their dragnet now extended beyond the city, into the suburbs and adjacent towns. Some twenty suspicious characters had been caught in this net and were being held by the police for investigation, but the real murderer, who taunted them with his notes and supplied them with all manner of clews, still remained at large.

Shumway, with his feet propped on a steam radiator, sat reading the papers and smoking cigarettes until a boy came in with the morning mail. Then he walked to the desk where the boy was sorting the letters. One stood out from all the rest and riveted his attention. He drew it forth, a long red envelope, addressed in angular handwriting to "City Editor, Herald."

After a momentary hesitation he tore it open and extracted the sheet of red paper within. On one side of the sheet was a huge black Z, on the other side this message was written:

Walter E. Hubbell, president of the Midland Trust & Savings Bank, will die before four p. m. to-day, Friday, and J. D. Hoyt, president of the State Bank of Oakdale, will die at nine fifteen a. m. to-morrow, Saturday.   Z.

CHAPTER XII.

KATHARINE CALLS.

IT was as if an unseen hand had dealt Shumway a blow in the face. He sank limply into a chair, staring with distended eyes at the bit of red paper between his trembling fingers.

For the first time the fog of terror, in which all were groping, pierced him personally. Hitherto he had sought to penetrate this fog in the detached, impersonal manner of a scientist. But J. D. Hoyt was Katharine's father!

For the first time, too, he experienced a sort of dazed helplessness. Stunned by the unexpected blow, he seemed powerless to think or act. But only for a moment. Swiftly emerging from his inertia and realizing the need for quick action, he got Carmody and Pierce on the telephone, told them of this new development and then went to his desk, evolving a new twist to his original plan.

He inserted a sheet of copy paper in his typewriter, wrote a "slug" and his name in the upper left-hand corner, spaced three times, and then he sat scowling at the typewriter keys, while the plan shaped itself in his mind. Suddenly he began writing and wrote steadily, without a moment's pause, until Carmody arrived.

When Carmody had read the note from Z, Shumway disclosed what he had written. "I've two special requests to make," he said. "One is that we run that story through all editions to-day, and the other is that you give me a letter to John Tyson, head of the publishing firm of Tyson & Sons, asking him to lend us a contract blank such as they sign for successful authors. You might tell him we want to use it in connection with a literary note on our Saturday book page."

An hour later, with the coveted blank in his pocket, Shumway telephoned Hoyt at the bank in Oakdale. "Yes, I got the 'death message,'" said Hoyt laughingly, "but I'm not taking it seriously."

"Does Katharine know?"

"No. I arrived at the bank only a minute ago and found it in my mail. You're the first person I've mentioned it to. I shall now turn it over to the postal authorities and forget about it."

"Whatever you do," said Shumway, "don't tell Katharine. No use worrying her unnecessarily."

Calling at the Midland Trust & Savings Bank, he found Hubbell quite differently affected.

"I received the thing this morning," said the banker, patently alarmed, "and I don't intend to take any chances. I've already retained two armed guards to remain with me constantly during the day, and as an added precaution I'm carrying this." He exhibited a loaded revolver. "Our fascinating Mr. Z," he said with grim humor, "will not catch me napping; I promise you that."

Shumway returned to his office and for the next forty minutes was busily employed with the publisher's contract in a secluded corner of the local room. Here he felt secure from interruption and prying eyes.

Meanwhile he learned from Carmody that the chief of police, the chief of detectives, every police captain and all the newspapers had received duplicates of the terrifying message opened by him that morning. As on the preceding day the newspaper publishers agreed to suppress news of the communication.

The man hunt grew in fury. Every den and crooks' hang-out, every dive and criminals' nest was being ruthlessly raided. Suspects were rounded up by scores. The police stations were crowded to the utmost. And still the fog remained impenetrable. Z, the arch murderer, could not be found.

Shumway was finishing his job on the publisher's contract when a copy boy brought word of "a lady waitin' outside to see you."

It was Katharine, and her first words, when she beheld him, were: "What on earth have you been doing to yourself? You look as if——" She checked her tongue and stared at his face, his clothes, as who should say: "You've been drinking!"

So engrossed had he been that he had forgotten his unshaved face and the ragged habiliment which he had not removed since yesterday morning. Now, however, instead of feeling embarrassed, he was conscious of satisfaction with his trampish appearance. Such an appearance was still essential to his plan. Preoccupied, he made a vague remark, in an absent-minded way, about "not having time to clean up."

"Well, I think it's time you were taking time," she said, piqued by his apparent lack of interest. "But what really brought me here," she went on, opening her reticule, "is this." She gave him a sheet of red notepaper. He opened it and read in the angular scrawl that had become familiar to him: "Twenty-four hours after you receive this you will be fatherless."

"It came in the mail this morning after papa left home," she told him. "I loathe anonymous notes. There's something peculiarly cowardly about them. I suppose I shouldn't worry about it, but do you think it really means anything?"

"It means nothing whatever," he promptly assured her and tore the note to pieces. "Just forget that you ever received it."

"Very well, I shall. Now do you get shaved and freshened up and meet me somewhere for lunch."

He shook his head. "Not to-day."

"Why not?"

He declined to give a reason, except to say he was "too busy." This, of course, was worse than no reason at all.

She chided him for looking like a vagabond and hinted, none too subtly, that he was guilty of insobriety. He, thinking of the big task ahead of him, remembering he was actuated largely by the hope of saving her father, made an effort to conciliate her. She construed this as indifference. The thought irked her. Their words grew acrimonious. All this, of course, could end in but one way: they quarreled and parted in anger.

CHAPTER XIII.

SHUMWAY'S VISITOR.

SHUMWAY walked back into the local room, got his overcoat and hat and started for his shanty, resolutely closing, or trying to close, his mind to Katharine. But the thought of her and their first quarrel lurked in his mind, ready to leap up in an unguarded moment and torture him anew.

Stopping at a drug store on his way to the cabin he bought a roll of absorbent cotton, a bottle of wood alcohol, a cob pipe, and a package of cheap smoking tobacco. At a hardware store he procured an aluminum sauce pan with a long handle. He also purchased another quart of whisky and two more gallons of kerosene.

An hour later he sat at the cheap pine table in the front room of the cottage, reading his book on banking. The jar of red apples was on the table, and on the floor beside his chair were the jelly glasses and a quart bottle of whisky.

He wore the discolored hat and threadbare overcoat, and these, with his unshaved face, soiled collar and frayed necktie, gave him a decidedly unkempt look. The cob pipe between his teeth completed the picture.

About four o'clock he went out and telephoned his office. He was told that Walter Hubbell had died twenty minutes ago.

"Poison," said Pierce succinctly. "A new variety of sanitary drinking cup was sent him in the mail, apparently a sample from a manufacturer. Hubbell took it to the water cooler. In half an hour he was dead. His guards were with him, but they might just as well have been in China."

Deeply troubled, Shumway returned to the cottage. The early winter dusk was setting in, and he lit the oil lamp on the table. Then he placed a wad of the absorbent cotton in the saucepan, thoroughly saturated it with alcohol and put the pan on the floor near the table, with the long handle toward him.

He then sat down and resumed his book. It was dull reading, and his eyes were heavy-lidded. If only he might sleep! But he forced himself to stay awake and plowed steadily on. Several times he dozed fitfully, and each time awoke with a jerk. At last, however, tired nature had her way. His head sank slowly forward. He slept soundly.

He was awakened by a hand falling heavily on his shoulder, and he looked up to find a tall, gaunt man towering above him, calmly eating an apple. The stranger unfolded a copy of *The Standard* and held it beneath the pale yellow light shed by the lamp. "What's the meaning of this?" he demanded and pointed a bony forefinger to a first-page story.

Shumway, rubbing the sleep from his eyes, leaned forward and made a pretense of reading the story. "It's true," he said, "every word of it."

The stranger seemed incredulous. "Prove it," he said.

"With pleasure," said Shumway, and took the publisher's contract from his pocket and gave it to him.

Deliberately the man drew a pair of steel-rimmed spectacles from a rusty case, adjusted them to his nose and, his lean jaws working methodically on the apple, carefully read the contract through. It specifically set forth that Tyson & Sons had agreed to publish a book "exposing the evils of the modern banking system," written by one Professor Hugo Zipf, and had advanced the aforesaid Professor Zipf five thousand dollars on his royalty account.

Clearly impressed, the stranger asked: "Would they care to publish another such book?"

"Perhaps. Do you know somebody who has written one?"

Vouchsafing no answer he crossed to the shabby bookcase and peered through his spectacles at the tattered volumes. "Rubbish!" he exclaimed. "Not a book in the lot worth reading! Any man who reads such trash can't write intelligently of banks and banking. I've written a book that will

startle the world. I've described how bankers make three thousand per cent on every dollar intrusted to them. I've exposed all their crimes, and I can prove every word."

"Sit down," said Shumway genially, "and tell me about it. But first," he added, hospitably placing the bottle of whisky and jelly glasses on the table, "let's have a nip of liquor."

"I've never touched liquor in my life," said the man, seating himself near the window. "I shan't start now."

"An apple then?"

"Thanks. Your apples are better than your books." He selected one from the glass jar, split it with his thumb, took a generous bite. "Odd flavor for a Baldwin," he remarked, munching thoughtfully.

"You like it?"

"Very odd flavor. Not bad, though." He again bit heavily into the fruit.

Shumway filled a jelly glass with whisky. "This is what gives it the flavor," he said, offering the glass temptingly. "Try it."

The man hesitated, chewing his apple and eying the glass suspiciously. Finally he took it in his hand, sniffed the whisky, tasted it, smacked his lips, sipped it, coughed, then emptied the glass at a gulp.

"Fire!" he exclaimed, coughing and sputtering.

Shumway leaned across the table, looked him steadily in the eye and said evenly in a confidential tone: "You look like a man who can hold his tongue, so I'm going to tell you a secret. I've done more for our cause than write a book. I believe in direct action. What would you say if I were to tell you it was I who killed Henry Reeves, Frank Eggleston, L. D. Ashfield——"

The man leaped to his feet, his eyes blazing. "I'd say you were a liar!" he declared. His lips were curled back angrily, revealing a missing front tooth.

"I've proof," said Shumway and

spread on the table his sheets of cherry-colored paper, the Z's uppermost.

"Forgery!" said the gaunt stranger and swept the bits of paper to the floor. "I say you lie!"

Shumway filled the cob pipe with tobacco and took a match from his pocket. "What makes you think I lie?"

His infuriated guest was striding violently to and fro. The fiery whisky, coursing hotly through his veins, lashed his fury. Suddenly he paused at the table. "You know you lie!" he said in thunderous tones and banged the table with his fist. "I am the man who put those crooks away. Don't lie to me! I am the man that America is talking about to-night. You are nothing! I"—he drew himself up proudly—"I am the celebrated Z!"

At this point Shumway lit his match, leisurely touched it to his pipe and dropped it, still lighted, in the saucepan on the floor. Instantly the cotton, soaked with alcohol, burst into flames. He seized the blazing object by the long handle, ran to the door and flung it far out into the street. It described a flaming parabola in mid-air.

When he closed the door and turned back into the room his guest was helping himself to the whisky. He quietly sat down in the chair near the window and watched him swallow three drinks in rapid succession.

It opened the floodgates of his speech. Moving nervously about the small room, now boastful, anon tearful, he told a rambling, disconnected story of how his life's savings had been lost in a bank failure, how he had vowed vengeance, and how he had cunningly planned and executed the murders that had struck terror to the city these last few days.

"Reeves and Ashfield were easy," he said. "I merely stepped up behind them at their desks, slit their throats and walked out. Eggleston was difficult. I needed all my nimble wit to

enter that vacant office, pick him off with a rifle and get away clean. To-day's job was simple, some prussic acid in a drinking cup sent to Hubbell with the compliments of the Sanitex Drinking Cup Co. A gamble, of course, yet I won.

"And to-morrow," he said with a flourish, pausing at the table for another drink of whisky, "I shall remove J. D. Hoyt of the State Bank of Oakdale. I shan't rest until I've killed 'em all! I will show up their vicious system, demonstrate that all bankers are leeches——"

"How will you kill Hoyt?" Shumway softly interrupted.

"Artistically. When he enters his automobile to-morrow morning a time bomb in the seat will explode and blow him to atoms."

The murderer had poured another drink of whisky. As he lifted the glass to his lips, Shumway reached behind the gunny sack at the window and rapped sharply on the pane.

In another moment the door burst open, and Detective Sergeants Michael Sullivan and Tom O'Shea, both old friends of Shumway, charged into the room.

The ensuing ten minutes were filled with violence, for they were dealing with a madman. The table was upset, the bookcase overturned, and everything was smashed, but when the struggle ended he was securely tied and handcuffed. The fog had passed. The hunt was over.

Some two hours later Shumway sat in the office of the chief of police, the center of a throng of policemen, detectives, reporters, and representatives of the Bankers' Association. Ambrose Niclow Zander, otherwise known as Z, had signed a complete confession and was now safely locked in a cell.

For what seemed the twentieth time,

Shumway was asked: "How did you do it?"

"When I saw that first sheet of red paper," he answered, "I put him down as a homicidal maniac, and when he committed the second murder, leaving another red sheet behind, I knew I was right. It was clear to me, then, he was obsessed by some real or imaginary grievance against bankers. It was also a safe bet that he had either written a book on banking, or was contemplating writing one, and was seeking a publisher. I was sure he would eventually seek my fictitious Professor Zipf, in whom he recognized a kindred spirit, for publishing advice. My only fear was that he would delay too long. But the story I wrote this morning fetched him."

"What about those apple seeds?" somebody asked.

"They were a symbol of his wrath. 'An apple a day' was the favorite maxim of the president of the bank in which he lost his savings, and he says he wanted to show that 'he eats apples best who eats them last.' In his confession, by the way, he boasts of having killed that man soon after the collapse of the bank. We're investigating this, and it is probable that in the indictment another murder will be charged against him."

Shumway paused, once more to gaze with dancing eyes on the three bright-colored checks in his hand, aggregating thirty-five thousand dollars, and all were made payable to him. One of these he promptly indorsed and gave to Captain Grimm of the Detective Bureau.

"I want you to divide that five thousand equally between O'Shea and Sullivan," he said. "They never lost faith in my plan, eccentric though it seemed, and they were right on the job when I needed them. Besides," he added, pocketing the thirty thousand, "I've plenty left on which to get married, if the girl will forgive me for not shaving to-day."

Chapter 9

AIMEE SEMPLE MCPHERSON

FUNERAL

Los Angeles Times
October 10, 1944

**Thousands at Aimee Rites
Evangelist Laid to Rest After Temple Services
Attended by Throngs**

"Aimee Semple McPherson, the Canadian farm girl who became a legend of evangelism around the world, was buried at sundown yesterday on a grassy hillside looking toward the Angelus Temple she built as a monument to her faith and the Foursquare Gospel."

Ten thousand attend services for Evangelist Sister Aimee McPherson

My George Hodel investigations continue to be forged and rebarred with irony. (Pun intended)

Time and time again, I have noted the many "beyond bizarro" twists of fate that keep presenting themselves in the life and crimes of Dr. George Hill Hodel.

I have frequently referred to these occurrences as "The Gods Must Be Laughing" or "Synchronicities."

Incredibly, in the death of Sister Aimee, we have THREE MORE to add to our long list.

The first is found, as shown above in the front page headlining of her funeral.

Note the date, October 10, 1944. That date happens to be the 37th birthday of Dr. George Hill Hodel. (My father was born on October 10, 1907, in Los Angeles.)

If I am correct (and I believe I am) Dr. George Hodel did force an overdose of the barbiturate *Seconal* on Sister Aimee in Oakland, just as he did with his secretary, Ruth Spaulding, some eight months later. The dramatic coincidence manifests when the world is informed of her funeral in page one headlines and showing the burial photographs on the very day of her killer's birthday!

The second comes with Sister Aimee's internment.

She is buried at Forest Lawn Cemetery, a *three hundred acre* mortuary in Glendale, California, just four miles north of her own Pentecostal megachurch, Angelus Temple, in the Echo Park district of Los Angeles. As of this date, there are more than 335,000 bodies buried at Forest Lawn, which was established in 1906.

As fate would have it and as presented in an earlier chapter of this book, my grandparents, George and Esther Hodel, are also buried at Forest Lawn Glendale. My grandmother, Esther Leov Hodel, was buried there after succumbing to tuberculosis in 1935. My grandfather, George Hodel, Sr., was buried next to her after dying from a heart attack in 1954.

I was astounded to realize that both of my grandparents are buried at the same cemetery as one of their son's probable victims. But, as indicated with a third of a million souls resting in peace on three hundred acres, it's understandable.

But, the "coincidences" do not stop there.

As shown in the following photographs, George and Esther Hodel are buried in the same section as Aimee Semple McPherson's, "The Sunrise Slope" Section. More than that, *they are interned approximately three hundred feet north of Sister Aimee's grave on the same slope.* (See photographs to follow.)

I'll repeat it, "You Can't Make This Stuff Up!"

1944 Forest Lawn (Glendale) gravesite/memorial of Aimee Semple McPherson
[Note: the rectangular memorial faces east and the rising sun. It extends left, southward and northward to the right with the monument's back facing west and the setting sun.]

The westering raking rays of the sun setting on the "Sunrise Slope Section" of Forest Lawn Cemetery behind Aimee Semple McPherson's burial monument.

Gravesites of George Hodel Sr. and wife Esther

<1944 Forest Lawn (Glendale) gravesite/memorial of Aimee Semple McPherson

This photograph shows the relationship of Aimee Semple McPherson's grave to that of George and Esther. The Hodel graves are approximately 300 feet north of McPherson grave, all three buried in the Sunrise Slope Section.

300 ft. away, gravesite monument of Aimee Semple McPherson

George Hodel (Sr.) Esther Hodel

Author points to the graves of his grandparents in the "Sunrise Slope Section" of Forest Lawn Cemetery

The author points at his grandparents' side-by-side graves situated on Sunrise Slope Section of Forest Lawn Mortuary. Plaques read: "Esther Hodel April 1873-August 1935 / George Hodel Feb 1873-June 1954 "Until the Day Break, And The Shadows Flee Away."

And, now for our **third** irony.

One cannot help but wonder if Dr. George Hill Hodel attended the services for Sister Aimee. Does a psychopathic killer mourn for his victim and show respect by attending her funeral? Somehow, at least in the case of GHH, I doubt it.

But he would most assuredly have celebrated his own birthday, yes?

How?

In George's case, we believe, based on a stack of circumstantial evidence as presented in BDA I and BDA II that on October 11, 1944, the day after the world was shown Aimee's funeral photographs and burial site, George likely went dancing at the famous wartime Hollywood Canteen.

And more.

I believe that George, after dancing with Georgette Bauerdorf, a pretty twenty-year-old, "Junior Hostess" at a military USO-type canteen, followed her home. He then forced entry into her West Hollywood apartment, and beat and strangled her to death. Placing her dead body in the apartment bathtub, he turned on the water, and left, taking her car from the basement carport, and abandoning it in downtown Los Angeles, not far from his medical office.

Girl, 20, Found Dead In Filled Bathtub In Hollywood Apartment; Probe On

Hollywood, Cal., Oct. 13 (*P*)— Georgette Bauerdorf, 20-year-old daughter of a retired oil executive, was found dead in a filled bathtub in her apartment yesterday.

The body, clad in the upper half of pajamas and apparently dead several hours, was discovered after the wife of the apartment house manager investigated an open door to the apartment.

A small piece of wash cloth or towel dangled from Miss Bauerdorf's mouth, Inspector William Penprase said.

He said her death probably resulted from an accident, but that the cloth in her mouth and the absence of her car from its garage warranted a further inquiry. He said a post-mortem examination would be held today.

A large quantity of jewelry was found undisturbed, and there was no evidence of a robbery. Penprase found among her effects a round-trip airline ticket to El Paso, Texas, indicating she had planned to leave

today and return next Wednesday. A notation in her diary said she had planned to attend the gradua-

GEORGETTE BAUERDORF
Hollywood girl found dead

tion there Monday of someone identified only as "Lou."

No Marks On Body

There were no marks on her body. Bloodstains on the tub, Penprase said, probably were from her nose or mouth which she may have injured in a fall.

She was the daughter of George Bauerdorf, former New York oil executive, who, with Mrs. Bauerdorf, the girl's stepmother, reportedly was in New York on a vacation.

Bauerdorf, reached at the Park Lane Hotel in New York, said he believed his daughter's death "was accidental."

"Lou" Identified

"We do know that she suffered from cramps and heartaches and refused to go to a doctor," he added, "and we think perhaps they might have caused it."

Bauerdorf identified the "Lou" mentioned in the girl's diary as an air cadet whom she had dated. He said that he planned to return to Los Angeles.

West Hollywood sheriff's detectives investigated the Bauerdorf Murder. Georgette was slain late-night on October 11, 1944. Her death was initially thought to be "accidental" but found to be a homicide after the autopsy, performed just days later. Examination revealed a medical ace bandage had been forced down her throat to suffocate her and her body placed in the bathtub.

Evidence Shows Heiress Waged Terrific Fight

Bruises and Fist Marks Found on Her Body; Light Over Door Found Twisted to Darken Place

FOUGHT FOR LIFE — Autopsy examination showed Georgette Bauerdorf put up terrific battle for life against man who attacked her in apartment at 8493 Fountain Ave.

SLAIN GIRL — Georgette Bauerdorf, 20, oil heiress, shown in beach scene, who was attacked and killed early Thursday and found in bathtub in her Hollywood home.

Los Angeles Times October 15, 1944, Bauerdorf death reclassified as Homicide post autopsy

The Early Years Part I.

In summary—

As indicated earlier, none of these crimes can be proven "beyond a reasonable doubt" without the aid of hard physical evidence such as a written confession or fingerprints or DNA linkage.

Yet, it remains my confident belief that my father, George Hill Hodel, did commit and or aid as an accomplice in each of these named crimes.

These six crimes committed in the 1920s in review are:

1. **Rev. Patrick E. Heslin**, August 2, 1921, Colma, California. Kidnap/Murder

THE REV. PATRICK E. HESLIN

2. **William Desmond Taylor**, February 1, 1922, Los Angeles, California. Murder

William Desmond Taylor

3. **Nina Martin**, August 23, 1924, Los Angeles, California. Kidnap/Murder

4. **May Martin**, August 23, 1924, Los Angeles, California. Kidnap/Murder

DA Investigator Capt. Hunter points to the location where the Martin sisters' bodies were found, 1925

5. **Aimee Semple McPherson**, May 18, 1926, Los Angeles, California. "Kidnap-Extortion"

Sister Aimee in hospital, Douglas, AZ
"Avengers" Ransom Note

6. **Aimee McPherson**, September 27, 1944, Oakland, California. "Accidental Overdose" or Murder?

September 28, 1944, *LA Times* reports
the death of Sister Aimee Semple McPherson

These crimes, (Rev. **Heslin**, the two **Martin sisters**, film director **William Taylor**, and the **two Sister Aimee McPherson crimes**, 1926 kidnap hoax and her later 1944 suspected murder), complete our investigation of George Hodel's suspected crimes in the 1920s.

Well, not quite. **There is one additional crime** that I believe my father may have committed in that decade, which I had initially intended to include in this book. However, upon further consideration and reflection, I have decided to omit it from this summary.

Depending on what my further investigation into that specific crime reveals, I may include it in a future, "Standalone book," should I uncover additional incriminating evidence.

~ ~ ~

Case in point, re: crime #5:

Aimee Semple McPherson, May 18, 1926, Los Angeles, California. "Kidnap-Extortion"

[additional evidence]

A recent revelation and announcement by third parties of additional linking evidence requires me to now include the following additional chapter.

402

Steve Hodel

Chapter 10

Aimee Semple McPherson
&
The "Celebrity Cypher" Postcard

A Sixty-Four-Year-Old Thoughtprint?

Upon completing *The Early Years-Part 1 – The 1920s* in the summer of 2020 I immediately began writing its companion edition. By year's end I was finishing, *The Early Years-Part 2 – The 1930s*.

As I wrote the closing chapter of *Part 2*, in December 2020, something quite extraordinary and unexpected occurred.

On December 3, 2020, an international three-man-team of code breakers (working to solve what was known as the "Zodiac 340 Cryptogram" written and mailed to the press by the infamous San Francisco serial killer in 1969) announced they had successfully "cracked the code."

A fifty-one-year-old enigma was—SOLVED.

The results of this discovery created a bit of a "time warp" in my narrative of *TEY-Part 1 – The 1920s*.

Just as we are about to enter the 1930s, I find that I need to present to you, my readers, information related to my father's criminal acts and events *that will not occur for some four and then seven decades into the future.*

Why?

Because I believe these current events relate directly back to criminal acts that occurred in 1926 and that we examined in Chapter 7 (page 272), as relates to Aimee Semple McPherson, her fake kidnap hoax and her probable sexual escapade with her radio station manager, Kenneth Ormiston.

With that understanding, let us temporarily jump forward to the present—to January 2021—and hopefully I can demonstrate how the present connects us to the past.

Author's Note: For those who are unaware of my previous investigations let me simply say that two of my published books, *Most Evil I (Dutton 2009) and Most Evil II (Rare Bird Books 2015)* link my father, Dr. George Hill Hodel, as the perpetrator of serial crimes committed in the San Francisco Bay area in 1968 and 1969.

In those two books I make a compelling case that George Hodel reinvented himself from being the "Black Dahlia Avenger" in the 1940s and assumed a new persona, giving himself a new name, "Zodiac." in the late 1960s.

December 11, 2020

So then, here is the beginning of my original blog documenting this historic new code breaking discovery on December 11, 2020.

Zodiac '340 Cipher' Cracked by International Three Man Team of Code Breakers

By Steve Hodel | December 11, 2020 | 21 💬

December 11, 2020
Los Angeles, California

Huge Kudos to the civilian team of code-breakers that have cracked the Zodiac 340 cryptogram. Truly, an international accomplishment.

David Oranchak
Virginia, USA

Sam Blake
Australia

Jari Van Eykcke
Belgium

Zodiac 340 Cipher Mailed to
The San Francisco Chronicle in
November 1969

The solution to the 340 cipher, according to Oranchak's team:

I HOPE YOU ARE HAVING LOTS OF FUN IN TRYING TO CATCH ME THAT WASNT ME ON THE TV SHOW WHICH BRINGS UP A POINT ABOUT ME I AM NOT AFRAID OF THE GAS CHAMBER BECAUSE IT WILL SEND ME TO PARADICE ALL THE SOONER BECAUSE I NOW HAVE ENOUGH SLAVES TO WORK FOR ME WHERE EVERYONE ELSE HAS NOTHING WHEN THEY REACH PARADICE SO THEY ARE AFRAID OF DEATH I AM NOT AFRAID BECAUSE I KNOW THAT MY NEW LIFE IS LIFE WILL BE AN EASY ONE IN PARADICE DEATH

Many had thought (hoped) that Zodiac would reveal his actual identity in this code, but as we see, that was not to be.

SFPD detectives working with sociologists back in 1969 determined the concept of "collecting slaves for paradise" originated in Negroes, Occidental in the Southern Philippines.

I included the fact that my father, George Hodel, and his wife, Hortensia Starke Hodel, owned a large Sugar Plantation in Negroes, Occidental in the 1960s forward. (Actually, my stepmother and her family owned the plantation for many decades preceding the Sixties and had become quite wealthy and she was elected a Congresswoman representing that region in Manila. While stationed in the Navy in Subic Bay, I visited the plantation with my father and Hortensia and spent a few days of R&R (Rest and Relaxation). No question that George Hodel would have been well aware of this island lore of "collecting slaves for paradise."

The cracking of the code, while itself was an amazing accomplishment, adds little to what we already knew, just more ramblings by Zodiac and his "collecting slaves."

Here is a link to an excellent YouTube video produced by David Oranchak explaining the team's work and "how they did it."

https://www.youtube.com/watch?v=-1oQLPRE21o&t=77s

The 340-Zodiac Code that had defied solution by eyes-on experts for over five decades, had finally been "cracked" by the three-man International Team of David Oranchak, Sam Blake, and Jarl Van Eykcke.

Sadly, the long hoped-for identity of the serial killer calling himself "Zodiac" was not revealed.

Or was it?

Here is the follow-up blog I posted on January 3, 2021, just three weeks after the above announcement:

James Valks and Luigi Warren Use Recent Zodiac 340 Cryptogram Solution To Sleuth Out Potential Anagram Linkage of Dr. George Hodel to Separate Zodiac Ciphers

January 3, 2021
Los Angeles, California

I am the first to admit I do not excel in the world of ciphers and cryptograms.

Fortunately, many of my readers have that gift.

Three weeks ago, I blogged on the recent developments of the International Team (David Oranchak, VA, USA; Sam Black, Australia, and Jarl Van Eykcke, Belgium) in cracking the Zodiac 340 Cipher.

As we begin the New Year, I would like to update what I believe are some dramatic new linkages that build on and from the solving of the 340 cipher.

The credit for this potential linkage goes to two separate individuals.

Here are their separate contributions as I received them in chronological order.

LINKAGE NO. 1
James Valks aka "No Excuses"

In December 2020, shortly after the Zodiac 340 cipher was solved, in reading the comments section of the team's YouTube solution I came across an entry by an individual* identifying himself as "No Excuses."

*(Permission given, his real name is JAMES VALKS.)

Using the 340-cipher solution, James applied it to Zodiac's "My Name Is..." Thirteen Letter cipher.

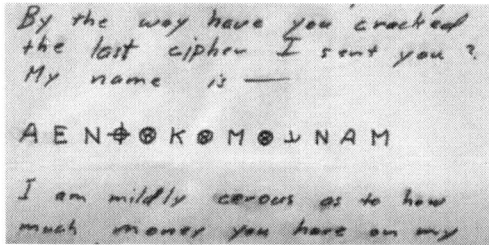

And per his email, believes it translates as indicated:

James Valks' Email No. 1

hi steve, i messaged you on facebook about the z13 cipher, I used the whole key from (lets crack Zodiac - episode 5 - the 340 is solved)... and it actually also works.. just have a look and follow the key for each letter u should get this as the answer...DREHGAROGLEDO - (drgeorgehodel) the only changes made were the zodiac sign changed to + sign..the number (8) two them have become the letter G and the other is an R..everything else is followed 100% by the key. thanks i hope i have made sense of through this

James Valks' Email No. 2

No Excuses 4 hours ago
@steve hodel i wasn't too sure before so I went back to look. I used the whole key from (lets crack Zodiac - episode 5 - the 340 is solved)...and it actually also works.. just have a look and follow the key for each letter u should get this as the answer...DREHGAROGLEDO if u can make sense of why it is scrambled it would help..but tell me this...how is it no other letters show up. follow the key and u will see it.. the only changes made were the zodiac sign changed to + sign..the number (8) two them have become the letter G and the other is an R..everything else is followed 100% by the key. please write back after you try it.
thanks.

steve hodel 2 hours ago

@No Excuses Could you contact me privately at my steve@stevehodel.com on this. Thanks

SKH Note - In my previous book publications and writings as relates to the "Zodiac Thirteen Letter Cipher" I had suggested that two potential signatures of my father could potentially fit: DR GEORGE HODEL or GEORGE HODEL MD.

Huge KUDOS to James Valks for this initial linkage to a separate Zodiac Letter as a potential anagram using Zodiac's 340 Code.

LINKAGE NO. 2
Dr. Luigi Warren

I have known and communicated with Dr. Warren (he has a Ph.D. in Biology from Caltech) for many years and his thoughts as relate to my father's history and actions have been invaluable. He also has communicated much of his thinking as relates to GHH crimes both as Black Dahlia Avenger and Zodiac in his public tweets through the years.

I approached Luigi with the following email on January 1, 2021:

> LW:
>
> Got this from a Zodiac reader. Don't know if it is actually correct as I get lost in the new cryptogram solution with the shifting, etc. But if he is correct pretty damn big anagram Thoughtprint wouldn't you say?
>
> Steve
>
> (I attached Valks' Email No. 1)

Luigi responded the following day:

Steve:

I'm not much of a cipher guy, but I couldn't resist trying to "fix" the problems with the intriguing 13-character cipher solve suggested by your reader. I did come up with an idea which might be helpful, although it still "needs work." I summarize it in the attached file. Perhaps your reader would be interested.

Best,

Luigi

Here is Luigi's additional response and analysis:

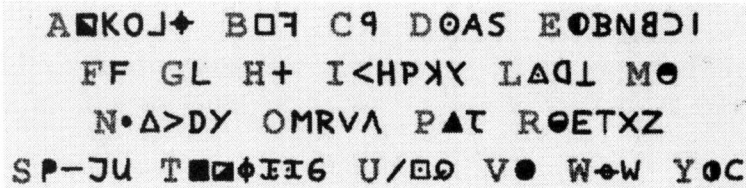

Recently deduced 340 homophonic substitution cipher key
13-Character "My name is" cipher

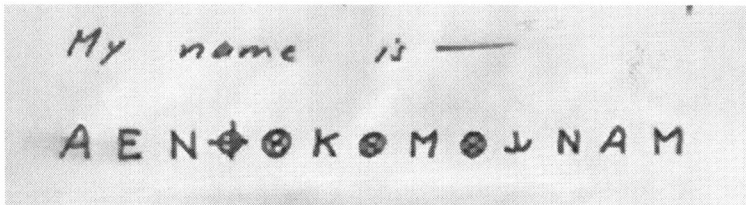

A POSSIBLE PARTIAL SOLUTION BASED ON THE Z340 KEY

Apply the 340 key & assume the novel 8-ball symbol (not used in the Z340) means wildcard (*). Gives:

DREA*A*O*LEDO

<u>Pro</u>: "DR" intro and "LEDO" fragment are suggestive of DRGEORGEHODEL, which as the right character count (13).

<u>Con</u>: Even with free rein to pick and desired letters to fill the three wildcard positions, we still don't get an anagram of DRGEORGEHODEL — at the very least, we're stuck with two As we can't use. We have to introduce somewhat artificial assumptions to make that problem go away.

AN IMPROVED PARTIAL SOLUTION?

Note that the Z340 cipher was identified in the newspapers as a homophonic substitution cipher, where multiple symbols map to the same letter to defeat frequency analysis. Generally, it would be a hopeless task to decode a 13-character homophonic substitution cipher without a key. The idea of the first solution described above is that by deciphering the harder Z340, also a long homophonic substitution cipher, we get the key and then it is just a matter of unscrambling a simple anagram to get the Zodiac's name. Only, as noted above, it doesn't quite work…

My idea to "bridge the gap" is inspired by the following observations:

1. Despite its short length, the 13-character cipher includes multiple repeated characters: 3 8-balls, 2 Ns, 2 Ms and 2 As. That seems strange for homophonic cipher—even if the idea is that we get the key by solving a different, much longer cipher, why use the same cipher character from a group representing a particular character repeatedly?

2. The multiple instances of the same symbol could be a hint that this is actually a simple substitution cipher. That's logical — the Good Lord giveth and the Good Lord taketh away. We have a simpler type of cipher, but much less text to work with.

3. The idea that a simple substitution cipher is hinted at is reinforced by the inclusion of the 8-ball symbol, not shared with the Z340. That is the most frequent symbol, occurring 3 times in the 13-character cipher. As every schoolboy knows, the commonest letter in the alphabet is "E."

4. If we assume that the 13-letter cipher is a simple substitution cipher, then the number of repeated symbols is a big help. GEORGEHODELMD is a better fit than DRGEORGEHODEL — it's got a 3:2:2:2 pattern of repeats like the cipher, versus 3:2:2:2:2 for the latter.

5. For our simple substitution key, we can keep four mappings from the Z340 key (A => D, E => R, M => O, inverted T => L) and we assume that the 8-ball is E. Then that leaves us three new mappings we need to get H, M, and G from the Zodiac symbol, K and N. It doesn't matter which is which because this (is) going to give an anagram. Would be nice if some reason drove those picks, but afraid I don't have anything to offer on that score as yet.

6. On that basis, we get the following clear text: DRGHEMEOELGDO. That is an exact anagram of GEORGEHODELMD.

7. On his blog, Richard Grinell has recently made a compelling case based on the Z340 solve that the Fairfield letters must be genuine and contain subtle hints to solving the 13-character cipher. I think the excerpt below might be a hint to think about repeated symbol counts. My thought is that the names of the places and the numbers themselves mean nothing — the idea is to prompt thinking on the lines I've suggested above.

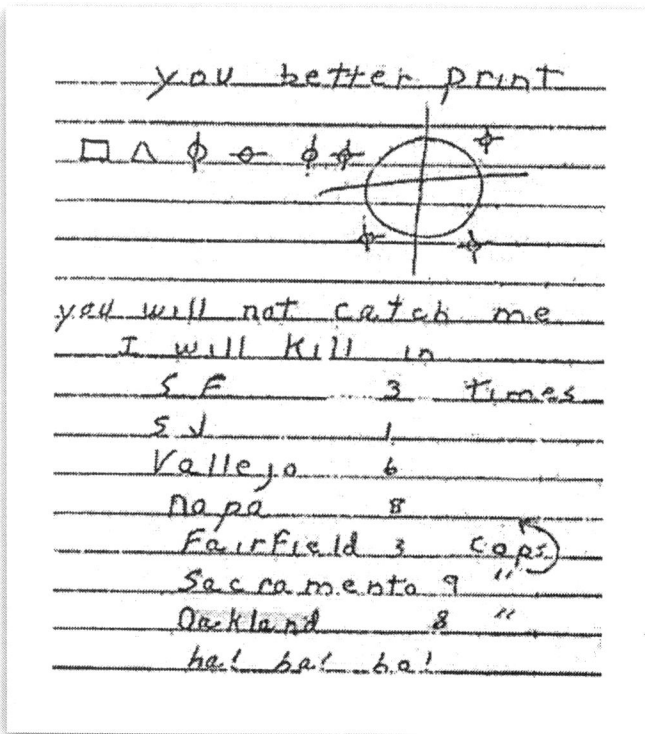

Luigi Warren's email continues:

Replying to @luigi_warren and @FBISanFrancisco

1/ I should note here that the idea of applying the Z340 key to the Z13 cipher & treating the clear text as an anagram came from a YouTube commenter with the handle "No Excuses." This poster suggested DRGEORGEHODEL as a possible solve. As I discuss above, I think this looks to be

Luigi Warren @luigi_warren - 1m

Replying to @luigi_warren and @FBISanFrancisco

2/ on the right track, but I think there's going to be extra wrinkles we have to figure out to get a fully satisfying solve for the Z13. OTOH, applying the exact same description strategy yields a plausible solution for the z38 without further ado...

The Fairfield Letters

Many self-proclaimed "Zodiac experts" have for decades opined that two letters allegedly sent by Zodiac back in December 1969 and postmarked from Fairfield, CA, were not written by Zodiac and were "copycat" letters and "not legit."

The first letter was mailed on December 7, 1969, and addressed to the "*San Francisco Chronicle.*"

San francisco Chronicle
5t misson
San francisco
94109

This is the zodiac speaking

I just need help I will kill
again so expect it any time
now the will be a cop
than I will turn my
self in . OK

HER>< ⊡ 0 ∅ ⊖ 0 L<
    △ T / ⊥   ω B I
    + + ⊉ φ ٩
    ⅂ U Z / ⊙ ⊙
        ⊿ ⌂   0 A I K I +

The second Zodiac letter followed and was mailed to the *San Francisco Examiner* on December 16, 1969. In addition to the letter, it contained a crude drawing of "the bleeding knife of Zodiac." (see top page 415)

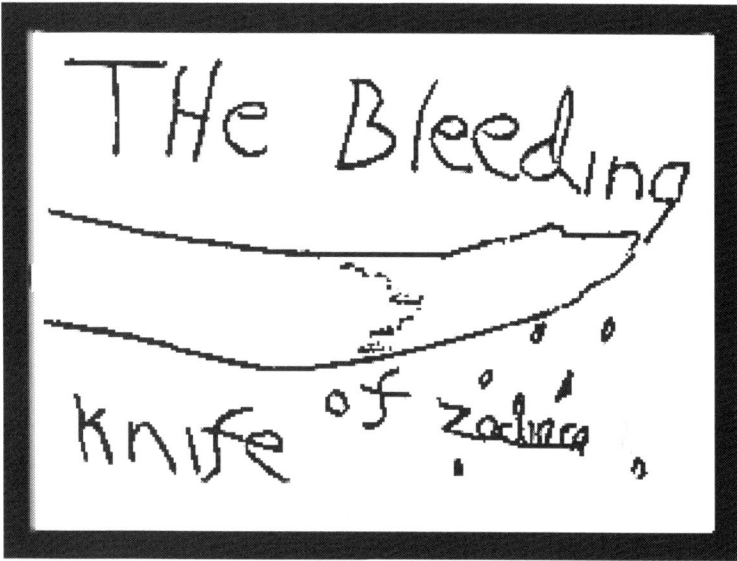

I have always maintained that both 1969 "Fairfield Letters" were legitimate, and Zodiac wrote both.

I believe the handwriting (printing) is that of my father, Dr. George Hill Hodel.

Further, compare the word "knife" written in the drawing "bleeding knife of Zodiac" to the word "knife" written on the car door at the Lake Berryessa Zodiac assault. See comparison below:

Zodiac Lake Berryessa
car door

Zodiac Fairfield Letter

Here is what I wrote in *Black Dahlia Avenger III* (*Rare Bird Books* 2018), as relates to the Fairfield Letter and linking "Zodiac's Bleeding Knife" to George Hodel.

It is my position that GHH, inspired by his hero "Jack The Ripper" and his crude sketch of a bleeding knife in his mailing of the "Boss Letter," copied JtR and his drawing in both his Black Dahlia Avenger and Zodiac letters to the press.

from **BDA III page 42**

George Hodel / Jack the Ripper - Identical Crime Signatures / MOs

- Showed extreme savagery and overkill toward his female victims
- Left victims in public places so bodies would be readily discovered
- Carefully posed victims' bodies and their personal effects at crime scene
- Sent numerous handwritten, cut-and-paste taunting notes to press & police
- Feigned illiteracy
- Drew crude knife dripping blood and mailed to press
- Taunted police with "catch me if you can"
- Mailed human body part to victims' relatives and / or police
- Used red ink and / or iodine in letter to authorities to imitate blood
- Signed mailings to police and press as, "a friend."
- Terrorized cities (London, Los Angeles, Chicago, Riverside, & San Francisco Bay Area) by promising to commit additional killings—"there will be more"—and also threatened to include "boys and girls" in his future murders

BDA III page 43

(Top) Jack the Riper original "Boss Letter" showing killer's "bleeding knife" sent to London Police. (Lower Left) Black Dahlia Avenger article indicating killer sent in, "A crude drawing of a dagger dripping blood." (Newspaper did not provide a reproduction of the actual drawing.) (Lower Right) FBI file showing a crude drawing of "the bleeding knife of Zodiac" believed to be mailed by Zodiac to press in the "Fairfield Letter." George Hodel as both "Black Dahlia Avenger" and "Zodiac" is taunting press and police with another "Jack the Ripper"—inspired "Bleeding Knife," further demonstrating his knowledge and familiarity with JtR's MO.

With this as background let us now return to the further analysis of the good Dr. Luigi Warren.

Luigi Warren @luigi_warren · 1m
Replying to @luigi_warren and @FBISanFrancisco

Applying the new Z340 key to the Fairfield letter cipher & assuming an anagram, below is the best I've come up with so far. Not bad at all!! This is using the pure, unadulterated key. Some symbols are indistinct in the reproductions—I have noted the ambiguity as best I can.

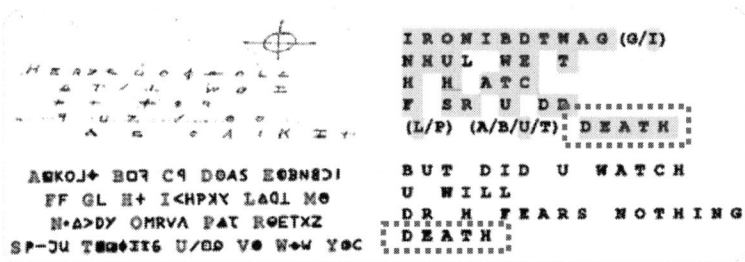

1:33 PM Jan 2, 2021 · Twitter Web App

NOTE - Both of the above solutions/translations end with (or if you will) are signed "**DEATH.**" Is there a correlation?

Here, Dr. Warren explores his correlative conclusion regarding the use of the word DEATH as a signature.

Luigi Warren @luigi_warren - 1m
Replying to @luigi_warren and @FBISanFrancisco

I've no doubt George Hodel was very familiar with the 1927 William Hickmans kidnap-murder case, where the ransom note was signed DEATH written in Greek characters, and we may be seeing an "homage" to that crime here.

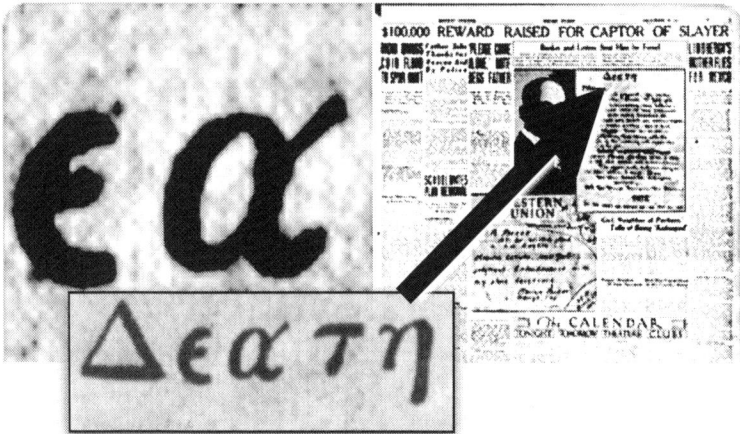

Luigi's email shows a newspaper article with examples from the ransom note where **Greek letters** were used to spell: "**Death**". Below are the letters (delta, epsilon, alpha, tau, & eta) from the **Greek alphabet** that spell "**Death**".

Δδ delta
Εε epsilon
Αα alpha
Ττ tau
Ηη eta

Δεατη

After his Fairfield Letter contribution, Luigi followed it up with one additional analysis of a separate Zodiac coded postcard.

But, first permit me to again quote from California State Historian Kevin Starr's *MATERIAL DREAMS: Southern California Through the 1920s (Oxford University Press 1990).*

(This partial excerpt was initially presented in Chapter 7 - Aimee Semple McPherson, beginning on page 272.)

> Once widowed, once divorced, Sister Aimee was in her mid-thirties, vital in every aspect of life, at the height of her fame. The object of one aspect of her vitality was Kenneth G. Ormiston, employed at the Temple as station engineer for KFSG, but unfortunately, a married man.

> The ensuing farce survives today as Aimee Semple McPherson's enduring claim to notoriety. On the afternoon of May 18, 1926, McPherson was last seen at Ocean Park, a swimming area near Venice. She was presumed to have drowned, but a massive search by police and Temple members failed to discover any body. In the search, two people, a diver and a Temple member, were themselves drowned. A little more than a month later, three days after an all-day memorial service at Angeles Temple, McPherson resurfaced on June 23 in the small Sonoran town of Agua Prieta, claiming to have been kidnapped and to have escaped from a shack in the Sonoran desert where she was being held captive. Researchers with a taste for American style *Grande Guignol* have patiently unraveled the entire episode.

> It is all but certain that Sister Aimee took a month's vacation in the company of Kenneth Ormiston, spending part of this time in a honeymoon cottage in Carmel. Los Angeles District Attorney Asa Keyes, produced a grocery list from the Carmel cottage in what was unmistakably McPherson's handwriting.

> For nearly half a year, Keyes gathered evidence preparatory to taking McPherson to trial on charges of conspiracy to produce false testimony. The embattled

minister defended herself vociferously all the while against the storm of scandal and innuendo that swept Los Angeles.

McPherson escaped going to trial when the District Attorney, fearing that his case fell short of the total conclusiveness needed to convict a person of McPherson's popularity, withdrew charges at the last possible moment. Her disappearance and feigned kidnapping, however, spiced by the motive of sexual adventure, rendered her a laughingstock. After a year and more of press scrutiny and legal investigation, Aimee Semple McPherson became that from which no public figure can ever recover momentum—an object of public ridicule.

~

In September 1990 "Zodiac" mailed another of his many taunting postcards. (The same year George and June Hodel relocated permanently to a penthouse suite at 333 Bush St. West in DTSF.)

Below is an example of the back of the "Celebrity Cypher" as written and mailed to the "*Vallejo Times Herold*" (sic) in September 1990.

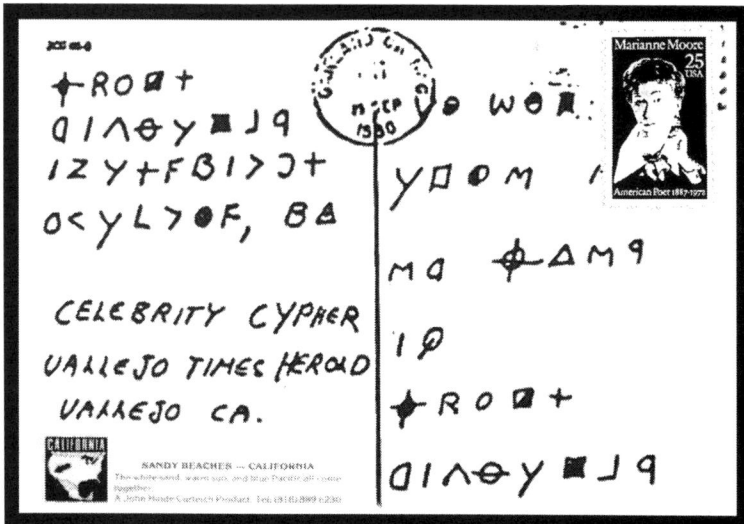

The postcard's front has a framed color photograph titled: "Sandy Beaches." In the foreground, growing out of the 'white sand,' are two wind-gnarled Cypress trees through which appears the white incoming surf with rolling blue waves fading into the deeper blue ocean to the horizon. Beneath dark blue clouds in a lighter blue sky. The sandy beach extends to the right (out of frame) and appears to encompass a cove or small bay on whose other side is a treed jut of land forming a point. Below the image, framed with an ocher-colored border, is the word: "CALIFORNIA."

This image is reminiscent of the famed Cypress Point and Carmel-by-the-Sea. (See image on page 429.)

On the back side of this taunting postcard is a cryptogrammatic message showing the addressee as: "Celebrity Cypher," and mailed to "*Vallejo Times Herold*, Vallejo CA." with an Oakland, California, postmark dated "25 SEP 1990." (See image page 430)

In the upper lefthand corner is a printed numerical mark in italics: "*2CG 66-B*." In the upper righthand corner is the canceled 25-cent Marianne Moore stamp with the caption: "American Poet 1887-1972." **Note:** the Moore stamp was issued April 18, 1990, in Brooklyn, New York. It was designed by Gregory Rudd and was the eighth stamp issued in the Literary Arts Series according to the Smithsonian's National Postal Museum re: Women on Stamps: Part 3.

On the postcard's back in the lower lefthand corner is a small imprinted logo. Below the word "CALIFORNIA" is a map of the US with an arrow pointed toward the west coast, ostensibly to its sandy beaches—such as those found at Carmel-by-the-Sea.

To the right of the small "map" is the caption & credit: "Sandy Beaches — California / The white sand, warm sun, and blue Pacific all come together. / A John Hinde Curteich Product. Tel: (818) 889 6230."

The cryptogrammatic message appears to have been penned first, leaving a space for the 'address' or the reverse: the addressee/address was written first and then the message added. In either case, the writer had to bunch up the letters of the addressee/address to avoid going over the printed vertical midline on the postcard. Second, the stamp was applied to the postcard. Then, third, the postcard was mailed where it received its postmark and the stamp was cancelled.

However, two areas are of concern: 1) on the top line of the cryptogram (top right) there are five letters or symbols with the first letter/symbol being partially obscured by the postmark. 2), it would appear that the stamp was affixed over the message, possibly obscuring the end-part of the first and second lines (dotted boxes) disappearing under stamp to the vertical dotted line indicating the approximate righthand margin of the cryptogram.

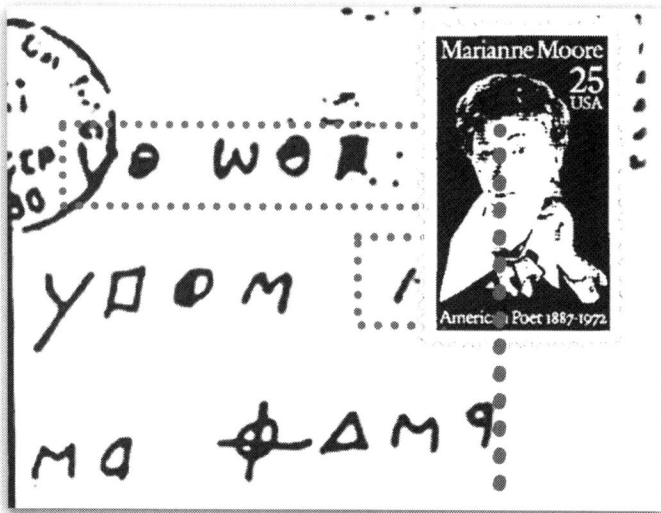

If true, how do those unknown symbols/letters add to or detract from the cryptogram's intended message?

Here is Luigi Warren's analysis of the postcard, in his own words.

Steve:

> Now looking at the 1990 Celebrity Cypher Card—the one with a picture of Carmel Beach*—using the Z340 key to get the clear text and assuming that is an anagram. It sure looks like a lot of interesting words are popping out. There are several ambiguities in the available image of the lettering, and I always end up with a few letters left over. Still, I believe the message may go something like this:
>
> POLICE
> BE NOT AFEARD (or NOW FREE?)
> HE (or HODEL?) CANNOT FUC (or WOO?)
> THAT WANTON WOMAN IN HELL
> THE AVENGER
>
> "THE AVENGER" really stands out. You can't miss it—look at the second and third lines of the clear text (below).
>
> The plot thickens…
>
> Best,
>
> Luigi

*Note: The image on the front of the "Celebrity Cypher" postcard is described by Luigi as being "Carmel Beach." Though the beaches of Carmel are likely scenes for photos of Cypress trees, sand and ocean, the postcard only refers to: "Sandy Beaches."

SKH NOTE:

My sincere appreciation goes to both JAMES VALKS and LUIGI WARREN for their contributions and anagrammatic insights into our ongoing investigation. I say to both of you—AMAZING WORK.

I want to reiterate my observation that the "Celebrity Cypher" postcard was mailed in September 1990, which means it was after my father and his wife June had permanently relocated to their thirty-ninth-floor condo at 333 Bush St. in DTSF.

During one of my visits in the early 1990s, June showed me her full-page collections of stamps honoring various major poets.

These were all of the major poets as recognized by the USPS. The stamp on the "Celebrity" postcard was that of poet "Marianne Moore 1887-1972."

(See **Note** on page 422 re: issue date.)

A few days later, I received the below email message from Luigi with his further revised analysis of the anagram using the three-man-team's new 340 Zodiac Code solution.

Luigi Warren on January 5, 2021, at 3:19 am

Steve:

Got my first "perfect" anagram solve for the Z62 (Celebrity Cypher) — one with no symbols left over. That's disregarding the ambiguous mark under or on the stamp, which it occurs to me might be a comma.

Here it is:

**WANTON WOMAN, FANATIC COCOTTE
HATE-HEWN AVENGER
BURN ALONE IN A HOLE OF HELL**

Not too bad as a shot on goal, I think. "HEATHEN AVENGER" is another interesting phrase that fits the anagram, but I've yet to find a perfect solution, including that one.

Best,

LW

Thanks to the fantastic work of the International Codebreaking team cracking the Zodiac 340 Code and James Valks and Dr. Luigi Warren's spring-boarding off of that solution—it would appear together they may have assisted in linking the distant past (1926) with the recent past (1990) to the present (2021).

How so?

Carmel-By-The-Sea — Celebrity Cypher

The word *celebrity* and Carmel, California, (its "lone cypress tree" *on page 428*, its beaches, its beach cottages) are often associated in people's minds. They may remember the election of the town's celebrity mayor, Clint Eastwood, in 1986.

Others with a farther reaching memory may remember the *celebrity*, Aimee Semple McPherson and her 1926 "Love Nest Scandal" with the manager of her radio station, KFSG (K Four Square Gospel), Mr. Kenneth Ormiston.

Carmel Beach Cottage where Sister Aimee and Kenneth Ormiston "vacationed." The rental agreement showed Ormiston used the name of "McIntire" to rent the cottage, and the couple moved into the residence on the day of Aimee's disappearance, May 18, 1926.

In Chapter 7, we reviewed all of the potential linkages of George Hodel to the 1926 Kidnap Hoax of Sister Aimee.

We read the 1926 typed ransom demand from "Steve and Rose," who identified themselves as "The Avengers."

>
1926 "Avengers" Ransom Note

Lone Cypress Tree - Carmel

Below is a second 1926 Sister Aimee "Avengers" note informing her mother to contact attorney S.S.Hahn in dealing with them. ("Steve and Rose") Eighteen years later, Dorothy Hodel will use S.S. Hahn as her divorce attorney after fleeing from George Hodel and meeting with Hahn on the very day (September 27, 1944) of McPherson's "accidental" death by "overdose of Seconal." There are no "coincidences." Clearly, to my mind, my mother awoke to the headlines, grabbed her three small children, and said, "We're out of here." Unfortunately, fate would return all four of us to our father's residence within a few months.

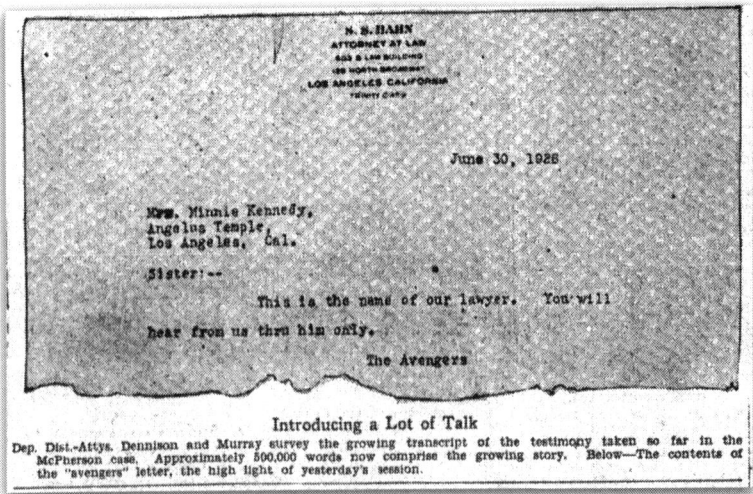

Thoughtprints
The Three Cryptograms

No. 1 "Celebrity Cypher"

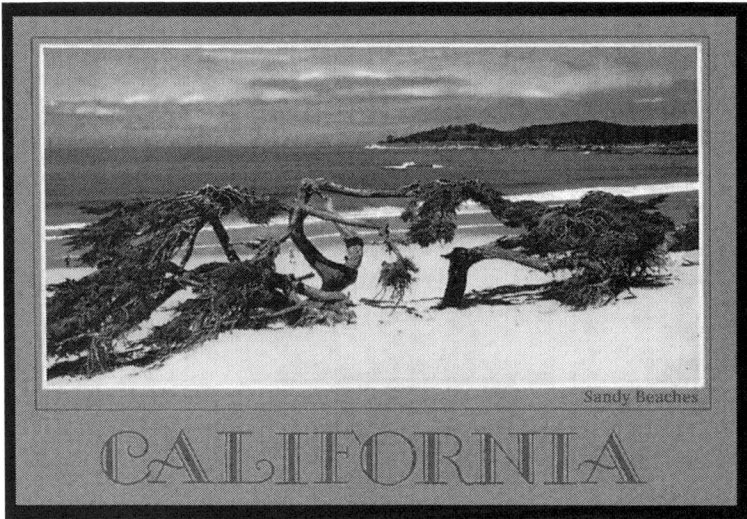

front

At first glance, a picture postcard is just that, a postcard, with a pretty picture on the front and blank spaces on the back for an address and message usually written in ink, in cursive or printed.

But the back of this postcard is more than it seems. It is festooned with Zodiac-style cryptographic symbols. Thankfully, the address on the back was immediately legible for mailing. But, again, it is more than it appears. It is not just a seemingly indecipherable coded message but has, when unscrambled or translated, mysterious connective tissue—links.

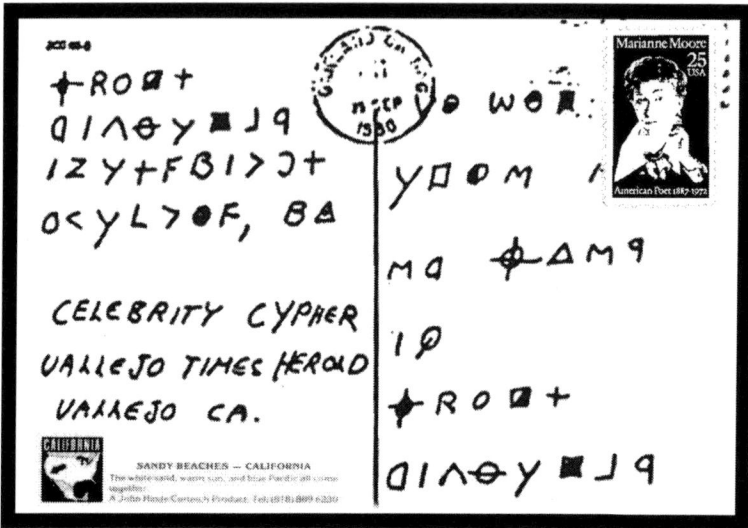

back

What was it he said in this 1990 Zodiac 340 "Celebrity Cypher Code" as translated by Luigi Warren?

Oh, yes, "Zodiac," said:

WANTON WOMAN, FANATIC
COCOTTE
HATE-HEWN AVENGER
BURN ALONE IN A HOLE OF HELL

The message suggests Zodiac, as an "Avenger," is expressing hatred for someone he considered a cocotte, a loose woman, a prostitute, who he hopes will burn alone in her private hell hole. And via the "Celebrity Cypher" postcard's image Zodiac suggests she is connected with the beach town in or around Carmel, California.

Which came first, second, third, or...?

- Was Dr. George Hill Hodel remembering a previous visit or was a new visit to the small town of Carmel-by-The-Sea [population 4000 in 1990 just ninety miles south of his new home in San Francisco], a trigger that made him unable to resist creating an historical taunt using his 340 Zodiac Code, by referencing his 1926 persona as one of the "Avengers" of yesteryear in a postcard?

- Or could GHH have seen and purchased, in San Francisco or Oakland, the popular "California - Sandy Beaches" postcard and been 'inspired' to use his 1926 "Avengers" personality to taunt the *Vallejo Times* as well as law enforcement with his relationship to McPherson?

- Was the timing—an anniversary?

Throughout GHH's criminal history he consistently created and sent to police, the press and the victim's family—written, printed or cut and pasted-style— taunting messages until, in the 1960s, he devised various cryptographic Zodiac codes to disguise both his messages and his identity.

In investigating the crimes of GHH, what to some may seem a coincidence or an ironic "fact," "clew," or "M.O.," time and again I have found with GHH, there are no coincidences. To me, they are thoughtprints.

For example:

Aimee Semple McPherson was found dead in her hotel room on **September 27**, 1944, in Oakland, CA.

Exactly forty-six (46) years later, "Zodiac" pens the "Celebrity Cypher" postcard & mails it on **September 25** in Oakland, California, with the expectation that it will arrive in the hands of the *Vallejo Times Press*, in time for it to be published in the paper on **September 27,** 1990, the actual anniversary date of Aimee Semple McPherson's death/murder. A crime I believe was perpetrated by Dr. George Hill Hodel.

Further, I have previously demonstrated, even given GHH's acknowledged 'genius IQ,' he was a copy-cat/plagiarist *par excellence*. Where, then, did GHH get the idea or inspiration for the **Zodiac-spelled "Celebrity Cypher"** postcard? As in the past, was his source a movie, a book, a magazine, or a newspaper?

Since 1983 "**Celebrity Cipher**" a column (created by Luís Campos) has appeared in newspapers around the world... most certainly in LA and the Bay Area and undoubtedly read by GHH. The gimmick is to challenge readers to "crack the code" and solve the quotation from a famous person, i.e., "celebrity."

Perhaps Zodiac didn't like Campos 'stealing his idea,' so to speak, of having newspapers publish his encrypted messages?

In my opinion, Zodiac, twenty-year attention-grabbing "celebrity" criminal mastermind, decided to play along. But instead of solving one of Luís Campos's cryptograms, Zodiac decided to mail in his own "Celebrity Cypher" to the *Vallejo Times Press*. All for the purpose of publicizing the anniversary of the crime he committed forty-six years earlier.

According to Andrew McMeel Syndication* **Luís Campos** authored "**Celebrity Cipher**" a syndicated newspaper column in which "**he published** more than 14,000 **cryptograms** and crossword puzzles—in English and Spanish...".

*andrewsmcmeel.com/puzzles/celebritycipher

As the text in the image below states: "Celebrity Cipher cryptograms are created from quotations by famous people, past and present. Each letter in the cipher stands for another."

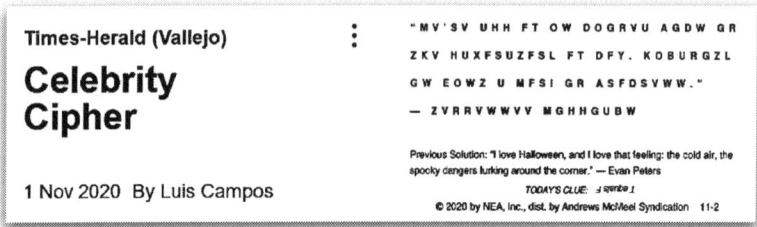

Times-Herald (Vallejo)   ⋮

Celebrity
Cipher

1 Nov 2020 By Luis Campos

"MV'SV UHH FT OW DOGRVU AGDW GR

ZKV HUXFSUZFSL FT DFY. KOBURGZL

GW EOWZ U MFSI GR ASFDSVWW."

— ZVRRVWWVV MGHHGUBW

Previous Solution: "I love Halloween, and I love that feeling: the cold air, the spooky dangers lurking around the corner." — Evan Peters

TODAY'S CLUE: J equals J

© 2020 by NEA, Inc., dist. by Andrews McMeel Syndication 11-2

Above is a recent "Celebrity Cipher" printed in the *Vallejo Times-Herald* on Nov. 1, 2020

That leaves the "celebrity" stamp of Marianne Moore on the back of the "Celebrity Cipher" postcard to discuss.

Was the use of the Moore stamp on the postcard another 'thoughtprint'?

I believe the answer is yes.

As mentioned, June Hodel's collection of stamps included those honoring major poets, etc. In addition to her full sheets of stamps she and Dad had many "singles" to affix to the hundreds of business letters they mailed.

Though I do not remember seeing the Moore stamp, on my visit, among the poet-stamp pages she showed me. It is likely that when the stamp was issued on

April 18, 1990, she acquired a full page of this stamp... and singles for use in their mailings.

I believe GHH saw the resemblance between the celebrity poet Marianne Moore and the celebrity evangelist Aimee Semple McPherson.

Two Look-Alikes -- Did George Hill Hodel see the resemblance?

He intentionally used the Moore stamp on the "Celebrity Cypher postcard" as a stand-in for the likeness of McPherson whom he had grown to hate.

No. 2 "Thirteen Letter Cryptogram"

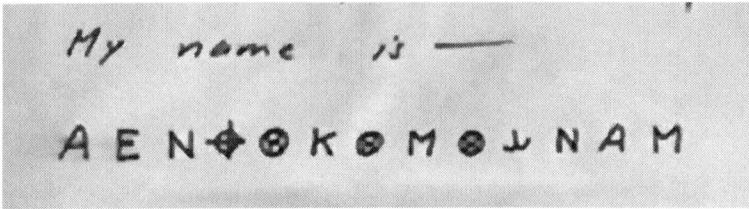

James Valks analysis: DREHGAROGLEDO

Which could potentially be an anagram for

DRGEORGEHODEL (?)

No. 3 "Fairfield Letter Cryptograms"

Luigi Warren's 2021 analysis of the 1969 letter:

The decoding above obviously focuses on:

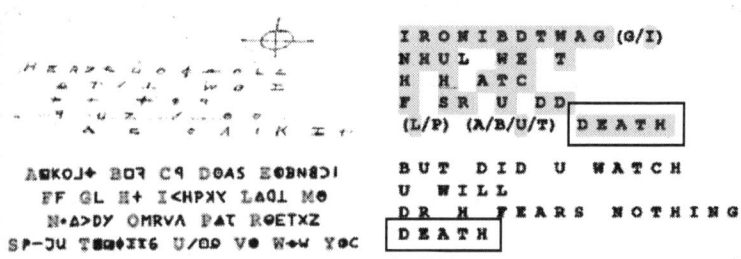

"DR H FEARS NOTHIN DEATH."

As previously mentioned, in Zodiac's second Fairfield Letter, he included a second page with the below drawing of a crude bleeding knife. (Ed. Border added.)

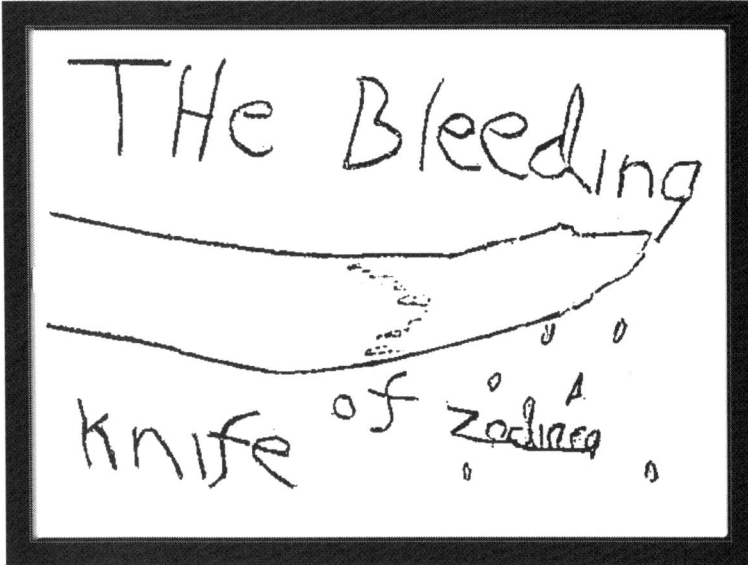

I believe this shows George Hodel's familiarity with Jack the Ripper lore [the Boss Letter contained a crude drawing of a bleeding knife] and his deliberate use of identical drawings George sent to the police in 1947 as "Black Dahlia Avenger" & again in 1969 as "Zodiac."

**Though this now concludes
The Early Years Part 1 ~ 1920s,
my continuing investigations did not stop there.**

**We now move forward to examine
a new decade of criminal activity.**

Next:

The Early Years

Part II - 1930s

ACKNOWLEDGMENTS

Firstly, I would like to acknowledge here my "partner" and good friend, Robert J. Sadler, retired Dallas Police Department officer, Poet, Photographer, Private Investigator, and author of the true-crime book *One Step from Murder, the Friendly Burglar Rapist* and now eighteen 'Michael Grant' novels.

Robert and I have been friends for the past ten years, and though he lives in Dallas, Texas, and I in Los Angeles, California, still we have stayed in regular contact, usually by phone several times a week over these past many years. Robert has been my long-distance partner, and my "Dr. Watson" providing sound advice and constructive criticism, always helping me to "stay on track" when I have the occasional urge to "derail."

Sadler comments of Hodel's True-Crime book In The Mesquite:

from *In The Mesquite*:

"As a collaborator with Steve in getting his book *In The Mesquite* into print, I am biased. However, that does not preclude me from offering my opinion:

My obseravtion of Steve Hodel's life's work, his investigations and his books is that he laboriously and meticulously gathers information and corroborates all the facts that can be corroborated. To those facts he brings to bear over 50 years of investigative know-how and experience to support every aspect of his suppositions and conclusions. His unquestioned integrity remains the cornerstone of his investigative ethos: discover the facts, analyze the facts, let the facts connect where they will and report those facts."

~

Robert J. Sadler, former Dallas Polices Officer, Crime Analyst, Private Investigator, Security Consultant and is author of the true-crime book: *One Step from Murder, the Friendly Burglar Rapist*, and fifteen novels.

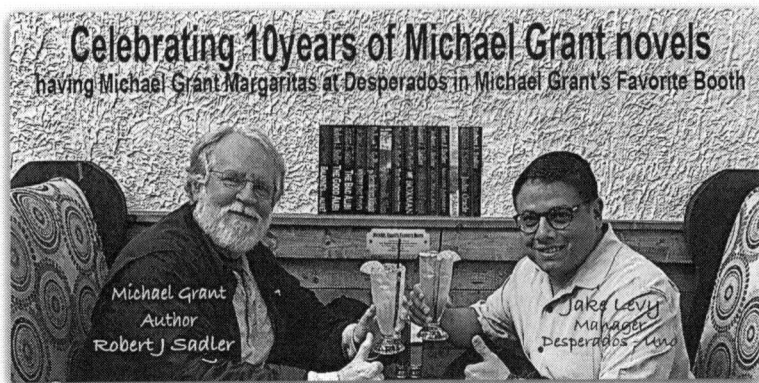

Robert J. Sadler and Jake Levy ~ 2018

The author's favorite Mexican Food restaurant is Desperados. He is shown above in "Michael Grant's favorite booth" at Desperados Uno in Dallas with manager Jake Levy. The second location, Dos, in Garland, Tx is managed by Jake's brother, Michael. Desperados is also the 'fav' of his novels' main character Michael Grant & home of the top shelf margarita "The Michael Grant" created by the author & enjoyed by thousands of Desperados' customers.

Secondly, I would like to thank and acknowledge Barbara Anderson for her careful grammatical review and fact-checking of many of the dates. Her keen eyes have caught and corrected many chronological inconsistencies.

Also, kudos and high praise to book cover artist, Hannah Linder, who designed both *The Early Years* covers.

I would like to thank my many friends here in Los Angeles that have provided sound advice and good counsel.

They include my good friend of twenty years and regular lunch partner, David Browning, and his wife, Suzie. David recently retired as Senior writer/ producer for *Sixty Minutes*. My ex-wife Carole and her husband, Ron Wong. Carole and I have remained friends for more than fifty years.

Finally, a mucho gracias to the many Internet "Friends" on *Facebook* and at my blog site and all readers "foreign and domestic" of my books.

My Sincere Best Wishes,

Steve Hodel
Los Angeles
December 31, 2020
www.stevehodel.com
www.stevehodel.com/blog
Email: steve@stevehodel.com

Hodel Biographies
Father: George Hill Hodel
Son: Steven K. Hodel

George Hill Hodel M.D. (1907-1999)

Dr. Hodel was born in Los Angeles, California, in 1907 and was the only son of Russian Jews who immigrated to the US through Ellis Island in 1903. Prior to immigrating to the United States at the turn of the century, his mother, Esther Leov Hodel, was a dentist in Paris, France. His father, George Hodel, Sr., arriving in Los Angeles became a prominent banker and sold Life Insurance.

George, Jr., a musical prodigy, performed piano concerts at the LA Shrine Auditorium as a nine-year-old boy. He attended South Pasadena High School and graduated at age 15 and attended the prestigious Caltech University. With an IQ of 186, he was one of Stanford University Professor Lewis Terman's "Termites" who were studied beginning in the 1920s with followups throughout their lifetimes.

Hodel attended pre-med at UC Berkeley and obtained his MD at UCSF, Parnassus campus in 1936.

Dr. Hodel served as the sole surgeon at one of FDR's CCC logging camps in Arizona, then became a District Health Officer for the State of New Mexico and doctor to the Navajo and Hopi Indian Reservations before returning to Los Angeles and joining the LA County Health Department.

He specialized in Venereal Disease control during WWII and was appointed as the Head of LA County Health Department's Social Hygiene Program.

The **CHINA LETTER** author joined UNRRA in August 1945 and was assigned to Hankow China in February 1946, where he served for nine months with the honorary rank of "Lt. General" before resigning and returning to his medical practice in Los Angeles. His "China Letter" was written during that time.

Three years after his return from China, Dr. Hodel was arrested for incest and child molestation by LAPD in 1949.

Tamar Hodel, his fourteen-year-old daughter, accused him (along with three additional adults) of having sexual relations with her at the family residence. This resulted in a high publicity jury trial in Los Angeles. Doctor Hodel was defended by famed criminal defense attorney Jerry "Get Me" Giesler and was acquitted of the charges in December 1949.

Hodel fled the country in 1950 just as he was about to be arrested by the DA as a suspect in the infamous 1947 "Black Dahlia Murder." The secret Hodel DA/LAPD Black Dahlia Files (which named him "the prime suspect") came to light in 2003, four years after Dr. Hodel's death, when they were found locked away in the DA's vault. George Hodel was married five times and fathered eleven children.

After fleeing the US, he resided in Manila, Philippines, and became one of the world's leading experts in Market Research throughout Asia.

He returned to the US in 1990, where he resided in a penthouse suite with his wife, June Hirano Hodel, in downtown San Francisco and died in May 1999 at the age of 91.

After his death, ongoing investigations over the past twenty years (1999-2019) have identified Dr. George Hill Hodel as one of the world's most active serial killers, and to date investigations have linked him to twenty-five separate murders committed between the years 1938-1969.

Included in those crimes were LA's 1947 "Black Dahlia" and other "LA Lone Woman Murders" and San Francisco's 1968-69 "Zodiac Murders."

Steven K. Hodel

Steve Hodel is the son of Dr. George Hill Hodel. He is a retired Los Angeles Police Department Detective III and *New York Times* bestselling author.

He spent twenty-four years with the LAPD, where, as a homicide detective, he worked on more than three hundred murder cases and achieved one of the highest "solve rates" on the force.

He is a licensed PI and author, and his first book, **Black Dahlia Avenger: A Genius for Murder**, a *New York Times* bestseller was nominated for an MWA Edgar Award in the Best Fact category.

Steve has written five additional books: **Most Evil**, a *Los Angeles Times* bestseller, **Black Dahlia Avenger II**, a sequel, and an eight-year follow-up to his true-crime investigations, **Most Evil II** (Rare Bird Books, 2015). A fourth book, **Black Dahlia Avenger III: Murder as a Fine Art**, published in November 2018.

His most recent publication is **IN THE MESQUITE**: *The Solving of the 1938 West Texas Kidnap Torture Murders of Hazel and Nancy Frome* (Rare Bird Books 2019).

His investigations, spanning two decades, have been featured on NBC Dateline, CBS 48 Hours, Court TV, A&E, Bill Kurtis Cold Case Files, CNN Anderson Cooper, and the Discovery Channel. Steve most recently appeared in March 2019 on the Today Show and Dr. Phil, where he, with other family members, discussed the making of the hit podcast, **Root of Evil: The True Story of the Hodel Family and the Black Dahlia Murder**.

Steve resides in his hometown of Los Angeles.

Press and Book Reviews for
Black Dahlia Avenger I, II & III — Most Evil I & II

T BONE BURNETT, Oscar, Grammy and Golden Globe Award-winning musician-songwriter; Music Director, *True Detective* says:

"From this distance, there is no doubt that George Hodel committed/ performed theatrical murders in several cities over several decades. That a mad doctor's son grew up to be a detective and solved a master criminal's surrealist crimes—and it was his father—is mind-blowing. But, there it is. My deepest and sincerest respect for [Steve's] fearless and brilliant investigation into a profound darkness that [he has] brought into a penetrating light."

~~~

STEPHEN R. KAY, L.A. Co. Head Dep. District Attorney (07/2001) said:

"The most haunting murder mystery in Los Angeles County during the 20th century has finally been solved in the 21st century."

~~~

MICHAEL CONNELLY, *New York Times* Bestselling author of *The Harry Bosch Series* wrote:

"Los Angeles is the construct of its mythologies good and bad, fact and fiction. The legend of Elizabeth Short is one of the most enduring. But now Steve Hodel has come to put the Black Dahlia painfully to rest. With the tenacity and patience of the veteran homicide detective he once was, Hodel goes from odd coincidence to rock solid conclusion. Taking us on the intriguing and unsettling journey every step of the way. (Steve) Hodel's investigation is thoroughly and completely convincing. So too is this book. As far as I am concerned, this case is closed. Elizabeth Short's legend is now shared with a killer who has been pulled from the shadows of time and into the light. Everybody counts or nobody counts, and that includes the people shrouded in our myths. Steve Hodel knows this. And now we do, too."

~~~

DAVID THOMSON, *New York Times* Book Review wrote:

"George Hodel, I think is fit company for some of noir's most civilized villains—like Waldo Lydecker in *Laura*, Harry Lime in *The Third Man*, or even Noah Cross in *Chinatown*."

Author's Note:

For those interested in discovering and reading Dr. Hodel's later serial crimes and my follow-up investigations linking him to them, here is a list of my books and their recommended reading order:

Steve Hodel's: 6 True-Crime Books (in reading order left to right)

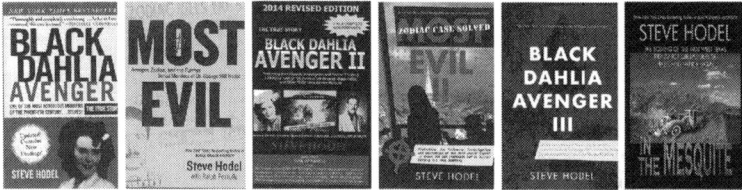

- in reading order -

Black Dahlia Avenger
Most Evil
Black Dahlia Avenger II
Most Evil II
Black Dahlia Avenger III
In The Mesquite
The China Letter
(by Dr. George Hodel - Introduction by Steve Hodel)

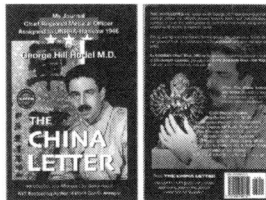

and now
The GHH Murders: The Early Years - Part 1

To quote Dr. George Hill Hodel:

"there will be more"

and there was—see:

The Early Years - Part II

Printed in Great Britain
by Amazon